*Human Rights,
Ethnicity, and
Discrimination*

Recent Titles in
Contributions in Ethnic Studies
Series Editor: Leonard W. Doob

Nations Remembered: An Oral History of the Five Civilized Tribes, 1865-1907
Theda Perdue

Operation Wetback: The Mass Deportation of Mexican Undocumented Workers in 1954
Juan Ramon Garcia

The Navajo Nation
Peter Iverson

An Unacknowledged Harmony: Philo-Semitism and the Survival of European Jewry
Alan Edelstein

America's Ethnic Politics
Joseph S. Roucek and Bernard Eisenberg, editors

Minorities and the Military: A Cross-National Study in World Perspective
Warren L. Young

The Emergence of Ethnicity: Cultural Groups and Social Conflict in Israel
Eliezer Ben-Rafael

Minority Aging: Sociological and Social Psychological Issues
Ron C. Manuel, editor

From Colonia to Community: The History of Puerto Ricans in New York City, 1917-1948
Virginia E. Sánchez Korrol

Human Rights, Ethnicity, and Discrimination

Vernon Van Dyke

CONTRIBUTIONS IN ETHNIC STUDIES,
NUMBER 10

GREENWOOD PRESS
WESTPORT, CONNECTICUT • LONDON, ENGLAND

Library of Congress Cataloging in Publication Data

Van Dyke, Vernon, 1912-
  Human rights, ethnicity, and discrimination.

  (Contributions in ethnic studies, ISSN 0196-7088 ;
no. 10)
  Bibliography: p.
  Includes index.
  1. Civil rights. 2. Minorities—Civil rights.
3. Discrimination. I. Title. II. Series.
JC571.V26   1985   323.1   84-10328
ISBN 0-313-24655-6 (lib. bdg.)

Library of Congress Catalog Card Number: 84-10328
ISBN: 0-313-24655-6
ISSN: 0196-7088

First published in 1985

Greenwood Press
A division of Congressional Information Service, Inc.
88 Post Road West
Westport, Connecticut 06881

Printed in the United States of America

10 9 8 7 6 5 4 3 2 1

To Dean
My Bride for Fifty Years

Contents

Series Foreword

Contributions in Ethnic Studies focuses upon the problems that arise when peoples with different cultures and goals come together and interact productively or tragically. The modes of adjustment or conflict are varied, but usually one group dominates or attempts to dominate the other. Eventually, some accommodation is reached, but the process is likely to be long and, for the weaker group, painful. No one scholarly discipline monopolizes the research necessary to comprehend these intergroup relations. The analysis, consequently, is inevitably of interest to political scientists, sociologists, historians, psychologists, psychiatrists, and all those concerned with human rights and equal treatment.

In our era we cannot fail to note that human rights of ethnic groups are being flagrantly or subtly violated in pluralistic societies on every continent including our own. This volume surveys the remedies that have been unsuccessfully or successfully attempted in modern states such as Belgium, Cyprus, India, Lebanon, and of course South Africa and the United States. American Indians, the Maoris of New Zealand, and other indigenous peoples are likewise included in the analysis. The appeal to majority rule as a justification is often only a cliché, not a compelling principle. The rights of blacks, for example, have been violated by a minority in South Africa but by a majority in the United States. As ever, every ethnic situation is somewhat unique for a host of historical, demographic, and political reasons.

The author contends that human rights are and should be associated not only with individuals but with groups. For it is in groups that individuals are socialized and thereafter realize or try to realize their significant values. The groups being examined here are those based upon language, religion, and race, variables that are usually intertwined. Documents that pervade modern thinking if not policies and actions, particularly those associated with the United Nations and the Genocide Convention, are cited and appraised. Like it or not, politics and ethnics are inseparable.

In each instance the author, a political scientist, first offers relevant and objective data. Then quickly and unobtrusively his analysis leads to a diagnosis and prognosis. The possible remedies are calmly implied or explicitly suggested. Sacrifices are frequently required by the dominant group that would rectify the damage to the subordinated group. The reader, while sharing the author's knowledge and moral impatience, thus gains additional insight into the perils of social and international relations. Nirvana? No, but one or more lights ahead appear visible.

Leonard W. Doob

Acknowledgments

I want to thank several institutions and a number of persons for making this book possible. The principal institution is the University of Iowa, which supported me not only in the usual ways but also with two research leaves. The National Endowment for the Humanities (NEH) granted me a senior fellowship and enabled me to direct two special seminars on the subject of the book. During the period of my NEH fellowship, the Woodrow Wilson International Center for Scholars provided me with a place to work and a stimulating environment.

Lane Davis and John Nelson, colleagues at Iowa, head the list of persons to whom I am grateful, for I have had a running discussion with them during the whole long gestation period. The book benefits, too, from what I have seen described as "inciteful" criticisms by anonymous readers, both of the book itself and of previously published articles. And the members of my NEH seminars were helpful.

Unfortunately I did not write the related articles in such a way that I could piece them together and call them a book, so the book is substantially new. Nevertheless, I am repeating a few passages from three of the articles and wish to thank copyright holders as follows for the necessary permission:

"Collective Entities and Moral Rights: Problems in Liberal-Democratic Thought," *Journal of Politics*, 44 (February 1982), 21–40. Permission granted by the editor.

"The Individual, the State, and Ethnic Communities in Political Theory," *World Politics*, Vol. 29, No. 3 (April 1977), 343–369. Copyright © 1977 by Princeton University Press. Reprinted by permission of Princeton University Press.

"Human Rights Without Distinction as to Language," *International Studies Quarterly*, 20 (March 1976), 3–38. Permission granted by the Executive Director of the International Studies Association.

*Human Rights,
Ethnicity, and
Discrimination*

1

Equal Treatment: The Individual and the Group

The Charter of the United Nations requires members to promote human rights "without distinction as to race, sex, language, or religion," and almost all the constitutions of the world include a similar rule. In the constitution of the United States the main statement of the rule is in the fourteenth amendment, specifying that no state shall deny to any person the equal protection of the laws. Few ideas are as widespread and as fervently championed as the idea that equal treatment is imperative and discrimination wrong.

Agreement on the general idea, however, does not include agreement on its meaning, and that suggests my purpose here: to contribute to thought about the meaning that ought to be given to the requirement of the Charter just quoted. I will pursue this purpose, in the main, by considering selected concrete circumstances and practices around the world that point up significant questions. I will select the circumstances and practices mainly for their heuristic value—that is, for their help in identifying problems and in suggesting possible and desirable solutions. It is not my purpose to assemble any kind of scientific sample, for I do not aim to prove that any one set of rules of interpretation is in fact followed. My assumption is that the information assembled and the questions raised will provide a basis for making interpretations of the Charter and of the equal protection requirement that are sounder than they might otherwise be. And with the assumption goes a hope of a normative sort: that I may also be able to contribute more directly to the development of a desirable conception of the requirement of the Charter and of the rule of equal treatment.

I will focus on distinction as to race, language, and religion, and will add another category: distinction applying to indigenous peoples. I will make no attempt to deal with distinction as to sex, important as that subject is. The reason for the choice concerns political possibilities. Groups identified by race, language, religion, or indigeneity are potential candidates for some kind of special political status (perhaps autonomy or independence), whereas groups identified by sex are not.

"DISTINCTION" AND "DISCRIMINATION"

The provision of the Charter quoted above requires members to promote human rights "without *distinction* as to race, sex, language, or religion." A problem of meaning thus crops up at the outset, for "without distinction" might mean either "without differentiaton" or "without discrimination." We can rule out the first of these meanings, for a ban on *differentiation* would lead to absurd results. In bilingual communities it would prevent the assignment of school children to classes according to the language that they know; and it would prevent the classification of students by race in order to bring about integration. And a ban on differentiation by sex, to refer briefly to that subject, would preclude separate public toilets for men and women, separate barracks for men and women in the armed forces, and separate facilities for confining male and female prisoners. Obviously, this is not the intent behind the requirement of the Charter.

There is no doubt at all that "distinction" is to be defined as "discrimination," not as "differentiation."[1] Human rights are to be promoted without *discrimination* as to the characteristics named.

This interpretation is confirmed by a look at international instruments other than the Charter, for some of them clearly accept "discrimination" as a synonym of "distinction." And implicitly they make a significant additional point—that nondiscrimination is to be associated with equal treatment. The

Covenant on Civil and Political Rights, for example, speaks in the principal relevant article of discrimination:

All persons are equal before the law and are entitled without any discrimination to the equal protection of the law. In this respect, the law shall prohibit any discrimination and guarantee to all persons equal and effective protection against discrimination on any ground such as race, color, sex, language, religion, political or other opinion, national or social origin, property, birth or other status.[2]

As this indicates, the ideas of nondiscriminatory treatment and equal treatment are counterparts of each other. In analyzing the idea of discrimination we will simultaneously be analyzing the idea of equal treatment. Note too that the Covenant prohibits discrimination "on any ground." Thus the grounds named are illustrative, and the list differs from the list in the Charter. In any event, the focus here will be on the three characteristics named—race, language, and religion—and on discrimination against indigenous peoples.

Several international instruments include definitions of discrimination. The International Convention on the Elimination of All Forms of Racial Discrimination, sponsored by the United Nations, says that the term *racial discrimination* applies to

any distinction, exclusion, restriction or preference based on race, colour, descent, or national or ethnic origin which has the purpose or effect of nullifying or impairing the recognition, enjoyment or exercise, on an equal footing, of human rights and fundamental freedoms in the political, economic, social, cultural or any other field of public life.

In other words, the purpose or effect of differentiating measures is the crucial consideration—the purpose or effect with respect to the equal enjoyment of human rights. Measures whose purpose or effect is to impair equal enjoyment are discriminatory, whereas other differentiating measures presumably are not.

The courts of the United States have struggled for many years over the question of the meaning to give to the equal protection clause of the fourteenth amendment, and thus to the idea of discrimination. I will analyze their interpretations in Chapter 6. Suffice it to say here that according to American courts differentiation as to race, language, or religion is discriminatory when it is unreasonable, arbitrary, unfair, capricious, or invidious; and, conversely, differentiation that occurs for a legitimate purpose and is rationally related to the purpose and necessary to its achievement is nondiscriminatory.

THE PROBLEM

Both of the definitions given above help start us on our way, but they leave many problems without a clear solution. The principal problem stems from the fact that in many parts of the world ethnic groups, identified by race, language, religion, or indigeneity, cherish and want to preserve a separate identity; or they have some other kind of legitimate interest that can best be protected or promoted if they are given special and differential treatment. But special and differential treatment for a group entails differentiation between members and nonmembers, automatically raising the question whether the differentiation should count as discrimination.

This is the main problem that we will be pursuing throughout the book: whether differentiating measures are to be justified in the name of a group right or interest or whether they are to be condemned as violating the right of individuals to equal treatment.

THE PROBLEM ILLUSTRATED: LEWIS, ON *POLITICS IN WEST AFRICA*

In our imagination we can range societies along a scale. At one end of the scale is an entirely homogeneous society, with everyone belonging to the same race, speaking the same language, and adhering to the same religion. At the other end is a plural society, with people deeply divided into distinct communities, each community differing sharply from the others in terms of race, language, and religion; the members of each community attach great importance to the differences, identifying themselves primarily with their own community and looking on other communities as enemies. In between are all gradations; differences as to one or more of the characteristics exist, some of them mutually reinforcing and others cross-cutting, and people give them varying degrees of significance.

The problem of assuring equal and nondiscriminatory treatment is bound to differ in these different kinds of societies. Given a homogeneous society, the problem is non-existent, for in the absence of any differences in the specified characteristics, there can be no discrimination based on them. Given a plural society, however, the problem may well be overwhelming.

It will be helpful to think of the problem at the most difficult extreme, and we can do it by looking at *Politics in West Africa*, written by W. Arthur Lewis. His concern is more with democracy than with discrimination, but his analysis is relevant to both subjects.[3]

Lewis focuses on the fact that the rhetoric of democracy emphasizes majority rule, which in elections really means that support by a plurality is enough. He points out that the plurality rule leaves large numbers of people—possibly even a majority—unrepresented. Moreover, associated with majority or plurality rule is the idea that one side wins ("winner-take-all") and the other loses, the idea that the winner is "in power" and the loser "out."

Lewis points out that practice in the more advanced countries differs from the rhetoric in that the winners do not literally take all, and the losers are not entirely "out." Instead, minority parties are permitted to play a role, with their members serving on legislative committees and appointed to this or that agency or office. And he points out that minority members of legislative bodies are treated with respect, the possibility being recognized that they may later become part of a majority. Different parties can alternate in power without disaster, and individuals can switch from one party to another at will.

As Lewis sees it, the rhetoric of the advanced countries, which he deplores, becomes tragic in plural societies like those of West Africa. There "people are mutually antipathetic, not because they disagree on matters of principle, like liberals and socialists, or because they have different interests, like capitalists and workers, but simply because they are historical enemies."[4] Political parties are ethnic, each representing one of the tribes that is the historic enemy of others. Individuals are not free to switch parties, their fate being bound up with the fate of their tribe. Any party that wins takes complete control of government, regarding victory as a tribal triumph that entitles it to use government as an instrument in advancing its own interests and perhaps in settling scores with other tribes. Possibly it will simply neglect them, but it is more likely to oppress or exploit them, or even destroy them. The losing tribes have no reason to give loyalty or support to a government that is the instrument of the enemy. Moreover, the tribe that gets into power has every incentive to manage things so as never to be thrown out, so democracy goes by the board.

Given his analysis, Lewis denounces the majority rule approach to politics (the zero-sum approach) as "immoral and impractical." As he sees it, "the democratic problem in a plural society is to create political institutions which give all the various groups the opportunity to participate in decision-making." And he gives reasons why they should have the opportunity: "only thus can they feel that they are full members of a nation, respected by their more numerous brethren, and owing equal respect to the national bond which holds them together."[5]

Instead of "majority rule," Lewis recommends coalition government, based on proportional representation and the single transferable vote. More significantly for our purposes, he wants all parties to be offered seats in all decision-making bodies, including the cabinet.[6] Government, he says, should not be regarded as an arena in which some win and others lose but as a forum in which negotiations occur for mutual reassurance and accommodation among groups: "Group hostility and political warfare are precisely what must be eradicated if the political problem is to be solved; in their place, we have to create an atmosphere of mutual toleration and compromise."[7]

Lewis's analysis and prescription have obvious implications for questions about equal treatment and discrimination. In the first place, he points by implication to a problem that cannot be corrected simply by a rule against discrimination. That is, he assumes that, given free elections, members of each tribe vote for their own kind, which can happen not only in societies divided by tribe but also in societies divided by race, language, or religion. In the secrecy of the polling booth, voters are free to discriminate as they please, and any tribe or group that commands a plurality becomes the winner that takes all. In the second place, Lewis makes it clear that when one tribe gets control over government in a deeply divided society, the equal enjoyment of human rights is not to be expected. Instead, the dominant tribe favors its own members and discriminates against the others, perhaps doing them in. In the third place, Lewis does not even mention a rule against discrimination as the solution to the problem. Quite apart from its irrelevance to voting, he does not find such a rule promising with respect to the operations of government. Instead of protesting differentiation on an ethnic basis, he pleads for it. His plan for proportional representation on a tribal basis requires that voters register on separate electoral rolls (communal rolls), and his plan to invite members of every tribe to take seats in all decision-making bodies requires that members be selected for those bodies on an ethnic basis; representation is to be communal.

Now it is reasonable to suppose that some country might want to give effect to Lewis's recommendations. In fact, as we will see in subsequent chapters, some have attempted to do it. And this raises the question whether, if differentiation on the basis of race, language, or religion occurs for the reasons that Lewis cites, it should be judged to violate the requirement of the Charter that human rights be promoted without distinction.

OFFICIAL ACKNOWLEDGMENTS OF THE PROBLEM, WITH SOLUTIONS INTIMATED

In effect, various official international actions and agreements acknowledge the problem to which Lewis refers and to which this book relates; and they point toward solutions. One of the actions was taken by the United Nations Commission on Human Rights when it established its Sub-Commission on Prevention of Discrimination and Protection of Minorities, for the name itself intimates that, though discrimination should be prevented, differential measures designed to protect minorities may be desirable. The reference is to national or ethnic minorities, not to partisan minorities. Now if you adopt differential measures to protect a minority, you need to differentiate between members of the minority group and the rest of the population.

In 1947 the sub-commission adopted the following statement:

1. Prevention of discrimination is prevention of any action which denies to individuals or groups of people equality of treatment which they may wish.
2. Protection of minorities is the protection of non-dominant groups which, while wishing in general for equality of treatment with the majority, wish for a measure of differential treatment in order to preserve basic characteristics which . . . distinguish them from the majority of the population.[8]

The intimation is that differential treatment may be justified in the name of enabling the minority to preserve its special characteristics. And if minorities are entitled to such consideration, the question also arises whether majorities have a comparable claim.

In 1962 the sub-commission just referred to adopted a set of "General Principles on Freedom and Non-Discrimination in the Matter of Political Rights."[9] The set included a list of "measures which shall not be considered discriminatory," among them measures taken to ensure:

1. The adequate representation of an element of the population of a country whose members are in fact prevented by political, economic, religious, social, historical, or cultural conditions from enjoying equality with the rest of the population in the matter of political rights;
2. The balanced representation of the different elements of the population of a country;

provided that such measures are continued only so long as there is need for them, and only to the extent that they are necessary.

Now the "elements of the population" referred to surely include ethnic groups, the suggestion being that it is not necessarily discriminatory to set them apart for purposes of representation. And the resolution permits the view that representation (quota representation?) of various elements may be thought desirable throughout the government—that is, in all decision-making bodies, as Lewis suggests, presumably including the civil and military services.

International agreements that call for affirmative action also acknowledge the problem with which we are concerned. The main relevant agreement is the convention on racial discrimination, quoted above. It says that "when the circumstances so warrant," parties shall take "special and concrete measures to ensure the adequate advancement of certain racial groups or individuals belonging to them, for the purpose of guaranteeing them the full and equal enjoyment of human rights." In other words, it requires preferential treatment. To be sure, it specifies that "these measures shall in no case entail as a consequence the maintenance of unequal or separate rights for different racial groups after the objectives for which they were taken have been achieved." But during a transitional period of unspecified duration, differentiation is permissible, and may be directed toward whole groups and not simply toward individual persons. So long as differential and preferential measures are directed toward the advancement of certain groups toward the equal enjoyment of human rights, they are not to be considered discriminatory.

Both of the Covenants on human rights include the same article on self-determination: "All peoples have the right of self-determination. By virtue of that right they freely determine their political status and freely pursue their economic, social, and cultural development." Here the implications for equal and nondiscriminatory treatment are not quite as obvious as in the other cases, but are nevertheless profound; and I expect to invoke the right of self-determination enough in subsequent chapters to justify laying the groundwork here.

The belief that the right of self-determination deserves emphasis in the present context rests on an assumption concerning the meaning of the word *peoples*. There are three possibilities: (1) that the word applies to the entire population of a sovereign state; (2) that it applies to the entire population of a political dependency; and (3) that in the case of multinational or multiethnic states and dependencies, it also applies to the national or ethnic subdivisions. I assume that the word has, and should have, all three meanings. Certainly it has the first, for according to common usage the right of self-determination is in one sense the right of a sovereign people to conduct its own affairs without external intervention. Certainly it also has the second, for it is regularly invoked as the right of the inhabitants of political dependencies (Namibia, for example) to become independent or to choose among possible relationships to an outside power.

The controversial question is whether the word also has, and should have, the third meaning, and my assumption is that it does and should. The idea of self-determination achieved its great prominence when Woodrow Wilson championed it at the close of World War I; and he championed it in part on behalf of nations that found themselves within the Austro-Hungarian Empire and in part on behalf of national minorities living in border regions. That is, though apparently thinking only of Europe, Wilson gave the term a broad application, and the world endorsed his stand. Once one rejects the view (which I will do in a moment) that the right of self-determination is an unconditional right to secede, there is no good reason to narrow the application down. If nations within multinational states have a right of self-determination, then so do sizeable, self-conscious ethnic communities within multiethnic states; and if minorities living in border regions have the right, then so do minorities living elsewhere.

The case for giving a broad meaning to self-determination rests not only on the historic record but also on additional considerations. It is not only in the states of West Africa, on which Lewis focuses, that people attach importance to their national or ethnic affiliation. In one degree or another, they do it all over the world. They think of themselves as Germans or Frenchmen, as white or black, as Christian or Muslim, or as speakers of English or Spanish. And identification with such groups has great significance for individuals. Their sense of their own worth, their dignity, and in some cases the opportunities open to them depend on the status of, and the circumstances surrounding, the group of which they are a part. Mutual respect is more likely to be shared, and to be shared more fully, within the community than across communal lines, and members of a community are likely to be more sensitive to the rights and interests of fellow members than to the rights and interests of strangers and aliens. We can all think of cases where government in the hands of one group has even denied the common humanity of other groups and has denied the most basic human right, the right to life.

Where the divisions within a society are not deep, it may well be possible to safeguard ethnic communities in a variety of ways that stop short of full self-determination. But in plural societies—societies where the divisions are deep and enduring—self-determination may well be vital, for in such societies, as Lewis said, the tendency is for one of the peoples to establish its political dominance and to subject the others, denying them not only equal treatment but other human rights as well. Those concerned about the equal enjoyment of human rights will want to build safeguards against this tendency.

The main problem with an emphasis on the right of self-determination arises from a tendency to think of it as absolute (that is, unconditionally available) and therefore as permitting the group exercising it to secede. But this kind of perspective is not tenable, either with respect to the right of self-determination or with respect to any other right. Theoretically, of course, it would be possible to pick out one right and declare it absolute, but this would surely be unwise; and it would be impossible to make more than one right absolute, for conflicts among rights are always arising, and adjustments and abatements are therefore unavoidable. The usual illustration is that your right to swing your fist must be interpreted compatibly with my right to keep my nose intact. Your right to free speech must be interpreted compatibly with my right to be free from slander. And so on. We enjoy rights on the condition that we interpret and apply them with due respect for the rights and fundamental interests of others. Ways should be sought, of course, to maximize the enjoyment of rights by all, but full and unrestricted enjoyment of every right is impossible. Thus the right of a people to self-determination must be interpreted in a way that gives due respect to other rights and interests that are at stake. If a multinational state has a right to maintain its integrity, this may override the right of a constituent nation to choose independence; but it does not necessarily override the right of a constituent nation to enjoy some degree of autonomy and self-government.

Now if a people has a right to self-determination, problems about equal and nondiscriminatory treatment may well arise, for the right is broad. Among other things it means that the people may "freely pursue their economic, social, and cultural development." Precisely what this entitles them to do is of course open to argument, but if it is taken to mean, for example, that a people has a right to preserve its culture, which the General Conference of Unesco and certain other international conferences have asserted,[10] then questions about discrimination may well come up, for measures by which a community seeks to preserve its culture may involve differentiation between members and non-members. For example, there may be separate schools for different ethnic groups, or guarantees of the kind that Lewis recommends for the representation of the different groups in all decision-making agencies of government. And this might entail quota systems and preferential hiring.

In sum, international actions and agreements of several sorts acknowledge the problem of reconciling the rule of equal treatment with differentiation aimed at protecting and advancing the rights and interests of ethnic communities; and the general rule endorsed is that when the purpose and effect of the differentiation is to promote the equal enjoyment of human rights it is not to be considered discriminatory.

THE QUESTION OF STATUS AND RIGHTS FOR GROUPS

In stating and illustrating the problem to which this book is addressed, and in describing official acknowledgments of it and intimated solutions, I have tacitly brought up another problem that ought to be explicitly identified, for it will come to loom large. It relates to the assumption that ethnic groups may have interests and a legitimate claim to status and rights. For example, it is implicit in what is said above that an ethnic group may have an interest in special measures that assure it representation in government, and may have a legitimate claim to a right of representation and to whatever status this implies. Or it may have an interest in and a right to self-determination, or to preferential treatment for its members. No problem of any moment arises if the group in question is conceived simply as an aggregation of individuals, for then a reference to the rights of the group becomes a kind of shorthand way of referring to the rights of the members. But it is also possible to think of the group as a collective entity, a unit, a whole, analogous to a corporation, it being understood that the corporation may have rights distinct from those of individuals associated with it. This conception sometimes raises objections. I will take up the question more fully in the final chapter, but need here at least to acknowledge it. Those who go through the book may want to keep the question in mind.

In common practice one encounters both of the conceptions just identified. One group may be treated simply as an aggregation of persons, and another as a collective entity; or the same group may be treated both ways for different purposes. The main point is that the second view is a distinct possibility. In fact, this book is written on the assumption that we can best develop an understanding of the problem of discrimination and the problem of the equal enjoyment of human rights if we take the view that a national or ethnic group may be an entity, a unit, with collective rights. In law we accept this view regularly, conceiving the state itself, for example, as a corporate person with collective obligations, rights, and interests, distinct from those of individual persons. Moreover, as I will indicate in subsequent chapters, the law in a number of countries formally accepts certain ethnic communities as collective juridical personalities.

Once we leave the legal realm and enter the moral realm the situation is not so clearcut, but my argument is that in some circumstances ethnic communities should be regarded as units with moral rights. The argument reflects an outlook that ought to be briefly stated.

One aspect of the outlook relates to the source or origin of rights. My assumption is that they come into existence on the basis of human choice—that any person or agency capable of making a judgment can decide that X is a human right, and that the judgment has greater or less significance depending on the standing of the person or agency making it and on the number and standing of those who concur. Actually, widespread agreement exists, as is attested by the adoption of the Universal Declaration of Human Rights, the Covenants, and a number of other international instruments. Those who make the judgments may do so on any ground they choose. Some claim that rights have a divine or natural source—a claim that I dismiss as an effort to attach undeserved authority to frail human choice. I endorse the view that rights reflect interests. We pick out certain interests that we consider morally entitled to respect, and we call them rights. We put into the category of human rights those interests that we judge to be of fundamental importance and that are shared (potentially at least) by all humankind.

It is arguable that human rights should be limited to the rights of individual persons, but I go along with the contrary decision that is reflected in the statement that all "peoples" have the right of self-determination. I think it clear that ethnic communities and "peoples" may have collective interests, and that some of them are of such fundamental importance and so general (universalizable) that they are and ought to be called rights. Further I think it clear that individuals sometimes have interests that can best be promoted and protected by granting a right to the community; or, to put it conversely, that some interests of individuals cannot be effectively served unless a right is conceded to the group to which the individuals belong. Further, if it be conceded that governmental action may make a community a juridical personality, then I think it logically necessary to grant the possibility that the community may have had a prior moral claim. I will offer support for these views here and there in the chapters that follow and will attempt to advance a coherent argument in support of them in the final chapter.

2

Distinction as to Language

Problems about distinction as to language arise wherever more than one language is spoken—in international organizations, and in virtually every country of the world. The object here is to identify and describe the problems and to assess the solutions. In the assessment we will take into account the definition of discrimination contained in the international convention against racial discrimination, quoted above, but will need to supplement it with other considerations. The definition developed in the United States, emphasizing the ideas of the reasonable and the arbitrary, is more flexible and thus more generally applicable. The focus will first be on the practices of the United Nations itself, and then on a series of territories or countries: the Aaland Islands, Belgium, India, and the United States.

LANGUAGE AT THE UNITED NATIONS

The United Nations differentiates as to language. Of all the languages spoken by delegates who attend its meetings, it designates a small number as "official" and a smaller number as "working," and gives no status to the rest. It publishes its documents in some languages but not in others; and when it hires people to work in certain offices, it takes their command of language into account. Obviously, some persons are favored by the decisions made, and others are disadvantaged.

Some of the choices about language in the United Nations are simply a matter of voting strength, and principle may or may not be much involved. If the Arabic-speaking states can muster enough votes, then Arabic becomes an official language, and that is that. Still, the issues can be discussed in terms of principles.

On the one side are considerations calling for equal status for all the languages that the delegates speak. Given such equal status, every delegate could speak and listen, and read the documents of the United Nations, in his own language; and everyone could enjoy the convenience and the pride that comes with a recognition of that language and avoid the mortification of having it treated as a language of limited currency or worth.

On the other side are considerations relating to cost and efficiency. Member states have an interest in the size of their budgetary assessments, and they know that it would be expensive to serve every delegate in his own language. For every additional language more translators would have to be trained and paid, more elaborate electronic systems would have to be installed for simultaneous translations, more equipment, facilities, and personnel would have to be devoted to the production and dissemination of printed materials, and so on. At some point, the effort to assure equal treatment as to language would impair the functioning of the organization. Further, the burden placed on those whose language is not classified as "official" or "working" is limited. If a delegate's language is not a working language, the odds are that he will know another that is; and, though learning an additional language is difficult, it is by no means impossible. Balancing these various considerations off, general agreement exists that at some point the benefits of classifying one more language as "official" or "working" do not justify the costs. Argument occurs over various questions (How many languages should be on the list? Which ones? What should the precise implications be?), but that the right to equal treatment as to language has to be balanced off against other compelling interests is a principle that all accept. That is, they find a balancing test reasonable and justifiable. Everyone accepts the rule that for a right to be implemented there must be a relationship of proportionality between the benefits and the costs.

We are on treacherous ground here. The balancing test puts all rights in potential jeopardy. It can be taken to suggest that respect for rights is a matter of convenience, or that the rights of one or the few should always give way when the interests of the many can thus be served. Nevertheless, the principle holds. As indicated in Chapter 1, no right can be absolute—or at least not more than one right can be, for conflict among rights is inevitable. Further, conflict is inevitable between rights and public interests of a compelling and fundamental sort. The appropriate view is that when X is classified as a right, a strong presumption is asserted in favor of respect for it, and a heavy burden is placed on anyone who wants to argue that it should be overridden. But in some circumstances it is reasonable and neither arbitrary nor invidious to hold that it must give way; and in such circumstances the overriding of a right should not be considered discriminatory.

The United Nations employs a balancing test not only in selecting official and working languages, but also in recruiting employees for the Secretariat, often with decisive results. Command of one or more of the working languages is imperative— a bona fide occupational qualification (bfoq).[1] By general consent the bfoq overrides any contrary right of the individual to be considered "without distinction." If some applicants have a working language as their mother tongue, that is their good fortune; and if some have learned a second or a third useful language, they add to the reasons for distinguishing in their favor. A decision that goes against a person because he fails to meet a bfoq is not considered discriminatory, and the rule is reasonable. If an institution is to operate effectively, those working in it must be able to communicate efficiently with each other and with those whom they serve.

Not only does the United Nations differentiate as to language in its own practice; it also prescribes differentiation to others. Thus when it recommended the partition of Palestine it specified that "the State shall ensure adequate primary and secondary education for the Arab and Jewish minority, respectively, in its own language and its cultural traditions."[2] Presumably the "adequate" education was to be equally adequate, in which case the General Assembly endorsed the principle of separate but equal treatment so far as language is concerned.

A point is implicit here that ought to be made explicit. To be equal, treatment does not necessarily have to be the same. On the contrary, differentiation is sometimes necessary. Put in broader terms, what the General Assembly did with respect to educational arrangements in Palestine can be justified by a principle associated with the definition of discrimination developed in the United States—the reasonable classification principle: that sometimes in order to treat people equally it is desirable and even necessary to classify them and to treat them differently depending on the class to which they belong. The question is whether the classifying is reasonable or has a rational basis, and the question has two parts, one asking about the purpose being pursued and the other about the criteria employed.[3]

The question about purpose is whether it is legitimate. If the purpose were to distinguish those who are to get an elementary education from those who are not, it would be illegitimate, for it is now agreed that everyone is entitled to such an education; it is a human right. But if the purpose is to make it possible for each child to get mother tongue instruction, it is surely legitimate; and this is no doubt one of the purposes that underlay the General Assembly's action. Presumably the General Assembly had another purpose as well. It spoke of minorities and their cultural traditions, suggesting a recognition of a group right: each minority had a right to preserve its culture, including its language.

The second part of the question whether classification is reasonable has to do with the criteria employed. Put in general terms, the criteria must be relevant (that is, rationally related) to the purpose, and must be such as to produce fairly neat results (that is, must actually get people into the classes proper for them without any undue over- or under-inclusion). If the purpose is "responsible voting," for example, and the criterion of classification is age, the purpose would be generally approved as legitimate and the criterion would be accepted as relevant. Everyone can name an age below which "responsible voting" would be unlikely. But everyone can also agree that an age requirement of 40 would be discriminatory, for it would exclude many who are just as capable of responsible voting as those included: it would be under-inclusive.

In the case of the General Assembly's recommendation that children in Palestine be classified as Arab and Jewish and be taught separately, all of these requirements were met. The purpose and the criterion of classification were acceptable, and the means were rationally related to the end. In truth, the recommendation called for a continuation of the policies fixed after World War I by the terms of the British mandate.

Lest these answers appear easy and obvious, let it be noted that a different conception of purpose in Palestine might also have been legitimate, calling for different methods. During the period of the mandate, a British white paper in fact bewailed the requirement that Arabs and Jews be educated in their own language, on the ground that the object should have been not to enable them to maintain their language and culture but to "bring the races together." Given this object, the wish was that both Arabs and Jews could have been taught English at the primary level and then have been put together in the same classes at the secondary level, with English as the language of instruction. "Had it been practicable in Palestine, such a system, adopted at the outset and consistently pursued, might have gone far in a generation to break down the barriers between Jew and Arab and to nourish a sense of common Palestinian citizenship."[4] In other words, different legitimate ends may call for and justify different means, and judgments about equal and nondiscriminatory treatment may need to vary accordingly.

The principle that it is acceptable to classify children by language for purposes of education later came to be included in Unesco's Convention against Discrimination in Education. It permits the separate but equal schooling of children from different linguistic communities. So, incidentally, does it permit separate but equal schooling by religion or by sex, though prohibiting it by race.

THE AALAND ISLANDS

The Aaland Islands got their independence from Russia along with Finland toward the close of World War I. Swedish-speaking, the islanders wanted to join Sweden, but since they had been historically tied to Finland, Finland insisted on its claim. A crisis developed, and out of the crisis came a compromise. The islands remained a part of Finland, and the islanders became citizens of Finland, but they were given a means of protecting their language and culture from the dangers that an influx of Finns might involve. An international agreement provided that if anyone not legally domiciled on the islands presumed to come in and buy real estate, he could be compelled to sell out. Repurchasing rights were given to all legal residents of the islands, to the Provincial Council, and to the commune in which the real estate was situated; and a local court was to be the arbiter if the parties directly involved were unable to agree on the price.

The significant feature of the agreement for present purposes was that it made a distinction between different citizens of Finland. Those already legally resident on the islands could buy real estate there and get a secure title, whereas other citizens could not.[5]

In the United States that kind of arrangement would be unconstitutional, for it denies the equal protection of the laws. It is as if property in Hawaii could be bought by anyone already resident there, but not by any citizen coming in from the mainland—an arrangement that the courts would strike down without hesitation. But good arguments can be made, appealing to either expediency or principle, that the arrangement was justified.

The expediential argument is that the agreement resolved an international crisis, peacefully, and on a basis mutually acceptable to the parties.

The principled argument rests basically on the proposition that established rights and interests are to be respected in the absence of good reason to the contrary. Finland had an established right to the islands, however tenuous, and Sweden had none. The islanders had at least an interest in preserving their language and culture and maintaining an established community, and I would argue that they had rights entitling them to do so. They had a right to freedom of expression, which includes the right to choose the language in which expression occurs. They had a right to equal treatment. And above all they had a right of self-determination, including a right "to freely pursue their economic, social, and cultural development." All of these rights would have been increasingly threatened or undermined the greater the number of Finns allowed to establish themselves on the islands.

As indicated in Chapter 1, none of these rights should be regarded as absolute. All of them had to be interpreted in the light of other rights that would be affected by the decisions made. In the end, the right of self-determination was given an interpretation compatible with Finland's claim, and the special repurchasing rights given to the islanders had minimal adverse effects on anyone, for prospective purchasers of real estate were warned away. There were no invidious implications for other citizens of Finland and the arrangement imposed no significant burden on them—presumably nothing more than restricted future opportunities.

We are back again to a balancing test. The individual and collective rights of the islanders are balanced against the right of other Finnish citizens to equal treatment. It is reasonable to suppose that the granting of the special right to the islanders was vital to the preservation of their language and culture, and that the equal right of Finns to get secure title to real estate on the islands was of minor significance to them. The benefits on the one side were far greater than the burdens on the other, which suggests that, given the conflicting rights, the choice made should not be classified as discriminatory. In Chapter 4 we will note that the United States has adopted a comparable rule with respect to American Samoa, which is classified as an unincorporated territory to which the fourteenth amendment does not apply.

Perhaps I should call attention to the fact that the agreement in the Aaland case gave repurchasing rights not only to individual residents but also to governmental units. In law, then, rights went both to individual persons and to communities as

corporate entities. Whether the agreement implied an acceptance of the view that the corporate entities had moral claims
is a question that we do not now need to resolve, though I might
note that those who approve the granting of the legal right to
the corporate entities are in an odd position if they hold that
the corporate entities had no moral claim to what they got.

BELGIUM

Belgium's population divides as indicated in Table 1. The
census has not included a question about language since 1947,
but the inhabitants of Flanders are overwhelmingly Dutch-
speaking and the inhabitants of Wallonia French-speaking.
Those in Brussels-Capital speak either language or both; some
four-fifths are thought to speak French.[6] All together, more
than half the population speak Dutch, and this has been the
case ever since Belgium came into existence in 1830. Nevertheless, through most of Belgium's history, French has been
the dominant language. To be sure, the 1830 constitution ap-
peared to be neutral on the issue, for it permitted individuals
to choose their language in dealing with the government; but
laws were officially published only in French and, except at
the local level in some areas, French was the language of the
bureaucracy. Moreover, French was the language of higher
education and, in general, the language of the elite. Dutch was
the language of the peasants—all the more disdained because
of its many dialects and the lack of a standard form. Dutch-

Table 1
Geographical Distribution of Belgium's
Population — 1980 Estimate

	Number	Per cent
Flanders	5,619,000	57
Wallonia	3,227,000	33
Brussels-Capital	1,009,000	10
German-speaking	65,000	0.6
Total	9,920,000	

Source: Belgium. Ministère des Affaires Economique. Institut National de Statistique.
Annuaire Statistique de la Belgique. Tome 100. 1980.

speaking persons who sought careers in government and politics, or professional careers of any kind, needed to take up French. The Flemish were thus left without an elite and were automatically marked as lower class and second class. Many resented the stigma. Moreover, many resented the francization of territory that had been Flemish, brought about not only by the shift of Dutch-speakers to French but also by the movement of French-speaking people into Dutch territory, which happened especially around Brussels. The result was that Flemish nationalism developed, focusing on the language problem.[7]

Concessions to the Flemish came at intervals, those made since 1960 being especially extensive.[8] As revised in 1970, the constitution starts right out asserting that "Belgium comprises three cultural communities: French, Dutch, and German. Each community enjoys the powers invested in it...." And, as we will shortly see, powers are in fact vested in the communities; they are corporate entities with a share in government. The Belgian constitution also says, "Belgium comprises four linguistic regions: the French language region, the Dutch language region, the bilingual region of Brussels-Capital, and the German language region." Boundaries of the regions are carefully drawn, and the requirements for changing them are such as to give each language community a guarantee of its territorial integrity. The territorial principle prevails—the principle that the treatment of a person as to language depends not on his own preference and skills but on his geographic location. "The cultural system must be French in Wallonia and Flemish in Flanders."[9] The conviction is that bilingualism would "debase the traditional character and individuality of the two communities." Even in Brussels (nominally bilingual, but overwhelmingly French) every effort is made to maintain the distinctiveness of the cultures and to see to it that children are brought up in the culture of their parents. The principle of personality replaces the principle of territoriality.[10] Measures reflecting these principles apply in the fields of politics and government, education, and business and commerce.

In politics and government a rule that was long followed voluntarily is now mandatory: that with the possible exception of the prime minister, the cabinet must include an equal number of French- and Dutch-speaking ministers. No matter if the best qualified persons are all French-speaking (or Dutch-speaking), half the posts must go to members of the other community. This means that so long as the members of parliament coming from a language community remain united, they have a veto on governmental action, for no one can form a cabinet or keep it in office without the cooperation of ministers from both language communities. No statement is made that cultural communities are units for purposes of representation. On the contrary, the constitution asserts that the members of parliament represent the nation. Nevertheless, the two communities are assured of substantially equal roles in representing the nation in the cabinet. Neither is to be permitted to achieve domination over the other.

Note that ("with the possible exception of the prime minister") numerical equality is called for and not representation in proportion to population. So far as representation in the cabinet is concerned, not persons but communities have equal weight. The model followed is the one that prevails at the international level rather than at the domestic level. Just as states enjoy sovereign equality, and just as each member state has one vote in the General Assembly regardless of population, so do the linguistic communities of Belgium have the same number of posts in the cabinet. The intimation is that the language communities are regarded as entities or units, and not as aggregations of individuals.

A similar arrangement exists for the civil service. The law requires that within the civil service a just equilibrium must be maintained between the linguistic groups, and this is interpreted to mean that above a certain grade the representation of the French and Dutch communities is to be equal. The parity rule is by law explicitly made to cover the foreign as well as the domestic service.[11] The principle of equality of opportunity for individuals, and selection according to merit, is thus again qualified; maintaining a just equilibrium (parity) between the language communities—by affirmative action if necessary— takes priority, and a better qualified applicant for a position may be passed over in favor of one who is less well qualified. Obviously, if the parity principle is acceptable with respect to groups identified by language, the question arises whether it is also acceptable with respect to groups identified by race, sex, or religion.

The struggle in Belgium has not only produced rules about the representation of the language communities in the central government but has also led to some degree of devolution of power to the regional level. A cultural council exists for each of the language communities, and in addition Flanders and Wallonia have separate regional councils, with Brussels slated to get one as well. In due course the cultural and regional councils are expected to have budgets of about 10 percent of the national budget and to exercise functions having to do with language and local and regional affairs.[12]

The principle of territoriality, mentioned above, applies rigorously to the language of instruction in the schools. The fact reflects unhappiness with experiences of the past, especially on the part of the Flemish. Until 1932 Flemish parents in many communities found it possible to have their children attend school where French was the language of instruction. This meant defection from the Flemish community and the acceptance of some degree of francization. An individualist would shrug at this, on the ground that freedom is desirable. But many self-conscious Flemings resented it. They attached value to the preservation of the linguistic and cultural community and to the enhancement of its status, and believed that this was important enough to justify overriding the claims of individuals to freedom of choice. In 1932 they obtained legislation going in the desired direction—legislation specifying that the language of instruction in all schools supported by the government must be the language of the region. In those instances where children from different language groups were in the same school, this meant that some got instruction in their mother tongue while others did not. The rule remains in effect, and a school loses governmental financial support if it teaches a single class in any language other than the one authorized. Even trans-mutation classes are forbidden—special classes to help children make the transition from one language to the other. In addition, if a school uses an unauthorized language as the language of instruction, its graduation certificates lose official standing.

Holders of such certificates may recoup their situation by passing a special examination administered nationally, but otherwise they are in effect barred from certain careers. In Brussels, fearing that some Flemish parents might contrive to send their children to French schools, Flemish leaders even insisted for a time that the word of the head of the family concerning the maternal or usual language was subject to verification.[13]

Rigorous insistence that the language of the region be the language of instruction extends through the university level. The University of Ghent switched from French to Dutch between the two world wars, and the ancient Catholic University of Louvain followed suit in the early 1970s—a French "section" choosing to move outside the Dutch language region.[14]

Insistence on the integrity of the Flemish language community extends into business and commerce. A decree of the Flemish Cultural Council in 1973 made Dutch the mandatory language of work in the Flemish region. Business enterprises are to use Dutch in company meetings, in internal communications, in negotiations between labor and management, in their records, and so on. The elite must adjust to the language of the workers, and not vice versa. Or, to put it differently, the burden of using a language other than the mother tongue is placed on those who come into the region from the outside and not on the native born. Management is denied freedom of choice, and thus an aspect of freedom of expression, and employees have their presumed choice reinforced by law.[15]

Not surprisingly, Belgium's policies have raised issues concerning discrimination. In particular, French-speaking parents in a number of cities and communes of Flanders applied to the European Commission on Human Rights, claiming that Belgian policies violated requirements of the European Convention for the Protection of Human Rights. They cited several articles. The two that concern us here specify that "no person shall be denied the right to education" and that "the enjoyment of the rights and freedoms set forth in this Convention shall be assured without discrimination on any ground such as...language...."

Both the European Commission and the European Court on Human Rights rendered judgment on the issues, employing similar criteria but not identifying them in any one succinct, coherent statement. Their concern was, of course, with acts or omissions attributable to public authorities. The acts or omissions concerned differentiation, the question being when differentiation or the failure to differentiate is discriminatory. Running through the comments on this question is the basic theme that reasonableness is to be approved and arbitrariness condemned. And the basic theme is elaborated in statements that the purpose pursued must be "legitimate and avowable," and that a "reasonable relationship of proportionality [must exist] between the means employed and the aim sought to be realized."[16] These criteria—already described above in the discussion of the General Assembly's recommendation on Palestine—led both the Commission and the Court to judgments that were largely favorable to Belgium's policies. Neither agency asserted that linguistic communities have rights as collective entities, but neither condemned policies predicated on the assumption that they do. Both considered it reasonable for the government to take measures designed to promote linguistic homogeneity on a regional basis; more particularly, both held that it is acceptable to select the language of instruction in schools on the basis of the principle of territoriality, even though this means that some pupils get mother tongue instruction and others do not. As the Court put it, the ban on discrimination

does not prohibit distinctions in treatment which are founded on an objective assessment of essentially different factual circumstances and which, being based on the public interest, strike a fair balance between the protection of the interests of the community and respect for the rights and freedoms [of individuals].[17]

The Commission and the Court disagreed on several lesser issues, thus implicitly testifying to the difficulties of judgment. The Court ruled against Belgium only with respect to a special arrangement applying to six communes on the periphery of Brussels.

With respect to the criteria of judgment, one aspect of the Commission's view calls for special comment. It concerns the implications of the fact that the provision of the European convention on education is stated negatively: "no person shall be denied the right to education." In the light of this, the Commission took the view that, in providing for education, the government extends a favor or privilege, and that the differential extension of favors or privileges is not discriminatory except under certain conditions: only if the object is to impose hardships or disadvantages on those not favored, or to damage their interests or weaken their position. And even then the differentiating measures can be excused if they are justified by administrative or other needs.[18]

The view is both questionable and dangerous. In the first place, the statement in the convention is not entirely negative. It acknowledges a right to education, saying only that the obligation of the state with respect to the right is negative. And a good argument can be made that, regardless of the European Convention, the state is under an affirmative obligation on other grounds. In the second place, and much more importantly, the idea that the ban on discrimination leaves the state free to give favors and privileges to one segment of the population while withholding them from the rest threatens to deprive the ban of much of its meaning. It would permit the establishment of a privileged class, or a division of the population into groups each of which is especially privileged in some respect. The equal protection of the laws is itself a right, limiting the behavior of governments even in granting favors. If the refusal of the government to assure mother tongue instruction to French-speaking pupils in the Dutch region is justifiable, the justification rests not on the ground that governments are free to bestow favors differentially but on the ground that they should respect the right of an ethnic community to preserve its language and culture—and perhaps its territorial integrity—even if conflicting rights of individuals have to be overridden or somehow abated.

It is plain from the above that Belgium treats its language communities as corporate entities with collective legal rights; they are units for purposes of government. The ultimate beneficiaries of the arrangements are individual persons, but the effort is to serve the interests of those persons by conferring legal rights on the community to which they belong. Group rights supplement individual rights, so that conflict can occur not only between individual rights but also between the rights of an individual and the rights of a group.

It would be foolish to argue that the specific measures adopted in Belgium are morally imperative, for others might serve approximately the same purposes; but I do argue that the language groups had a good moral claim that some such measures be adopted. In order to state the case, it is convenient to divide the measures roughly into those relating to participation in the cabinet and the civil service, on the one hand, and those relating directly to the language regions and rights, on the other.

With respect to the first of these categories, we should recall the analysis of *Politics in West Africa* by Lewis, described in Chapter 1. Relationships between the linguistic communities of Belgium were perhaps not as extreme as those that Lewis assumed among the African tribes, but what he has to say is relevant nevertheless. The basic premise is that, once ethnic groups develop an acute self-consciousness on a we-they basis, the odds are that members of each group will be especially sensitive to the needs and interests of fellow members; and their attitude toward members of other groups may range from indifference to enmity. Given this premise, the danger is that, if one group is permitted to become politically dominant, it will use government to advance its own interests, neglecting and even oppressing other groups. Moreover, prestige and pride are usually associated with the role of a group in government, those possessing power enjoying both, with others probably suffering the humiliation of second class status. If the differentiation goes far enough and lasts long enough, the second class group may disappear as an identifiable entity. In a few cases a dominant group has even sought to exterminate a subordinate group.

It is possible, of course, to take a Darwinian view, and to let a struggle for dominance and even for survival proceed. Those taking such a line would presumably also find it acceptable if the struggle seriously interferes with orderly, cooperative governmental processes, possibly leading even to the break-up of the state. But it is also possible to say that members of both groups are likely to be better off if an amicable arrangement can be made that is fair to those involved and provides reasonably for their mutual well-being. This is substantially what happened in Belgium, which is tantamount to saying that the arrangement is reasonable and neither arbitrary nor invidious, responding to morally legitimate claims of right.

With some strain, it might be argued that the claims of right were those of individual Belgians: each person had a moral claim that his or her group get half the posts in the cabinet and in the civil service. It is simpler, however, to say that, in effect, each group comprised the equivalent of a corporate entity, and that the corporate entity had the moral claim.

A seemingly alternative contention might be advanced: that Belgium adopted its various measures simply as a way of adjusting conflicting interests and that moral claims were irrelevant. The thought suggests two comments. The first is that the fact that X is an interest does not preclude it from also being a right. That interests were adjusted is inconclusive on the question whether a matter of right was involved. As indicated in Chapter 1, what happens is that we identify certain interests as being of fundamental importance and declare them to be rights, which seems to be what happened implicitly in the Belgian case. The second comment is that moral rights may develop prescriptively just as legal rights do. Once a morally unobjectionable practice is followed consistently for a number of years, like the practice of dividing cabinet posts evenly between the two language communities, a legitimate moral claim develops that it should continue to be followed.

Similar considerations are relevant to the measures relating specifically to language. What is said above with respect to the Aaland Islands applies here again. In addition, I might call attention to the obvious fact that language plays a central role in life, doing much to contribute to one's sense of identity and to determine which doors to opportunity will be open and which closed. Those who do well in life given the dominance of one language may find themselves cast off and seriously disadvantaged if a different language comes to prevail. And questions of prestige and pride arise here, just as they do in relation to political power, with a sense of humiliation as the lot of those whose language is scorned. Moreover, language is usually central to feelings of nationalism, and thus contributes to a sense of belonging that is so much prized. It is therefore understandable that people would want to preserve their language and assure it a place of respect if at all possible, and as a practical matter the measures necessary and desirable for this purpose can be taken more effectively on a communal than on a purely individualistic basis. Again one need not argue that the specific measures taken in Belgium to protect the two languages were the only possible ones, but that they responded to good moral claims seems clear. This means that the differential treatment provided for in the law should not be considered discriminatory.

INDIA

India illustrates in an extreme way the problem of equal treatment in a multilingual situation. According to the census of 1971, the largest language community, speaking Hindi, consisted of 154 million persons, or 28 percent of the population. The eleven next largest language communities ranged in size from 45 million (8 percent) down to 14 million (3 percent). Eighty-five percent of the population spoke one of the twelve leading languages, and the remaining 15 percent spoke a minimum of 269 more. (The number of other languages is much higher, but the census report gives statistics only on the 281 languages spoken by 5000 or more persons.) The 1961 census indicated that 93 percent of the population knew only their mother tongue; and it indicated that, of those knowing a second language, about 11 million knew English and 9 million knew Hindi.[19]

Like the United Nations, then, India faces a plethora of languages; and, as in the United Nations, a balancing of gains and costs leads everyone to the conclusion that the twelve leading languages (to say nothing of the 269-plus others) cannot have equal status in political life. A selection must occur—a selection that has confronted the Indians with a cruel dilemma ever since they achieved independence after World War II. To some at that time, the continued use of English meant a loss of self-respect, an acceptance of "a symbol of slavery." Gandhi himself took the view that "to get rid of the infatuation for

English is one of the essentials of *Swaraj*" (freedom), and he pressed "for banishing English as a cultural usurper as we successfully banished the political rule of the English usurper."[20]

But what indigenous language would substitute for English? Those who spoke Hindi had a ready answer, and in terms of the size of the various language communities everyone had to agree that Hindi had the strongest claim. But a decisive switch to Hindi would have given special status and prestige, together with concrete advantages, to one language community, implying mortification and concrete disadvantages for others. There was talk of a new imperialism, of an aggrandizement of one language community at the expense of the others.[21]

The problem was all the more difficult because of the lack of sensible criteria for selecting one or two indigenous languages in addition to Hindi. The Hindi community had 109 million more members than the second largest language community, but the second largest was not much larger than the third or the fourth or the fifth. Apart from the Hindi community, four others had between 38 and 45 million members, and five more had between 20 and 30 million.

Difficulties attending the selection of one or a few indigenous languages worked in favor of English despite sentiment against it. English could continue to be used without throwing the advantage so decisively one way or another in the rivalries of the domestic language communities. Moreover, the 2.5 percent of the population who knew English as a second language had a vested interest in maintaining its role; this gave them an advantage over the remaining 97.5 percent—including an advantage over fellow members of their own language community. They were already in the elite, and might or might not be able to maintain their status in the face of wider competition.

The result of the conflicting motives and pressures is that the constitution both reassures all language groups (and minorities) and makes a choice as to language. It reassures by specifying that "any section of citizens [with] a distinct language, script, or culture [has] the right to conserve the same." It also reassures by specifying that "all minorities, whether based on religion or language, shall have the right to establish and administer educational institutions of their own choice," and that in granting aid the state shall not discriminate against such institutions.[22]

At the same time, the constitution says both that Hindi is the "official language of the Union" and that the use of English for official purposes may continue—for fifteen years. Acting within the limits of the constitution, parliament later authorized the use of English indefinitely. Individual states are free to choose their own official language(s), and those that do not choose Hindi are by law free to insist that communication between them and the central government be not in Hindi but in English. Moreover, any non-Hindi state may veto the displacement of English by Hindi in connection with various activities of the central government.[23]

The arrangement differentiates, whether or not it should be called discriminatory. Those who know Hindi are favored, for they are not obliged to learn a second language in order to have a career in government, while others must. And those who know English have an advantage over those who do not. But in the situation that confronts India, what arrangement would distribute advantages and disadvantages equally without being prohibitively expensive? A three-language formula has been endorsed, partly with a view to making the burden of learning languages as great for the speakers of Hindi as for others. The different versions of the formula are all suggested by the possibility that those who achieve a certain level of education would all know not only Hindi and English but also a regional language. But the formula has not flourished for a variety of reasons, among them the cost and "the lack of motivation for the study of an additional modern Indian language in the Hindi areas as well as the resistance to the study of Hindi in some non-Hindi areas."[24] In at least some non-Hindi areas the determination to prevent Hindi from becoming dominant is strong.[25]

The problem of language figures not only in the operations of government but in recruitment into government service. Given the many languages, how can equal opportunity for employment in the civil service be assured? India has rejected the principle of quota representation for the different language communities.[26] It depends on civil service examinations ad-

ministered in English, which raises the question whether opportunities to learn English are equal. Pressures are strong to
administer the examinations in Hindi and in various regional
languages, implying inequality for those who do not speak any
of the languages selected.[27] The determination to prevent Hindi
from becoming dominant shows in the provisions of the Official
Languages Act that those in the civil service who know English
shall not be penalized if they do not also know Hindi.

The problem of language also figures in the very structure
of the state, for the question inevitably arises what the relationship should be between linguistic divisions and the boundaries of the provinces into which India is divided. The reasoning
that carried the day in the first years of independence was that
paramount emphasis must be given to making India a nation,
and that the establishment of linguistic provinces would not
promote this goal. Linguistic homogeneity might be considered
as a factor making for administrative convenience, but was not
to be considered as a value in its own right.[28] In any event,
full homogeneity would be impossible, for nowhere could linguistic provinces be formed with more than 70 to 80 percent
of the population speaking the same language.[29] Sizeable linguistic minorities everywhere were inevitable.

Some language groups were not appeased by these kinds of
considerations, and sporadically through the years boundaries
have been redrawn, and new provinces have been created, on
the basis of language. The Telegu-speaking state of Andhra
came into existence in 1953. Bombay was divided in 1960 between those who spoke Gujarati and those who spoke Marathi.
Nagaland came into existence in 1962. Punjab was divided in
1966, partly for linguistic and partly for religious reasons.[30]
And no one can be sure that fission by language has ended.
Whatever is done or not done, some kind of differentiation by
language is inevitable.

What of the language of instruction in the schools? The constitution of India says that "it shall be the endeavor of every
state and of every local authority to provide...instruction in
the mother tongue at the primary stage...." This seems to call
for the training of teachers and the preparation of teaching
materials in upwards of the 281 languages already referred

to—a gargantuan task, unlikely to be completed, especially since many languages exist only in oral form.[31] In fact, in the case of dozens and probably even hundreds of the minor languages, little has been done. Sophistry has it that these languages do not even count as "mother tongues."[32] Generally speaking, the regional languages have become the media of instruction at every level, from elementary school through the university.[33] This necessarily means unequal treatment for students from the smaller language communities—just as the choice of a few working languages in the United Nations means unequal treatment for those whose languages are not chosen.

Obviously, India's response to the language problem contrasts with that of Belgium. The contrast can be put most sharply by saying that India puts more thorough-going emphasis on the rights of minorities. Belgium, too, of course, prevents the Flemish majority from imposing its language on the rest of the population, but it rejects the idea of minority rights within the linguistic regions. India accepts pluralism everywhere, but Belgium wants to make and keep Flanders and Wallonia as homogeneous as possible.

THE UNITED STATES

According to a 1979 survey, persons in the United States 14 years old and over divide as follows with respect to mother tongue: English, 77 percent; Spanish, 4 percent; German, 3 percent; all other languages, 12 percent. This means that at least 19 percent of those 14 and over have a mother tongue other than English. (The mother tongue of 4 percent was not reported.)[34] Like almost all other countries, then, the United States faces questions concerning equal treatment as to language.

The main question concerns the use of language not in the home or in connection with private affairs but for public purposes—principally in connection with politics and government and in connection with education. Do those who speak English have a right to insist on a monopoly for English, or does respect for the right of equal treatment require recognition of the fact that some people, including some citizens, speak other languages? Do those who speak English have a group right to maintain the language? Do those who speak Spanish? How about those who speak one of the Indian languages?

Questions about language have arisen in connection with elections. For long the tendency was to hold, in effect, that only those who knew English could vote, but in the last two decades that tendency has been reversed. As recently as the 1960s, 20 states of the United States (scattered from Maine to Hawaii and from Georgia to Alaska) had literacy requirements for voting.[35] Thirteen of them specified that the requirement must be met in English. Five said nothing about language, apparently taking English for granted; a Wyoming court made this explicit, holding that the requirement of an ability to read meant an ability to read in English. As an alternative to English, Hawaii accepted Hawaiian, and Louisiana accepted the voter's native language.

Attacks on the test developed especially in the 1960s in conjunction with the movement against racial discrimination. All too often the test was used as a device to keep blacks from voting, and in addition it deprived members of foreign language minorities (Puerto Ricans in New York, for example) of their rights of political participation. Specifically for the purpose of enforcing the equal protection clause, Congress—in the Voting Rights Act of 1965—barred an English-language requirement in the case of those with six years of education in American-flag schools in which the predominant classroom language was other than English; the measure was for the benefit of the Puerto Ricans. The Supreme Court upheld the right of Congress to enact such legislation without itself interpreting the equal protection clause.[36]

In a companion case, two of the justices made it a point to declare that the equal protection clause alone, independently of any congressional action, forbids the distinction that New York was making between Spanish- and English-speaking citizens.[37] Similarly, the Supreme Court of California ruled that an English language requirement for voting denies equal protection; it rejected the claim that a knowledge of English could reasonably be required as a means of promoting more intelligent voting.[38] In 1970 Congress went farther, suspending the enforcement of literacy tests—and therefore of the language requirement—until 1975, and then in 1975 it prohibited them permanently.[39] Moreover, by 1975 half of the states with a literacy requirement had repealed it, and in others it was under attack.[40]

What the literacy and language test did was to give exclusive control over government to the English-speaking, permitting them to use government for their own advantage and for the disadvantage of others. It deprived others of an opportunity to hold government accountable. It left government without any compelling reason to tend to the interests of those who did not know English, even if they were citizens. It opened the way to favoritism for one group and neglect and oppression for the rest. It thus discriminated in such a way as to lead to more discrimination.[41]

Not only is the literacy/language requirement now prohibited, but the principle is established that elections shall be bilingual in districts where a language minority is of substantial size; that is, whenever anything is provided to the voters in English (e.g., notices, instructions, assistance, ballots), it must also be provided in the language of the minority. A few states have made their elections bilingual voluntarily (for example, New Mexico).[42] Others have done so because of orders from federal courts.[43] Now all must do so to conform with federal law. In 1975, finding that "voting discrimination against citizens of language minorities is pervasive and national in scope," Congress required bilingual elections in districts where more than 5 percent of the citizens of voting age are members of a single language minority, if their illiteracy rate (measured by failure to complete the fifth primary grade) is higher than the national illiteracy rate.[44] Five percent is also the figure that the courts have tended to adopt in deciding whether a language minority is substantial enough to justify a requirement that elections be bilingual; New Jersey, however, specifies 10 percent and California requires that bilingual election officials be recruited in those precincts with a non-English speaking voting age population of 3 percent or more.[45]

The congressional requirement is limited to a ten year period, but various considerations—most notably the court decisions based on the equal protection clause—make it highly unlikely that those who speak English will again restrict the suffrage to themselves. They never made a clear-cut claim to a group right to a political monopoly, and have now renounced tendencies that went in that direction. The right of the individual to equal treatment, regardless of language, prevails over any claim that the English-speaking group might theoretically assert to exclusive political control.

Elections aside, those who speak English come closer to asserting a group right—implicitly—in connection with other aspects of politics and government, and the necessities of the situation reinforce their attitudes. Whether or not legally required, a command of English is a bfoq for public employment, including employment in police and fire departments, and the holding of elective office. Civil service examinations are given in English only. Since court proceedings are in English, knowledge of it is prerequisite to jury service. Courts do, however, use interpreters in case a defendant is unable to follow the proceedings in English, and federal funds are available for improvements in this respect.[46] As a general rule, government documents are in English only. A notable exception exists in New Mexico, where the Spanish surnamed population comprises 28 percent of the total. There, if 75 percent or more of the population served by a local government is in one language community, certain public documents are printed solely in the language of that community; otherwise, they are printed in both English and Spanish.[47]

Obviously, the English-speaking in the United States have advantages in government and politics, but the balancing test and the principle of the bfoq caution against a general judgment that the practices followed are discriminatory.

Language policies in the public schools of the United States have varied, which is not surprising in view of the fact that choices have been made at the local and state levels as well as at the national level. The rule that is winning out, however, is that (except perhaps in Indian schools) instruction is in English. Pupils whose command of English is deficient are entitled to special measures to help them remove the deficiency, which gives evidence of a concern for the right of individuals to equal treatment. Moreover, bilingual and bicultural instruction is endorsed to a limited extent, which is suggestive of a recognition of the right of a group to preserve its culture. But the dominance of English is the overwhelming fact, and those who speak English are seeing to it that it remains the overwhelming fact.

Through most of the nineteenth century, choices as to language (in the states, as opposed to the territories) were made in the main at the local level. Although English was naturally the overwhelming favorite, a number of communities made other languages (notably German) the language of instruction, and a number chose to provide bilingual instruction. Contemplating this record, Kloss credits the country with relatively benign policies.[48] The record is different, however, with respect to linguistic groups other than those coming from Western Europe, and Leibowitz explains the difference in terms of the political and social acceptability of the language group in question:

If the group is in some way (usually because of race, color or religion) viewed as irreconcilably alien to the prevailing concept of American culture, the United States has imposed harsh restrictions on its language practices; if not so viewed, study in the native language has gone largely unquestioned or even encouraged.[49]

The harsh restrictions show up in the treatment of the Indians, the Mexican-Americans, the Puerto Ricans, the Oriental and other inhabitants of Hawaii, and the Filipinos.

Policies toward the Indians were long oppressive. An Indian Peace Commission recommended in 1868 that schools be established which Indian children would be required to attend: "their barbarous dialects would be blotted out and the English language substituted."[50] The federal government followed the recommendation, and when it later developed that Indian children kept on using their native tongues, the government took them away from home and family and sent them to off-reservation boarding schools designed to acculturate them to white civilization, naturally with English as the language of instruction.

Similarly, the Mexican-Americans got little respect. Their difficulties became serious after the Anglos achieved dominance in the Southwest and insisted in effect on the principle of territoriality. California adopted a law in 1870 requiring that "all schools...be taught in the English language." New Mexico did the same in 1891, and when Congress admitted New Mexico to statehood the enabling act specified that "school shall be conducted in English." If children arrived at school knowing only Spanish, they were nevertheless to be taught in English only.[51]

The Puerto Ricans had a comparable experience once they came under American jurisdiction. The only question was at what point instruction in English-only would begin—whether in the first grade or at the beginning of secondary education or at some point in between. Different choices were made at different times. President Roosevelt took note of the problem in 1937, declaring it "an indispensable part of American policy that the coming generation of American citizens in Puerto Rico grow up with complete facility in the English tongue. It is...the official language of our country." Only in 1949, after Puerto Rico obtained a greater degree of self-government, did Spanish become the language of instruction not only at the primary but also at the secondary level.[52]

In the light of the above, it is not surprising that Congress prescribed English as the language of instruction in both Hawaii (prior to statehood) and the Philippines, insisting on the requirement in the Philippines even in the years after independence was promised but before it became effective.[53]

Further, the early indulgence toward the languages of Western Europe declined toward the turn of the century and through the period of World War I. By 1903, 14 states had enacted laws requiring English as the language of instruction in both public and private schools, and by 1923 the number had increased to 34.[54] In some cases the laws imposed criminal penalties for teaching in a language other than English, but the Supreme Court declared them unconstitutional on the ground that they denied liberty without due process; at the same time, according to the Court, the power of the state to require that all schools "give instructions" in English was not questioned.[55]

Sharp changes in American policies are in process, stimulated by greater sensitivity to questions of equality and discrimination that has developed in recent years. The changes might have come entirely on the basis of the equal protection clause of the fourteenth amendment, but in fact its requirements have been supplemented by statutes. The first of the relevant statutes is the Civil Rights Act of 1964, Title VI of which specifies that:

No person in the United States shall, on the ground of race, color, or national origin, be excluded from participation in, be denied the benefits of, or be subjected to discrimination under any program or activity receiving Federal financial assistance.

The reference to national origin is in point here, for differences of national origin sometimes imply differences of language. Whether or not it was the intent at the time, the provision has been interpreted to forbid a strict application of the principle of territoriality—that is, to forbid an English-only policy in teaching students with an English language deficiency. This is indicated by guidelines that the Department of Health, Education and Welfare (HEW) issued in 1970:

Where inability to speak and understand the English language excludes national origin-minority group children from effective participation in the educational program offered by a school district, the district must take affirmative steps to rectify the language deficiency in order to open its instruction program to these students.[56]

I should acknowledge that the proper interpretation of the requirements of both the equal protection clause and Title VI has been clouded by judicial decisions that put stress on purpose or intent.[57] But given the principle that a governmental agency can be assumed to intend the natural and obvious consequence of a policy that it adopts, an English-only policy is surely ruled out in the presence of students who do not know English.

Congress took an additional step in adopting the Equal Educational Opportunities Act of 1974, which includes the rule that no educational agency of a state "shall deny equal educational opportunity to an individual on account of his or her race, color, sex, or national origin by [failing] to take appropriate action to overcome language barriers that impede equal participation by...students in its instruction program."[58] This language avoids the question of purpose or intent. It clearly indicates that simply an act of omission may deny equal educational opportunity—that is, a failure to take "appropriate action." Again the focus is obviously on the individual person with a language deficiency, and the goal endorsed is the removal, or at least the reduction, of the deficiency. There is no suggestion that groups speaking a language other than English have a right to preserve that language. As one court has put it, "Congress has determined that a school system which fails to overcome language barriers that handicap its students denies them equal educational opportunity."[59] Such students are to be put into a position to play a role in the activities of an English-speaking community.

In 1968 Congress took still another step when it enacted a Bilingual Education Act, and since then approximately a dozen states have followed suit; moreover, Congress renewed the Act in 1974, declaring explicitly that the object is to promote equality and offering grants-in-aid to support state programs. As noted above, a program of bilingual and bicultural education might be evidence of a concern for the preservation of the culture in question, and thus might suggest recognition of a group right. But it would be a mistake to interpret American practices in this way. Concern for the individual, not concern for the group, lies behind the adoption of such programs, just as it lies behind the adoption of the rule concerning the reduction or removal of English language deficiencies. Moreover, bilingual and bicultural programs are everywhere limited to only a few years, the expectation being that by the end of those few years the students will be in a position to continue their education in English. It is obviously not the thought that any constitutional right exists to bilingual and bicultural education, for a constitutional right would hold in all the states (not simply in those that enact the necessary legislation) and at every level of the educational system.[60]

A qualifier should be added to these statements about group

rights, for a group right of a sort is assumed—the right of the whole population to be prudent in the use of tax money. The right shows up in connection with the question of the number of students who have English language deficiencies or who qualify for bilingual and bicultural education. The relevant statement of the Commission on Civil Rights is as follows:

It should be noted that non-English speaking students' right to equal educational opportunity does not vary with their number in a school system. The constitutional principle is not invalidated because there may be but a single or just a few non-English speaking students attending a particular school. Schools must still take some measures to assure that such students have access to the educational curriculum. Numbers are important, however, in determining the most appropriate program.[61]

At the same time, it might be noted that the HEW guidelines of 1970, mentioned above, were addressed to "School Districts with More than Five Percent National Origin Minority Group Children," implying that the guidelines were designed only for such school districts and leaving it unclear what guidelines or rules might be applicable in school districts in which those speaking a language other than English comprise less than five percent of the total. State legislation providing for bilingual instruction commonly specifies that 20 or more students in the same school district must be of limited English-speaking ability in order to justify such instruction, some specifying that the 20 must be at the same grade level.[62]

The United States has thus given two different answers to the question of what constitutes equal and nondiscriminatory treatment with respect to the language of instruction. The first answer, and long the dominant answer, is that the principle of territoriality suffices. If Indians, Mexican-Americans, Puerto Ricans, Orientals, and Filipinos are all taught in English, they are all treated alike and so are not discriminated against, even in those school districts containing English-speaking students who of course are taught in their native tongue. The second answer, given in the Civil Rights Act of 1964 and subsequently, is that those with English language deficiencies must be given special instruction, whether it be in English as a second language or in full-fledged bilingual programs.[63]

The language policies of the United States reflect the individualism of the constitution and of the liberal tradition. The fact suggests a comment and a question. The comment is that individualism in the matter of language is no doubt rendered acceptable in part because those who speak English are secure in their predominance. Except perhaps in some localities, their status and pride are not at risk, and generosity toward the weak costs relatively little. If the risks and costs were greater, the same policies might or might not be followed. At crucial points in the nineteenth century, when more nearly equal status was sought for German, the speakers of English voiced firm and decisive opposition.[64] And, as already indicated, Congress made sure that Spanish did not prevail in the Southwest. Should Puerto Rico be admitted as the fifty-first state, English would still be overwhelmingly dominant, of course; but pressures for greater recognition of Spanish and the Spanish-speaking community would no doubt develop. The United States might well experience difficulties comparable to those of Canada, where the effort first was to make the operations of government fully bilingual and where, in more recent years, the emphasis in the province of Quebec has been on exclusive official status for French and on a greater degree of political autonomy.

It is interesting to ask about the implications if Congress, or possibly the Supreme Court, were to take the stand that a common language is a compelling public interest. Perhaps this would make no difference, for English already gets great emphasis. Even so, if the focus were on the nation and its interests rather than on the individual and his circumstance or preference, different judgments might be made, raising difficult questions about equal treatment and discrimination.

OTHER ILLUSTRATIONS

Let it be noted once more that no effort is made here to be comprehensive. The language problems and practices of many other countries might be described. Switzerland might get special mention both because of its linguistic and ethnic mix and because its problems and practices have already been so thoroughly described and explored.[65] Canada is mentioned above, and the policies of both the central government and of the provinces might get major attention here. For example, in 1981 the Legislative Assembly of New Brunswick enacted the following measure:

1. ...[T]he English linguistic community and the French linguistic community are officially recognized within the context of one province for all purposes to which the authority of the Legislature of New Brunswick extends, and the equality of status and the equal rights and privileges of these two communities are affirmed.
2. The Government of New Brunswick shall ensure protection of the equality of status and the equal rights and privileges of the official linguistic communities and in particular their right to distinct institutions within which cultural, educational and social activities may be carried on.[66]

New Brunswick thus makes explicit what is left largely implicit in legislation adopted elsewhere in Canada. In a legal sense, the language communities of New Brunswick are corporate entities and not simply aggregations of persons. Implicitly a measure of self-determination is conceded to them, a right of the communities to maintain their culture being intimated. The legal right granted corresponds to the moral right asserted in the international covenants on human rights.

CONCLUSION

The fact that people speak different languages leads to some of the most difficult questions concerning equal and nondiscriminatory treatment. Differences of race, sex, and religion can in many circumstances be literally ignored, but if communication is to occur in words, differences of language cannot be. Some kind of differentiation is inevitable, raising the question whether the differentiation is discriminatory.

Basic to the answer is the proposition that rights are not absolute. In decisions about language (as well as in many other kinds of decisions), rights and interests of several kinds are likely to be at stake, calling for action in different directions. Various legitimate claims must be balanced off against each other, and a judgment must be made as to which is overriding or what kind of adjustment is most appropriate. The need for this can be stated as a rule: that rights are to be interpreted reasonably, with due consideration for other rights or interests that may be affected. Danger lurks in the rule, for it deprives rights of an imperative quality and opens the way to erosion. But to treat rights as absolute would lead to impossible contradictions.

The question is whether principles exist that give helpful guidance, and the answer is that they do. We will be looking for them through the book. One was suggested in Chapter 1, and is reinforced in the present chapter. It is that individuals are not alone in possessing rights and interests. Groups (corporate actors or the equivalent) possess them too. We are accustomed to this in connection with the state, for it is everywhere acknowledged as a corporate actor with rights and interests. What is not so generally acknowledged is that other kinds of groups may have rights too; and if this is conceded, the possibilities of conflict obviously increase.

This leads to a second principle: that the costs and gains—the consequences of different courses of action—must be assessed, and a judgment must be made in the light of the assessment. The easiest situation is one in which the factors on one side of this balance are obvious and immediate and the factors on the other side are hypothetical and putative.

The arrangement described for the Aaland Islands illustrates the situation: the islanders can safeguard their culture by excluding outsiders as purchasers of real estate, but the outsiders lose nothing except an abstract right. The principal effect on them is to discourage a choice that relatively few would ever think of making anyway; and those few are left with alternatives that also appear satisfactory: they can buy property elsewhere. Moreover, any great influx of outsiders would have a visible social impact, changing a culture, whereas the denial to citizens scattered over Finland of an opportunity to hold property on the Aaland Islands has no social impact at all.

Since the gains are concrete and the costs are hypothetical, the case is good for concluding that the arrangement is justifiable.

Approximately the same pattern of thought applies to the Belgian arrangement dividing cabinet posts half and half between French- and Dutch-speaking ministers. The gains are obvious and immediate: political dissatisfaction that might readily produce a crisis is reduced if not eliminated. More generally, members of both communities (and especially the Walloons, who are a numerical minority) gain psychological satisfaction, for the arrangement symbolizes equality of status and respect, and assures each community against domination by the other; and members of both communities are assured that their rights and interests will be considered. The costs are hypothetical and putative, though perhaps not so markedly so as in the Aaland Islands case. Perhaps the average level of ability in the cabinet is reduced. Perhaps the principle of treatment according to personal merit is somewhat undermined. Surely some political careers are promoted and others handicapped, though the individuals involved may or may not be aware of the fact that linguistic considerations tip decisions that would go the other way if merit alone counted. These gains and costs cannot be reliably calculated, but surely the judgment that the gains outweigh the costs is plausible.

The problem is more difficult when the determination of the community to preserve its language leads to a requirement that the language be used for all public purposes, including instruction in the schools. This deprives individuals of a choice, and ignores their language skills. The problem arises in so many kinds of circumstances that generalization is difficult. The common attitude is that people who choose to migrate into an area where the language is foreign to them have no right to special consideration; they should either learn the new language or accept the consequences. The case for this is especially strong when their migration threatens to expand the territory of one language community at the expense of another. The danger to peace and harmony (that is, the danger to a legitimate collective goal or compelling public interest) may then be so great as to justify adamant insistence that the traditional language of the place prevail for public purposes. Language rights of the individuals who move give way to the communal goal of maintaining territorial integrity. And if this is the rule for border regions between linguistic groups, it is likely to have to be the rule for linguistic regions in their entirety, as in Belgium.

The absence of a territorial issue does not necessarily mean the absence of a problem. What of immigrants who form communities as enclaves within the country into which they move, maintaining their language and customs? If the answer is that they should accept the implications of their decision, what of their children and grandchildren—native-born citizens? It would surely be wrong to make the dominant language the language of instruction in the schools if they do not know that language, and it would surely be wrong to let them go through school without learning the dominant language, for they would then be handicapped for life. They must at least be taught the dominant language as a second language, and perhaps they should get bilingual and bicultural education, though this might become prohibitively expensive in the upper educational levels.

As for public purposes outside the schools, two considerations deserve emphasis: numbers make a difference, and so does the importance of the language policy to the fate of individuals. Given the greater number of Hispanics in New Mexico than in North Dakota, it should be expected that language policies in the two states would differ. And given the prospect that the fate of an individual is more likely to be affected by a criminal trial in which he is the defendant than by debates in Congress, the language policy relating to judicial proceedings can well differ from the language policy governing the printing of the *Congressional Record*.

Admittedly, these formulations are in general terms, and do not point unerringly to specific decisions. Problems such as those faced in the United Nations and in India are particularly intractable—where many languages have a good claim to status but where the costs prohibit giving status—or at least equal status—to all of them. Fortuitous circumstances may help resolve the problem, as in India where the gap is so great between the size of the group speaking Hindi and the size of the next largest groups and where Britain bequeathed English as the *lingua franca* of the elite. And fortuitous circumstances are likely to be supplemented by more or less arbitrary judgments and by considerations of power.

3

Distinction as to Religion

Problems relating to religion are almost as ubiquitous as problems relating to language. As in Chapter 2, treatment of them will be organized largely on a country by country basis, but here we will do it within a broader topical framework. We will focus first on formal arrangements for the representation of religious communities in government and then on arrangements for the extension of governmental support or cooperation to them. Formal arrangements for representation raise questions about discrimination because they make individuals eligible or ineligible for political positions depending on the religion to which they adhere; and the extension of support or cooperation raises similar questions because the cooperation and support go to some religious communities and not to others.

REPRESENTATION FOR RELIGIOUS COMMUNITIES IN GOVERNMENT

A number of countries require the head of the state to be a member of a specified religious community, and a smaller number treat religious communities as units for purposes of representation.

Britain is among the countries in which a favored religious community is assured that one of its members will be head of the state, for no one is eligible to wear the Crown unless he or she is willing to take communion with the Church of England.

The Church of England and all of its members thus have status and prestige denied to all others, which is discrimination on a grand scale. And discrimination against a few members of the royal family is possible in that a member otherwise eligible to wear the Crown may be rendered ineligible solely for religious reasons. The Scandinavian countries follow a similar rule, and so do the many countries where Islam is established.

Now obviously these states did not intend to condemn their own practices when they accepted the Charter rule requiring the promotion of human rights without distinction as to religion or when they accepted (as some of them have done) the rule of the Covenant on Civil and Political Rights that all persons are to enjoy the equal protection of the laws "without distinction of any kind, such as...religion...." The same comment no doubt applies to the draft Declaration on the Elimination of All Forms of Intolerance and of Discrimination Based on Religion or Belief, approved by the United Nations Commission on Human Rights in 1981. It specifies that "no one shall be subject to discrimination by any State, institution, group of persons or person on grounds of religion or other beliefs," and it goes on to require all states to "take effective measures to prevent and eliminate discrimination on the grounds of religion...."[1] For that matter, we might note parenthetically that monarchical countries presumably do not intend to condemn a hereditary rule of succession when they vote against distinction as to birth. Nevertheless, an inconsistency obviously exists. The outcome of historic struggles between religious communities was a favored political position for the winner; and that favored position survives despite the more recent growth of an insistence that everyone is entitled to equal and nondiscriminatory treatment regardless of religion.

In some countries, distinction as to religion in political life extends well beyond the office of head of the state. Colonial India and Ceylon, Cyprus, the Maldive Republic, and West Germany provide salient illustrations.

I mention colonial India and Ceylon because religious communalism is generally associated with them. When Britain established legislative councils in its dependencies, its practice was to see to the representation of "interests" in them—religious, racial, linguistic, commercial, and so on.[2] Given this precedent, the step was short to the establishment of communal electorates when elective bodies were established. In India the step was taken at the request of spokesmen for the Muslims, who complained that as a minority (14 percent of the population) they were unable to elect candidates in competition with the Hindus. Just as the whites of Rhodesia spoke through the 1970s of majority rule as black majority rule, so the Muslims spoke of Hindu majority rule. The Muslims and Hindus were all subject to Britain, so their communal rivalries were contained; but as between the two groups, the Hindus were dominant, and the Muslims resented the fact. Their solution was to delimit electorates on a communal rather than on a strictly geographical basis, with each communal group assured a quota of seats. Britain accepted the solution, making a comparable arrangement in Ceylon.[3] And in some legislative bodies Britain went farther, accepting the rule that "no bill or resolution concerning a community could be passed if three-fourths of the representatives of that community were opposed to it."[4]

In providing for the representation of religious communities, Britain obviously shifted away from individualism as a basis for political life and it shifted away from the idea of "majority rule." It implicitly took the view that the communities were entitled to representation, and that differentiation between individuals could appropriately occur to make this possible. The rationale for the policy is similar to the rationale for the division of cabinet posts in Belgium between the two main language communities. The underlying assumptions are that the society is permanently and deeply divided into more or less hostile elements; that people have little or no choice about their relationship to the political process, this being fixed by their ethnic affiliation; that minorities are therefore permanent minorities, doomed by "majority rule" to be excluded from government and left unable to protect or promote their interests by political means; and that, if permitted to do so, the winners can therefore make government their tool, advancing their own interests and neglecting, oppressing, or even destroying minorities.

A contrast exists when such cleavages as exist in the society are cross-cutting, so that those who win politically share some kinds of interests with those who lose; when individuals on the losing side are free, if they wish, to shift to the winning side; when a reasonable expectation exists that those who lose now may win later; and when those who lose are nevertheless included somehow in government, as in the committees of the Congress of the United States.

Britain's adoption of communalism in India and Ceylon is often denounced as evidence of a divide and rule policy, but whatever may be the truth about that charge, a more justifiable motive may well have operated: Britain may genuinely have sought to assure due consideration for the rights and interests of minorities.

I cite communalism in colonial India and Ceylon more as a significant fact than as a recommendation. Though communalism persisted and was expanded in these colonies, it was also deplored. Even British commissions that recommended the continuation and extension of the system deplored it. The much-quoted statement of the Donoughmore commission with respect to Ceylon was that

communal representation is, as it were, a canker on the body politic, eating deeper and deeper into the vital energies of the people, breeding self-interest, suspicion and animosity, poisoning the new growth of political consciousness, and effectively preventing the development of a national or corporate spirit....[T]here can be no hope of binding together the diverse elements of the population in a realisation of their common kinship and an acknowledgment of common obligations to the country of which they are all citizens so long as the system of communal representation, with all its disintegrating influences, remains a distinctive feature of the constitution.[5]

The commission took the view that "communal representation is least desirable when on a religious basis," for religious groups tend to subdivide, and once the principle of separate representation is accepted, each division comes forth with its separate claim.[6] Nevertheless, communalism continued in both India and Ceylon as long as the British were there; and in a sense it got its ultimate expression in the demand of the Muslims of Pakistan for independence within a separate sovereign state.

Religious communalism is also identified especially with Lebanon. During the period of the mandate, the French High Commissioner issued a decree legally recognizing the historic religious communities as corporate personalities and accepting their spiritual leaders as their political spokesmen.[7] He required the inclusion in the constitution of an article calling for the equitable representation of the religious communities in public employment and in the cabinet (Article 95).[8] (At the same time, the constitution specifies in Article 12 that "every Lebanese shall have the right to public employment without distinction except on the basis of merit and competence according to the conditions established by law.")

In connection with the gaining of independence, Lebanese leaders themselves concluded a National Pact accepting the principle that the various religious communities should each have its quota of representatives in the government. The census of 1932 had shown that the population divided between Christians and others at a ratio of six to five, and that ratio became the basis for allocating political positions. To permit adherence to the ratio, the number of members in the legislature of independent Lebanon has always been a multiple of eleven.[9]

In the ninety-nine member Parliaments of 1960 and 1964 the Maronites were allotted twenty seats, the Greek Orthodox eleven, the Greek Catholics six, the Armenian Orthodox four, the Armenian Catholics, Protestants and Christian minorities one apiece for a Christian total of fifty-four. The forty-five non-Christian seats were distributed as follows: Sunnites twenty, Shiites nineteen, and Druzes six.... The formula, furthermore, provides that the President of the Republic be a Maronite, the Prime Minister a Sunnite, the Speaker of the Chamber of Deputies a Shiite, and the Deputy Speaker and Deputy Prime Minister Greek Orthodox. Cabinet portfolios are carefully distributed among Christians and non-Christians, and key ministries are reserved for particular sects.... Furthermore every sect has a fixed share of important administrative posts.[10]

The civil war that began in Lebanon in 1975 makes it obvious that the arrangement was frail. Among other things, no provision was included for a reallocation of political posts as the distribution of the population changed. In fact the issue was so delicate that the Lebanese did not dare to take a new count of the number belonging to each sect, but the prevailing view is that the Muslims came to be relatively underrepresented. The breakdown of the arrangement is proof of its shortcomings; but it is not proof that a strictly individualistic, non-communal arrangement would have fared better. It may be fatal to organize government according to sectarian divisions, but it may also be fatal to refuse to take such divisions into account.

When Cyprus obtained independence in 1960, 78 percent of the population were Greek-speaking and Greek Orthodox, 18 percent were Turkish-speaking and Muslim, and the remaining 4 percent divided into various linguistic and religious groups. Members of the different communities were interspersed over the island. Individual villages or areas might be either Greek or Turkish, but no line could be drawn dividing the island geographically into Greek and Turkish parts. The two main communities were historic enemies. Distrust and animosity prevailed between them, exacerbated by the presence of Greece and Turkey in the wings.

Liberal democratic theory, and the provisions of the Charter banning distinction as to language or religion, suggest that Britain should have conferred a democratic constitution on Cyprus providing for the equal protection of the laws but doing little other than that to take the divisions of the society into account. This would have been welcome to the Greeks, for their numbers would have enabled them to dominate—either within Cyprus alone or within a larger Greece had *Enosis* occurred. Those in a majority can be expected to support the idea of majority rule. But the situation in Cyprus was comparable to situations in West Africa that led Lewis to decry majority rule and plead for coalition government, as indicated in Chapter 1. For that matter the situation was comparable to the situation in the United States during the period of Jim Crow, when the whites found "majority rule" so congenial to their racial interests.

Turkish attitudes on the acceptability of such prospects can easily be imagined. Some members of the Turkish community even objected to the use of the concepts *majority* and *minority* in Cyprus on the ground that these terms implied the existence of a whole that could be so divided; from their point of view, the population of Cyprus consisted of two separate communities entitled to equal treatment, like sovereign states.[11]

The constitution that Britain in fact conferred reflected negotiations with Greece and Turkey. It starts right out defining "the Greek community" and "the Turkish community," indicating that the smaller minorities, as groups, should affiliate with one or another of these communities and thus gain status and rights. It provides for the registration of voters on separate Greek and Turkish electoral rolls. According to it, those on the Greek roll elect the president and those on the Turkish roll the vice president. Ministerial posts, seats in the House of Representatives, and posts in the civil service (including the gendarmerie and police) are all allocated communally on a 7:3 ratio. In contrast, the ratio applicable to the armed forces is 6:4. In the House of Representatives, concurrent majorities of the Greeks and Turks who vote must be obtained for any measure imposing duties or taxes; in other words, each community has a veto. The High Court of Justice consists of two Greeks, one Turk, and one neutral person with two votes—the neutral person being nominated jointly by the Greek president and the Turkish vice president. Each community elects a Communal Chamber with the power to tax, exercising authority "in all religious, educational, cultural and teaching questions and questions of personal status" as well as questions "where the interests and institutions are of a purely communal nature...." The five largest towns have parallel municipal governments, one for Greeks and one for Turks, with coordinating bodies to supervise activities that need to be carried on jointly.

Much more quickly than in Lebanon the arrangements in Cyprus broke down. They lasted only three years. I do not mention them to illustrate success. Rather, I mention them to illustrate an extremely difficult problem—the problem of what to do when those participating in a political system are divided into distinct communities that are highly self-conscious and hostile to each other. When the people in any society attach great importance to ethnic differences, it becomes absurd to say that in connection with arrangements for government these differences should be ignored. No rule prohibiting discrimination is going to prevent individual voters from discriminating when they go into the polling booth, and to ignore this is to concede a political monopoly to whatever ethnic group commands a plurality of the votes. Other ethnic groups are then likely to be done in.

The method of seeking to handle the problem in Cyprus was to assign status and rights to ethnic communities as such. The fact that this happened is plain. No question arises of individuals having rights that they delegated to the community as a collective entity. The collective entity is treated as a right-and-duty-bearing unit whose existence does not depend on the identity of the specific individuals composing it. It continues as new members are born into the community and old members die off. Moreover, the constitution implicitly recognizes that treatment of the communities as right-and-duty-bearing units entails "discrimination" against individuals. It specifies that "every person shall enjoy all the rights and liberties provided for in this constitution without any...discrimination...on the ground of his community,...religion, language,...or on any ground whatsoever, unless there is express provision to the contrary in this constitution." The assumption is that if rights for the community mean discrimination among individuals depending on their membership, the discrimination is beyond constitutional challenge. I would myself rather say that differentiation among individuals should not be considered discriminatory when it is occasioned by the justifiable assignment of rights to a collective entity.

Both the Council of Europe and the General Assembly of the United Nations have recognized that the Cypriot constitution attributes rights to the communities. A resolution of the Council of Europe, after speaking of a certain right of "any individual" in Cyprus, goes on to speak of "other rights belonging to the communities...."[12] And a resolution of the General Assembly, after the invasion of Cyprus by the armed forces of Turkey, calls for "negotiations between the representatives of the two communities, to be conducted freely on an equal footing...with a view to reaching [an] agreement based on their fundamental and legitimate rights."[13] These resolutions reflect the view that any settlement reached must be acceptable to both sides. No settlement is to be imposed that would permit one side to dominate the other. Rights of persons to equal treatment are adjusted to the right of each of the communities to protect its communal interests.

After the Turkish occupation of the northern portion of the island, a sorting of the population occurred, Turks moving into the portion controlled by Turkey and Greeks moving out; and in 1983 the Turks carried communalism to the ultimate point by declaring themselves to be a separate sovereign state.

The Maldive Republic offers another illustration of religious communalism. Its constitution requires that the president be not only a Muslim but also a member of the Sunni sect; and it imposes the same requirement for ministers in the cabinet. Members of the Citizens' Majlis (parliament) must also be Muslims, but in this connection the reference to the Sunni sect does not appear. Obviously, those who formulated the constitution simply ignored the question of discrimination against individuals. They wanted to make sure that Muslims had a political monopoly. They said nothing about freedom of religion. In fact the original constitution included a requirement, subsequently deleted, that "every citizen" must learn "to recite the Holy Quran."

The Iranian constitution of 1907 included similar requirements. The Shah was obliged to "profess and propagate" the true Jaifariya doctrine. Only Muslims could serve in the cabinet. One Jew, one Christian, and one Zoroastrian, who were "sound in their respective beliefs," could represent their communities in parliament, but all other members had to be Muslim. Apostates from "the orthodox religion of Islam" were denied the vote.

I see no justification for the arrangements in either the Maldive Republic or in Iran. They do not protect the weak. They do not give the weak a means of holding government accountable or inducing government to be considerate of their interests. Rather they guarantee and perhaps accentuate the political power of the most numerous groups, groups that have no need for special protection. They therefore classify as discriminatory.

Lest it appear that religious communalism occurs only in third world countries, the Federal Republic of Germany might be noted. Before World War II, Protestants were preponderant in the German government, including the civil and military services, just as they were preponderant in the population of the country. But in the truncated post-war Federal Republic the distribution of the population is more nearly equal, and Catholics are a majority in the political party that has been dominant during many of the post-war years—the Christian Democratic Union (CDU). Emphasizing religious concerns and wanting to promote Christian unity in politics, they tend to think of confessional groups and not of individuals as the units of representation both in the party itself and in the government. In both they have sought fair representation, which generally means equal representation, for the two main confessions. In the government after 1949,

confessional parity at the top level was relatively easy to establish and was popularly accepted with little difficulty. The chancellor was of one confession and the president of another; the cabinet was evenly balanced, and a minister of one confession had a state secretary of another. The presidents of the eleven federal courts and the judges of the federal constitutional courts were kept in confessional near-balance.

The CDU had more difficulty establishing balance in the hith-erto overwhelmingly Protestant civil service, but by the middle 1960s it had substantially achieved its goal.[14]

The CDU pushed for confessional parity despite a constitu-tional injunction that "enjoyment of civil and political rights [and] eligibility for public office...shall be independent of re-ligious denomination. No one may suffer any disadvantage by reason of his adherence or non-adherence to a denomination or ideology." Still another provision of the constitution specifies that "no one may be prejudiced or favored because of...his faith...." Thus the constitution seems to reject the possibility that religious communities might be regarded as aggregations or entities entitled to representation. Nevertheless, this is how the CDU has regarded them, and its view can be endorsed or condemned depending on how deep and significant religious divisions in the population are judged to be. At least the CDU limited itself to a demand for parity and did not seek a monopoly for one religious group.

In the United States religion is clearly one of the factors influencing nominations and elections and influencing the president and others who have appointive offices to fill. During most of American history, Protestants have seen to it that only Protestants were elected to the presidency. A Catholic broke through the barrier in 1960. A Jew might or might not be able to do the same. In connection with the Supreme Court, the common reference is to the question of a Catholic or a Jewish seat, the unspoken assumption being that the appointment of Protestants is the rule to which exceptions are made. In elections, political parties concern themselves with the problem of a "balanced" ticket, meaning that they take into account considerations in addition to the personal merits of individuals; among other things, a "balanced" ticket takes religious differences into account.

Differing appraisals can be made of practices in the Federal Republic and in the United States. If a purely individualistic view is taken, the practices can be condemned, for concern for religion may lead to the selection of the less well qualified person for a given position. And if religion is genuinely insignificant in relation to government, or if cross-cutting cleavages cancel out its significance, the individualistic view should prevail. But the more significant religion is, the more attention to it is justified. The search for some kind of balance is a kind of affirmative action, an effort to compensate for tendencies toward discrimination that might otherwise prevail. Far from accentuating the power of the most numerous group, it works in the other direction. And the other direction is less likely to lead to abuse—more likely to lead to the equal enjoyment of human rights.

GOVERNMENTAL SUPPORT FOR, OR COOPERATION WITH, RELIGIOUS COMMUNITIES

Questions about discrimination and about the interrelationships between the rights of individuals and the rights of groups are raised not only by arrangements assuring certain religious communities a role in governmental affairs. They are also raised by the status and rights accorded to them for the conduct of their own affairs. The questions come up in connection with governmental support for specifically religious activities, in connection with education, and in connection with prohibitions of proselytism.

Religious Activities

The Federal Republic of Germany and Malaysia provide illustrations of governmental support for religious activities.

In the Federal Republic, almost 97 percent of the population formally belong to one of the two main denominations—about 51 percent to the Evangelical church and about 46 percent to the Catholic.[15] The government registers children as church members at birth, and they are thereafter officially considered as members unless they formally resign, which few do. The two main churches are corporate bodies under public law; and the constitution says that other religious societies must be granted like status upon application, if their constitution and the number of their members assure their permanence. Those recognized as corporate bodies are authorized to tax their members, and the government collects the taxes on their behalf. For that matter, financial relationships between them and the government are close in other ways, government subsidies being extended for a variety of purposes. The government provides for the education of the clergy. It appoints some ecclesiastical officials and concurs in the appointment of others. In such cases the officials "are considered civil servants and are paid by the state.... The state also pays in part for the construction and upkeep of a bishop's residence and even some of his entertainment allowance."[16] Both the federal and the state governments make what they call treaties with the two churches concerning their "joint responsibilities." These responsibilities relate mainly to social welfare, where state and church are "partners."[17] The state grants money for programs that its partner administers.

Earlier, in describing special measures to assure the representation of religious communities in government, I offered a justification: the measures make it less likely that the interests of the religious community will be persistently ignored or neglected—less likely that government will be regularly biased against it. Nothing comparable can be said on behalf of the support and cooperation that the state extends to certain churches, for the presumed object is to strengthen them; and discrimination occurs. Some churches are given a status and get support that the others do not enjoy; the state collects taxes from some persons but not from others depending on whether they hold membership in a church that is a corporate body under public law; and the tax rate differs depending on the church. Further, German practices raise questions about freedom of religion, for some of the subsidies that go to the churches come from general tax funds, which means that taxpayers have no choice but to suppport a religious activity: they are not free to withhold support from religion. At the same time, it should be acknowledged that the burdens associated with the discrimination are light. Additional churches can become corporate bodies under public law if they choose to apply; individuals can withdraw from their church if they choose; and differences in the treatment of taxpayers are minor.

Although some of the arrangements in the Federal Republic are unique to it, others have counterparts elsewhere. In Malaysia, for example, Islam is officially the national religion, and both the federal and the state governments support it. The constitution specifies that "no person shall be compelled to pay any tax the proceeds of which are *specially* allocated in whole or in part for the purpose of a religion other than his own" (italics supplied), but this does not prevent the use of public funds raised by taxes not especially allocated.

In 1957 about 4.6 per cent of state expenditures went for the support of Islam, the total doubling about five years later. In addition, the Federal Government has invested large sums of money for the construction of mosques and prayer houses. . . . The government also subsidizes the pilgrimage by Muslims both through direct subsidy and through a system of paid leave for public servants when they travel to Mecca on the *haj*. Public funds devoted to Islamic religious purposes and institutions [have] been steadily rising, but the total cannot be accurately determined because many funds for Islamic purposes are concealed within regular budget allocations.[18]

State governments in Malaysia likewise devote substantial sums to the support of Islam.

The case of Malaysia differs from that of the Federal Republic of Germany mainly in that only one religion is supported, and it is the religion of only about half of the population. About a third of the population are Chinese and almost 10 percent have Indian ancestry and are mainly Hindus. The naming of Islam as the official religion, however, precludes comparable status for any other religion. Thus discrimination occurs as between religious communities. Moreover, in so far as Islam is supported out of general tax funds, non-Muslims are compelled to contribute to a religion that they do not share.

Many states are like Malaysia in having an "official" or "established" religion, which automatically indicates discrimination. How serious the discrimination is depends on the kind and the extent of the special support given to the selected church and on the number of persons adhering to some different religion or to none.

Education

In the field of education various kinds of relationships exist between church and state, made understandable and expedient by historical developments. The general view in Europe once was that education was the function of the Catholic Church.[19] With the Reformation, Protestant churches came into existence that also took up educational functions, and with the development of the sovereign state, nationalism, and secularism, government came to play an increasingly important role. Now, in general, government is dominant—or at least it is the main if not the sole source of funds for educational purposes. But many governments have made an accommodation in the matter with organized churches.

Colombia and Spain illustrate an accommodation that permits Catholic influence and principles to prevail even though government pays the bills. In Colombia relationships between the state and the Catholic Church are still governed by a concordat of 1888, renegotiated but little changed in 1973.[20] The concordat requires the recognition of the Church as a juridical personality. It requires that in schools and universities, education "be organized and directed in conformity with the dogmas and morals of the Catholic religion." It obliges government to "prevent...the propagation of ideas contrary to Catholic dogma," and gives ecclesiastical authorities the right to "inspect and revise" textbooks and to "restrain" professors whose teaching does not conform to Catholic doctrine. The government subsidizes the Church. In 1953, in conformity with the requirements of a treaty with the Vatican, the government gave the Catholic Church quasi-governmental powers and a monopoly over missionary activities in certain portions of the country.[21]

In Spain, too, the Catholic Church has special status and rights, and those who go to school cannot avoid Catholic influence and instruction. A decree of 1954 provides that in public establishments of higher education it is "serious misconduct" for a student or teacher to express himself against the Catholic religion; in the case of a student the offense is punishable by expulsion.[22]

I do not see how arrangements such as these can be reconciled with the requirements of the Covenant on Civil and Political Rights concerning freedom of speech, freedom of religion, and equal treatment. The policies in question are not designed to enable each people composing the population of the country to preserve its culture. Rather, they give special protection and privilege to one religious community.

Though a few countries reinforce what amounts to a monopoly by the Catholic Church, most permit some degree of diversity. The United Kingdom offers one of the illustrations. An Education Act of 1944, applying to England, requires religious instruction in all primary and secondary schools, but it also permits pupils to be excused on the request of a parent; and it says that no pupil shall be excluded from any state-supported school on the ground that he does or does not attend a given Sunday school or place of worship. Another section of the act specifies that in schools over a certain size, a portion of the teachers are to be "selected for their fitness and competence to give...religious instruction."

Scottish schools at the primary and secondary levels are regulated by the Scottish Act of 1918. Among other things, the act provided for the transfer of "voluntary" schools to county and municipal school boards "without diminishing their denominational character."[23] Teachers appointed to a transferred school must be "approved as to their religious belief and character by the representatives of the Church or denomination in whose interests the school is conducted."[24] In line with these principles, Scottish newspapers carry notices of openings for teachers that include such statements as "Preference will be given to Roman Catholic candidates."

In the Federal Republic of Germany a struggle developed after World War II over religion in the schools, Catholics insisting on "parents' rights," that is, "the right to have their children educated in state-financed schools where they [are] taught by Catholic teachers and given instruction in history, literature, and so on, in a 'Catholic spirit.' "[25] Those insisting on "parents' rights" succeeded in getting a provision included in the constitution saying that "religious instruction shall form part of the ordinary curriculum in state and municipal schools, except in secular (*bekenntnisfrei*) schools. Without prejudice to the state's right of supervision, religious instruction shall be given in accordance with the tenets of the religious communities." Methods of implementing this constitutional injunction differ in the different provinces of Germany. In some areas, three school systems are maintained—Catholic, Evangelical, and non-denominational—and parents choose among them.[26] A comparable arrangement exists in the Netherlands, Belgium, and France.[27]

In Canada, education is a matter for the provinces, which follow somewhat different policies. I will use Alberta as an illustration. There public schools are denominational. "If the majority of the ratepayers are Roman Catholic, the trustees may be Catholic and the teacher Catholic. But religious instruction is limited to the last half-hour of the school day, and from this any Protestant children may be excused."[28] In this kind of situation, the Protestant taxpayers may take a vote among themselves on the question of establishing a separate school and we will assume here that they decide to do it. The vote binds all members of the Protestant community. "The majority of the minority have the right to compel the entire minority to join the separate school division."[29] School taxes paid by members of the minority then automatically go to the separate school, and members of the minority are considered legally resident not in the public but in the separate school district. Should a Protestant want to send his children to the public school, he is liable to a charge for tuition unless he switches religions. The appellate division of the Alberta Supreme Court so ruled in 1976, reversing a judgment of a lower court that this involved illegal discrimination.[30]

Some of the arrangements described above can perhaps be explained and justified on a purely individualistic basis. They may be designed to respect the rights of parents or to enable individuals to follow the dictates of their conscience or their religion without violating the law. In the main, however, if the arrangements are to be justified, it has to be on the basis of the argument that religious communities as collective entities have rights that override the right of individuals to be treated without distinction as to religion. The most likely proposition is that the right to freedom of religion includes freedom to maintain the religion, and maintaining the religion is more fully assured if children in the religious community are taught in their own schools.

Part of the problem is taken care of if we accept the rules of Unesco's Convention Against Discrimination in Education. The first article of that convention says in effect that separate schools are discriminatory, but then the second lists exceptions; and among the exceptions are separate schools established for religious reasons. They are not to be considered discriminatory unless the education they provide is inferior. The convention specifies, however, that participation in separate educational systems or institutions, or attendance at them, must be optional, which raises questions. Nothing at all is optional about the arrangements in Colombia. Those in school have no choice but to receive a Catholic education, and those who pay taxes have no choice but to support the Catholic Church. And it would

strain the truth to say that in Alberta participation or attendance is optional, for the individual has no choice about the
school that his taxes support (unless it be by switching religions), and the choice of the school to attend is not really optional since tuition payments may be entailed.

Once it is granted that a religious community can have a
separate school, it follows that religion may be taken into account in selecting teachers. Knowledge of the religion—and
probably adherence to the religion—become bona fide occupational qualifications; and if a Scottish Catholic school passes
over a better qualified Presbyterian applicant in order to hire
a Catholic, the differentiation is not to be considered
discriminatory.

A distinction should be made between different kinds of special measures concerning religious communities. Generally
speaking, special measures are justified if they can reasonably
be considered necessary to assure the fair representation of
religious communities in political and governmental life, and
they may well be justified if they can reasonably be considered
necessary to enable a religious community to maintain itself.
But special measures conferring advantages on one or more
religious communities and requiring people to support the religion or submit themselves to its influence surely go counter to
the spirit and probably also to the letter of bans on discrimination as to religion.

Proselytism

Some countries protect religious communities against proselytism. The fact has already been illustrated by the description
of arrangements in Colombia. Malaysia and Israel provide additional illustrations.

The constitution of Malaysia authorizes both federal and state
legislation to "control or restrict the propagation of any religious doctrine or belief among persons professing the religion
of Islam," and in fact all of the states "prohibit any religious
teaching or proselytizing by non-Muslims among Muslims";
even more "public religious preaching is prohibited... where

Muslims are present,"[31] and restrictions are imposed on the printing or distribution of books repugnant to Muslim law and doctrine. Such measures appear to violate the Covenant on Civil and Political Rights, which says that the right of a person to freedom of religion includes the right "either individually or in community with others and in public or in private, to manifest his religion or belief in . . . teaching." And they violate the requirement of equal treatment.

Malaysia's policies are no doubt inspired at least in part by the rule that a Muslim has no right to abandon his religion, which itself denies freedom of religion. Moreover, Malaysia in effect reinforces this rule not only by safeguarding Muslims from dangerous thoughts but also by making adherence to Islam one of the criteria for determining who is a Malay. If a Malay turns apostate, he ceases to be a Malay; and thus he ceases to be eligible for the benefits of the affirmative action program that the government sponsors, designed to promote the equal enjoyment of human rights by Malays.

Israel has legislation that falls in the same broad category. The legislation is general in its terms, not naming a specific religion that is to be protected; but it is clearly intended to protect Judaism. One piece of legislation restricts the conditions under which the religion of a minor can be changed, and it fixes criminal penalties for anyone who "performs the ceremony of the change of religion of a minor" contrary to the provisions of the law. It also specifies that "a person who instigates a minor, by directly addressing himself to him, to change his religion is liable to imprisonment for a term of six months."[32] In 1977 the Knesset adopted another law restricting efforts to convert adults. It prohibits giving or promising another person anything of material value in order to persuade him either to change his own religion or to induce someone else to do so; and it likewise prohibits the acceptance of material benefit offered for this purpose.[33]

Malaysia and Israel are by no means the only states with such legislation. Comparable measures in Colombia have already been mentioned. India bars foreign missionaries from certain tribal areas, and at least one of the states of India has legislation similar to that of Israel.[34] Greece forbids proselytism directed at the Greek Orthodox Church,[35] and Turkey affords the same protection to Islam.[36]

A VIGNETTE ON A THEOCRACY

One of the clearest illustrations of a conflict between individual and group rights concerns Mr. Delfino Concha of the Taos Pueblo Indian Reservation. Testifying before a Senate committee in 1969, he described deprivations inflicted on him "simply because I did not conform to the religious function."

I was denied the use of the community property, such as using the community threshing machine to thresh my wheat. I was denied the use of community water rights, ditch rights, even after expressing my desire to share in the upkeep of the ditches on the reservation. On several occasions when the community ditches were being cleaned by the community, I was forcefully told to go home because I had no rights. I was denied the use of the community pasture by the war chief....I was threatened, excommunicated from social affairs, and spat upon by some individual members of the council.[37]

Argument on the issue posed by Mr. Concha can go along either of two lines. The communal line is that Mr. Concha got about what he deserved. Religion was a central feature of the life of the pueblo, inextricably bound up with and vital to the preservation of the traditional culture. It enjoyed broad and willing acceptance, playing a significant role in people's lives. Individuals have claims to freedom, but they also have obligations to the community that makes their lives possible and gives their lives meaning. Anyone who abandons a communal religion defaults on his obligation; he weakens the community by his action and threatens it by his example. The potential cost to the community of permitting open and defiant apostasy is greater than the burden the individual would bear if he concealed his apostasy and conformed at least minimally to communal customs. Perhaps the pueblo could not compel Mr. Concha to conform, but it was justified in holding that his refusal to do so was tantamount to a withdrawal from the community and an abandonment of the rights that membership entailed. The pueblo was generous in allowing Mr. Concha to continue to farm communal land, and should not be faulted for inflicting the kinds of deprivations it chose.

The individualist line of argument is that Mr. Concha was wrongly treated. He should have been morally free to abandon the communal religion without impairing his claim to share in community property and community rights; the claim to share rested not on his religious beliefs or his performance with respect to religion, but on his membership in the pueblo acquired at birth, and it was reinforced by the contribution that he and his family and his forebears had made to the community's economic well-being. Granted that the pueblo had a right to try to maintain its culture, including its religion, the methods that it employed in Mr. Concha's case encroached so severely on his individual rights that they must be condemned. And this judgment would hold even if the pueblo had compensated him for the material losses that ostracism entailed. Once Mr. Concha took his unpopular stand, he could not reasonably expect to be elected or appointed to any office under the control of those remaining faithful to the religion, but no claim of right is here involved. Furthermore, the right to freedom of religion should be upheld as a matter of principle. To condone a pueblo for rejecting or violating the right and insisting on religious conformity is to abandon one of the fundamental achievements of Western civilization, and is to take a long step back toward the Inquisition.

Presumably the kind of treatment inflicted on Mr. Concha violates the Indian Bill of Rights that Congress enacted in 1968. It does not forbid the establishment of a religion by an Indian tribe, but does forbid the enactment or enforcement of any law prohibiting the free exercise of religion; and free exercise includes freedom to convert to a different religion or to reject all religion. Moreover, the bill of rights forbids any denial of the equal protection of the laws. In the main, however, it is for the Indian tribes, and not for the courts of the United States, to interpret and enforce these prescriptions, for the purpose of Congress is to further Indian self-government and to protect tribal sovereignty from undue interference.[38]

As between the communal and the individualistic lines of

argument outlined above, choice is difficult. It probably should turn on the relative importance of the communal and the individual interests at stake. The communal claim becomes stronger when religion suffuses all aspects of social life and the social structure, the distinction between the sacred and the secular disappearing; and the communal claim is weaker when a distinction between the sacred and the secular is maintained and when individuals can exercise freedom without seriously threatening the very foundations of the social order. Conversely, the individualistic claim becomes stronger for those who insist on the vital role of religion in their own lives; and it is weaker in the case of individuals who give religion no more than peripheral concern.

AUTONOMY FOR RELIGIOUS GROUPS

Practices in the Ottoman Empire through World War I illustrate autonomy for religious groups. Muslims were politically dominant, and were unwilling to accept adherents of other religions as equal citizens. But they were willing to allow Jews and the members of various Christian sects to organize as *millets* and to maintain their own laws and customs in the personal realm, operate their own courts, administer their own schools, and impose taxes on their own members. The central feature of the system was the differential treatment of individuals depending on their religion. The religious sects had status and rights as collective entities, and the rights of individuals were adjusted and modified depending on the sect to which they belonged. There was differentiation, but it was designed to recognize the right of religious minorities to maintain their distinctive characteristics.[39] It was an application of the right of self-determination in advance of Woodrow Wilson.

Vestiges of the millet system remain in the Middle East. Israel, for example, recognizes the corporate existence of a number of religious communities, which implies that they can have their own courts and apply their own laws and customs in personal matters, such as marriage and divorce.[40] Individuals may or may not even have the option of escaping the arrangement by renouncing their faith; Muslims, for example, do not.

The differential arrangements necessarily mean that individuals are treated differently depending on their religion. Jews, for example, are not free to marry outside the faith, whereas others are.[41]

In a limited way, even the United States grants autonomy to religious communities. The Old Order Amish of Wisconsin established the point when, though willing to send their children to public schools through the eighth grade, they refused to continue them in school until their sixteenth birthday as Wisconsin law required. One of their contentions was that obedience to the law would "ultimately result in the destruction of the Old Order Amish church community."[42] The Supreme Court accepted the argument, and declined to uphold the enforcement of the law. The court obviously took the view that freedom of religion assured in the constitution includes freedom of the religious community to preserve itself, and that the constitutional guarantee superseded the conflicting Wisconsin law. It thus permitted distinction as to religion.

CONCLUSION

This account shows that the law of many countries calls for distinction as to religion. In numerous respects religious communities are treated formally or tacitly as corporate persons with rights, and differentiation occurs among individuals depending on the religious community to which they belong. This happens in connection with arrangements for elections, the holding of public office, and representation in the civil and military services. Some governments support one or more churches or religions, perhaps giving one a status that others do not have or perhaps conferring differential benefits and imposing differential burdens in other ways. Distinction as to religion occurs in the activities of many states in the field of education. Some states permit preaching and other activities designed to promote one religion while restricting comparable efforts on behalf of other religions. Some theocracies exist, meaning that the status and even the acceptability of the individual in the community depends on adherence to the faith. Some religious communities have a measure of political autonomy, from which it follows that the law applying to their members differs from the law applying to others.

As in the case of differentiation with respect to language, what is done does not necessarily indicate what ought to be done. Where legal differentiations based on religion occur, international legal obligations may be violated. And differentiations may be morally unjustifiable even if they conform to both domestic and international law. In general, I would argue that the granting of either exclusive or special privilege or benefit to one religion or church (or to individual adherents thereof) is at best questionable, above all when the purpose or effect is to strengthen the position of one church in comparison to others or to compel people to submit to the influence or rules of a church. Laws restricting government office to members of a selected religious community are in this category. I assume that those who formulated the requirement of the Charter that human rights be promoted without distinction as to religion, and those who inserted comparable provisions in the Universal Declaration of Human Rights and other international declarations and agreements, did not intend to act contrary to their traditions or to call for a change in their constitutions; and perhaps the intent of the parties should override the clear meaning of the words to which they agreed. But if the words are binding, then the British rule limiting the Crown to Anglicans, and comparable rules in many other countries, violate the international standards endorsed.

In contrast, differentiation as to religion is justifiable in either or both of two circumstances. It is justifiable most notably when it can reasonably be considered necessary to assure fair representation in government. Above all when a society is deeply divided along religious lines, with a record of distrust and animosity between the religious communities, it may be fatal to the human rights of members of one of the communities if another is permitted to gain untrammeled political dominance. And it may be fatal to orderly political processes as well, for oppressed people who see no chance of justice through peaceful procedures sometimes resort to terrorism or rebellion. It is also justifiable when special measures can reasonably be considered necessary to enable a religious community to maintain itself, as in the case of the Old Order Amish of Wisconsin. A proviso attaches to each of these propositions: that exclusive privilege is not conferred; in other words, that the rule in accordance with which one ethnic community is treated shall be equally applicable to other ethnic communities that are similarly situated.

4

Equal Treatment and the Indigenous

The population of almost every state includes peoples at different levels of advancement. In the United States—and in most countries of the western hemisphere—the whites and the Indians are at different levels; in the Soviet Union, the Russians and some of the peoples of central Asia; in India, the main body of the population and the "scheduled tribes"; in South Africa, the whites and the black peoples of the "homelands"; and so on. Usually the less advanced are the indigenous people—the aborigines—already there when another people came in as colonists if not also as conquerors.

Few contend that the indigenous should be treated as so many individuals, without differentiation.[1] In those cases where this has been the rule, the indigenous have almost always proved unable to defend and promote their own rights and interests. In some areas they have simply been killed off, in others despoiled or enslaved. Barbaric treatment of them has been widespread. And a revulsion in the dominant communities against the practices of the past has led to a general consensus that the indigenous are entitled to special measures of protection—special status and rights, and special limitations on their transactions with others. The special status and rights are not to be permanent. They are to be extended only during a transition period, pending the full integration or assimilation of the indigenous into the dominant society. Nevertheless, the approved kinds of measures differentiate and therefore raise questions about discrimination.

The indigenous themselves agree in rejecting treatment as so many individuals. They want differentiation too, but for a fundamentally different reason. Those in the dominant society who favor protecting the indigenous tend to think in terms of conferring the benefits of civilization on them and then receiving them into advanced society. But the indigenous generally have a different conception of their own well-being. They have traditions and values of their own, which they cherish. Far from wanting to join an advanced society, they generally want to stay apart. And so they speak of self-determination and of the preservation of their separate identity. They welcome, in fact they want, special status and rights—on a permanent basis and not simply as protective devices during a transition period. And, like the differentiating measures that the dominant society may be willing to extend, those sought by the indigenous raise questions about discrimination.

Taking up these questions, we start with the Genocide Convention, for it assumes and asserts that peoples as collective entities have a right to survive—or at least a right not to be destroyed by certain kinds of acts. We go on to the Indigenous and Tribal Populations Convention and to the reaction of the indigenous to it. Then we take up the policies pursued toward the indigenous by a series of countries: policies of the United States toward the Indians and the Samoans; policies of New Zealand toward the Maoris; and policies of Fiji with respect to the Fijians. Finally, we will formulate standards to be used in judging whether measures differentiating for the benefit of the indigenous should be considered discriminatory and thus incompatible with the rule of equal treatment.

THE GENOCIDE CONVENTION AND THE RIGHT OF PEOPLES TO SURVIVE

We start with the Genocide Convention because it recognizes that a collective entity may have a right as a corporate body. The convention prohibits genocide, and defines it as any of the following acts committed with intent to destroy, in whole or in part, a national, ethnical, racial or religious group, as such:

a. Killing members of the group;

b. Causing serious bodily or mental harm to members of the group;

c. Deliberately inflicting on the group conditions of life calculated to bring about its physical destruction in whole or in part;

d. Imposing measures intended to prevent births within the group;

e. Forcibly transferring children of the group to another group.

Note that the concern is with the *group as such*. The acts listed count as genocide not because of their inherent nature, but only when the intent is to destroy the group as such. The killing of an individual person may be murder, but if the killing is intended as a step toward the destruction of the group it also becomes an act of genocide. The other acts listed might also be crimes against individuals, but the intent behind them may make them genocidal too.

Originating in the horror of the Holocaust, the Genocide Convention is relevant to the indigenous peoples of the world. Many of them were victims of genocide before anyone thought to coin the word. The American Indians are a case in point, as indicated by the notion that there is no good Indian but a dead Indian and as indicated by Wounded Knee and other massacres. The Bushmen of South Africa and the aborigines of Tasmania are also cases in point. In recent years in Brazil the Service for the Protection of the Indians was actually found to be destroying them. The genocide convention has never been formally invoked in international relationships, and may or may not be of practical significance. But the principle is clear that it recognizes national, ethnic, racial, and religious groups as entities with a right to be spared various kinds of acts intended to bring about their destruction.

We might note, too, that the African states have formulated a Charter on Human Rights and Peoples' Rights. The very name assumes that *peoples* have rights, and the Charter spells some of them out, including the right to exist and to develop.[2]

THE ILO CONVENTION AND THE
ATTITUDES OF THE INDIGENOUS

The introduction to this chapter refers to the willingness of the advanced to be paternal in treating the indigenous and the reactions of the indigenous themselves. The contrast is brought out by focusing on the Indigenous and Tribal Populations Convention and on the declarations of the indigenous relating directly or indirectly to it.

The convention was adopted by the General Conference of the International Labor Organization (ILO) in 1957 and has been ratified by 27 states.[3] By its own terms, it applies to

members of tribal or semi-tribal populations in independent countries whose social and economic conditions are at a less advanced stage than the stage reached by other sections of the national community, and whose status is regulated wholly or partially by their own customs or traditions or by special laws or regulations.

Another statement is that the convention applies to populations

regarded as indigenous on account of their descent from the populations which inhabited the country...at the time of conquest or colonization and which...live more in conformity with the social, economic and cultural institutions of that time than with the institutions of the nation to which they belong.

The convention calls for the special and differential treatment of the indigenous. "So long as [their] social, economic and cultural conditions...prevent them from enjoying the benefits of the general laws of the country to which they belong, special measures shall be adopted for the protection of [their] institutions, persons, property, and labor...." They are to be "allowed to retain their own customs and institutions," and due account is to be taken of their values and the problems that face them "both as groups and as individuals" when they undergo social and economic change. At the same time, "the primary objective...shall be the fostering of individual dignity, and the advancement of individual usefulness and initiative," and the special measures are not to prejudice the enjoyment of the general rights of citizenship. "Progressive integration" is to be the goal (though not "artificial assimilation"). The special measures are not to be used "as a means of creating or prolonging a state of segregation," and are to be dropped when the need for them is gone.

As these terms suggest, the convention combines a collective and an individual approach. The collective approach is to be taken at first, and is to be dominant for a time; but the long term objectives are individualistic. Individual dignity, individual usefulness, and integration are the goals.

These goals the indigenous reject. The reasons for the rejection are epitomized in a declaration adopted in 1980 by the Indian Council established by the Congress of Indian Movements of South America. The ILO treaty, the Indian Council complains,

does not consider in its articles the right to self-determination. It seeks integration and assimilation, with total lack of respect for the dignity of every people and its right to freedom. Its aim is the destruction of our culture, of our traditions and of our languages.... It seeks to promote the individual, which is contrary to the communal spirit of our peoples.

The same themes show up elsewhere. The World Council of Indigenous Peoples in 1977 adopted a Declaration on Human Rights, claiming the "right to self-determination," the "right to maintain our culture, language, and traditions in freedom," the "right to occupy land collectively," and the "right to an appropriate education in accordance with our culture and our traditions." "Under no circumstances," it declared, "should indigenous people be subjected to policies of integration and assimilation...." The demand is for recognition as nations, implying at least autonomy within the state if not status under international law.[4] The International Conference on Discrimination against Indigenous Populations in the Americas (1977) adopted similar sorts of resolutions.[5]

If the indigenous are accepted as "peoples," the article on self-determination in the human rights covenants, quoted in Chapter 1, makes their entitlement to self-determination clear.

Further, other international pronouncements reinforce the claims of the indigenous—again assuming that the indigenous count as "peoples." The General Conference of Unesco, as noted in Chapter 1, has adopted declarations asserting that "every people has the right and duty to develop its culture," and that all peoples have the right to "preserve" their culture.[6] If every people has a right to self-determination and to preserve its culture, orientations toward the group rather than the individual and to separatism rather than to integration ought to be acceptable.

INDIGENOUS PEOPLES AND RACE

Indigenous peoples differ from others not only in terms of their history but also in terms of race. This means that special measures to protect them necessarily involve racial differentiation, which in turn means that issues calling for judgment are bound to arise: whether the special measures are to be approved for the protection that they give to an indigenous people or condemned as racially discriminatory.

Though such issues cannot be entirely avoided, they can in many instances be resolved by appeal to the International Convention on the Elimination of All Forms of Racial Discrimination. The definition of discrimination included in that convention, quoted in Chapter 1, is indecisive on the issue, but a supplementary provision is clear, however badly worded:

Special measures taken for the sole purpose of securing adequate advancement of certain racial or ethnic groups or individuals requiring such protection as may be necessary in order to ensure such groups or individuals equal enjoyment or exercise of human rights and fundamental freedoms shall not be deemed racial discrimination....

Since indigenous peoples are regularly less advanced than others, they can readily be thought to need special measures to secure their advancement; and according to the convention, such measures are not to be considered discriminatory even if those already more advanced are treated unequally. It should be noted that the convention is concerned with the treatment of both groups and individuals; presumably the groups might be either collective entities (corporate units) or aggregations of individuals.

Not only does the convention permit such special measures, but in another article it requires them:

States Parties shall, when the circumstances so warrant, take...special and concrete measures to ensure the adequate development and protection of certain racial groups or individuals belonging to them, for the purpose of guaranteeing them the full and equal enjoyment of human rights and fundamental freedoms.

This means that special measures for the advancement and protection of an indigenous people are potentially compatible with the convention on racial discrimination even if the indigenous people are at the same time treated as a race apart.

The provisions just quoted are qualified. The qualification is that the special measures are not "to lead to the maintenance of separate rights for different racial groups [or] be continued after the objectives for which they were taken have been achieved." Here the same problem arises as in the case of the Indigenous and Tribal Populations Convention. Though the convention on racial discrimination is perhaps not quite as explicitly individualistic as the convention on indigenous peoples, implicit individualism is there. Separate rights for different racial groups on a permanent basis are to be avoided. If an indigenous people that is racially distinct wants to keep apart permanently and live in its own way, a government that goes along with that desire runs the risk of being condemned for racial discrimination.

In many instances, special measures are so clearly designed to protect the indigenous, and the indigenous are so clearly less advanced, that no significant problem of principle arises, even if the indigenous are also racially distinct. But in other instances, even if the people are indigenous, the common references to them are in terms of race, and they may be politically powerful and almost as advanced as the rest of the population. I have Malaysia especially in mind, and will discuss it in the next chapter. In such cases, judgment is sometimes difficult on the question whether special measures are to be approved or condemned, and on what grounds.

THE AMERICAN INDIANS

The American Indians are indigenous and are less advanced than the main body of the population, which suggests that differentiating measures on their behalf are at least permissible, if not required, according to the terms of both the Indigenous and Tribal Populations Convention and the convention on racial discrimination. But a problem already described comes up again. Whereas these conventions assume the desirability of ultimate integration or assimilation, the dominant wish of the Indians seems to be separatism on a permanent basis. And regardless of international standards, differential and separate treatment involves problems in domestic law and policy.

Evidence is abundant that the dominant wish of the Indians is for a permanently separate existence. The fact has been noted by various writers, among them Frances Svensson, herself an Oglala Sioux.

Where the Black goal has seemed to be equal participation in the benefits and privileges of American society, the fundamental Indian objective is best summed up as the right not to have to participate and still maintain an autonomous Indian identity, legally rooted in the historic treaty relationship and the traditional land base.[7]

Vine Deloria, Jr., also an Indian, makes the same point. He speaks of the Indian nations and asserts that they have "an inherent right to political and cultural existence comparable to any other nation."[8] And he advances a general philosophy on the matter:

Unless a society can find a means of integrating the rights of groups with the broader and more abstract rights of individuals, it will succeed in creating its own barbarians who will eventually destroy it.... The sovereignty of tribalistic-communal groups is more than the conglomerate of individual desires writ large. It is a whole new way of adjusting to the technology which dominates life in this century.[9]

As Deloria sees it, "the massive corporate organizations have driven us well into the era of neofeudalism." He objects to this, and speaks of the need "to reorient social goals more in line with a tribal-communal life style." In his eyes, "the contest of the future is between a return to the castle or the tipi."[10]

A desire for a permanently separate existence is also expressed in the manifesto of the Indians who made the Longest Walk (1978):

How do we convince the U. S. government to simply leave us alone to live according to our ways of life?. . . We have the right to educate our children to our ways of life. . . . We have the right to be a people. These are inherent rights. . . . Our fight today is to survive as a people.[11]

Individual Indians have, of course, chosen to abandon their tribes and enter the mainstream, and it is to be expected that some who remain tribal are nevertheless dubious about the wisdom or practicality of a separate course; no one knows how numerous those holding doubts may be. What is known is that a great many tribes persist, determined to preserve a distinct cultural identity and to pursue a separate existence insofar as possible.

White Americans have not agreed, and do not now agree, on policies to pursue toward the Indians. The actions of private parties and of lesser agents of the government have run the gamut from the benign to the genocidal. Purposes officially endorsed are suggested by the two themes of separation and assimilation.[12] At first, of course, the Indians were in fact separate, and governments of colonizing countries made treaties with them, as they did with foreign powers. When the United States became independent, it followed suit. Chief Justice Marshall made the classic statements concerning the status of the Indian tribes. Considering a dispute between the Cherokee nation and the state of Georgia around 1830, he held that since the Indian tribes or nations were located within the boundaries of the United States they could not with strict accuracy be called foreign; but neither were they ordinary members of the body politic. "The Indian nations," he said, "had always been considered as distinct, independent political communities, re-

taining their original natural rights...," and the Cherokee
nation specifically was

> a distinct community, occupying its own territory, with boundaries
> accurately described, in which the laws of Georgia can have no force,
> and which the citizens of Georgia have no right to enter but with the
> assent of the Cherokees themselves, or in conformity with treaties
> and with the acts of Congress.... [13]

Marshall's judgment was that Indian tribes should be described
as "domestic dependent nations."[14]

In the main, the principles that Marshall laid down still hold.
Since 1871 the United States has not dealt with the Indian
tribes through treaties, but it nevertheless still regards them
as separate political entities. One of the landmark decisions
describes the tribes as "semi-independent," and the Indians as
"a separate people."[15] Another points out that "the powers of
local self-government" of the Indian tribes existed prior to the
adoption of the United States constitution, and "are not operated upon" by it.[16] A federal district court in 1959 said that
the tribes

> have a status higher than that of states. They are subordinate and
> dependent nations possessed of all the powers as such [except insofar
> as] they have expressly been required to surrender them by the su-
> perior sovereign, the United States.[17]

And the Supreme Court at about the same time spoke of "the
right of reservation Indians to make their own laws and be
ruled by them," insisting that this right be respected.[18]

But respect for the Indians as "a separate people" has not
always prevailed. Sometimes assimilation, even forced assimilation, has been the goal. A Commissioner of Indian Affairs
said in 1890 that his object was "to break up reservations,
destroy tribal relations, settle Indians on their own home-
steads, incorporate them into the national life, and deal with
them not as nations or tribes or bands but as individual citizens."[19] Later another Commissioner of Indian Affairs pled that
the Indian be given "a white man's chance."

Educate him in the rudiments of our language. Teach him to work. Send him to his home, and tell him he must practice what he has been taught or starve. It will in a generation or more regenerate the race. It will exterminate the Indian, but develop the man.[20]

Among the efforts going in this direction was the forced separation of Indian children from their parents and (as indicated in Chapter 2) their assignment to boarding schools off the reservations, where the object was to teach them English and to "civilize" them.[21] In line with such policies, Congress enacted legislation making all Indians citizens, and as recently as 1953 it adopted a resolution saying that

it is the policy of Congress...to make the Indians...subject to the same laws and entitled to the same privileges and responsibilities as are applicable to other citizens of the United States, and to grant them all the rights and prerogatives pertaining to American citizenship....[22]

The resolution inaugurated what is known as the termination policy; and the special status of a number of tribes, and special federal relationships with them, were in fact terminated—with such disastrous consequences for the Indians affected that the policy was abandoned. The shift away from termination was indicated by congressional enactments and by a presidential statement.

The congressional enactments were the Indian Bill of Rights of 1968 (the Indian Civil Rights Act)[23] and the Indian Self-Determination and Education Assistance Act of 1975. The first of these measures has an element of ambivalence about it. It aims to protect individual Indians against their tribal governments, assuring them rights like those enjoyed by other citizens on the basis of the first ten amendments. In this respect it goes in the direction of termination and assimilation. The alleged need for protection is illustrated by the case of Mr. Delfino Concha, described in Chapter 3—the member of the Taos Pueblo who was denied tribal rights when he ceased to conform with respect to religion. Nevertheless, although Congress clearly sought to impose limitations on tribal governments when it enacted the Indian Bill of Rights, it also showed respect for tribal autonomy. It omitted the ban on the establishment of religion, and it departed from the precedents set in the first ten amendments in several other ways out of respect for the special position of the Indians.[24]

Discussion of the Indian Bill of Rights showed no intent to use the statute as an instrument for modifying tribal cultural attitudes in order to facilitate assimilation of Indians into the non-Indian community. In fact, the committee showed a positive intent to avoid requirements injurious to the tribes' capacity to function as autonomous governmental units.[25]

The case of a member of the Santa Clara Pueblo further illustrates the point that the Indian Bill of Rights, though ambivalent in its implications, was not intended to contribute to termination and assimilation. The bill includes a stipulation that "no Indian tribe in exercising powers of self-government shall:...(8) deny to any person within its jurisdiction the equal protection of its laws...." Among the laws is one concerning the hereditary acquisition of membership in the pueblo. It says that male members who marry females from outside the pueblo can pass membership on to their children, but that female members who marry males from outside cannot. A female member went to court about this, and she obviously had a *prima facie* case. But though she carried her plea to the Supreme Court, she lost. The Supreme Court pointed out that Indian nations are exempt from suit, just as sovereign states are, unless Congress provides otherwise, and it held that in enacting the Indian Bill of Rights Congress had not provided otherwise except in connection with habeas corpus proceedings. The ruling was that tribal courts are the appropriate forums for Indians wanting to vindicate their rights, and that federal courts should play no role.[26]

The proper inference from all this is that Congress has sought to balance respect for the rights of individual Indians with respect for the desire of the tribes to maintain their distinct cultural and political identity.[27]

Not long after the adoption of the Indian Bill of Rights, President Nixon recommended that Congress repeal the resolution of 1953 and instead "explicitly affirm the integrity and right to continued existence of all Indian tribes and Alaska native governments, recognizing that cultural pluralism is a source of national strength."[28] In effect the recommendation called for a formal abandonment of the termination policy.

Congress did not act precisely as requested, but instead enacted the Indian Self-Determination and Education Assistance Act, mentioned above.[29] In it Congress spoke of the "special legal relationship between the federal government and the Indian people," and it found that "the prolonged Federal domination of the Indian service programs has served to retard rather than enhance the progress of the Indian people...." It committed itself "to the maintenance of the Federal Government's unique and continuing relationship with and responsibility to the Indian people through the establishment of a meaningful Indian self-determination policy...."

In the light of previous reversals of policy toward the Indians, no one can say how enduring the policy honoring the right of self-determination will be or precisely what the policy will come to include. The policy is clearly compatible with provisions of the Charter of the United Nations and declarations of the General Assembly concerning self-determination, and fully compatible with declarations of the General Conference of Unesco concerning the right of a people to preserve its culture. It is not so clearly compatible with provisions of the conventions on indigenous populations and on racial discrimination specifying that differential treatment is to be temporary or transitional. At some point this issue will need to be resolved, and one of the themes of this book is that it ought to be resolved in such a way as to permit continued separatism on the part of peoples who desire it. This is one of the meanings and implications of the right of peoples to self-determination, and action honoring that right ought not to be classified as discriminatory.

Policies toward the Indians raise questions not only about compliance with international conventions and standards but also about compliance with the equal protection clause of the constitution of the United States. Both in periods when separatism has been accepted and in periods when assimilation has been pursued, the federal government has treated individual

Indians differentially and preferentially. It has long imposed restrictions on their freedom to alienate their property.[30] Until 1953 it prohibited the sale of liquor to Indians.[31] For almost a century and a half it has given preference to Indians in filling positions in the Indian service; currently the policy applies to the Bureau of Indian Affairs and the Indian Health Service, and it is imposed on private employers under contract with the Bureau to do work on or near reservations.[32] Further, organizations of the Indians themselves also hire on a preferential basis, having been specifically exempted from federal prohibitions of discrimination based on "race, color, religion, sex, or national origin."[33] Thus an advertisement soliciting applications for the post of Dean of Instruction at a Navajo community college includes the statement, "Navajo, or other Indian, preferred."[34]

Differential and preferential policies necessarily mean that individuals must be classified as either Indian or non-Indian, and various tests are employed. Sometimes it is the tribe that decides who is a member and who is not. Sometimes the rule is that to be classified as an Indian a person must be one-fourth or more of Indian blood. And sometimes in effect the two criteria are combined: the person must be one fourth or more of Indian blood and be a member of a federally recognized tribe.[35]

One of the issues raised by the differential and preferential policies, and by the tests for determining who is an Indian, is whether race is the basis for classification, and in some instances it is difficult to avoid an affirmative answer.[36] This creates a special problem with respect to the equal protection clause, for classification by race is "suspect," requiring "strict scrutiny," and putting the burden of proof on those supporting the classification. This will be discussed more fully below in Chapter 6. For present purposes, however, it is enough to say that distinctions need to be made, sometimes subtle ones. The Supreme Court has done so, holding that neither a legislative ban on discrimination in federal employment based on race nor the due process clause operates to forbid the preferential hiring of Indians. In its view,

this preference does not constitute "racial discrimination." Indeed it is not even a "racial" preference. Rather, it is...similar in kind to the constitutional requirement that a United States Senator, when elected, be "an Inhabitant of that State for which he shall be chosen,". . . or that a member of a city council reside within the city governed by the council. . . . The preference. . . is granted to Indians not as a discrete racial group, but, rather, as members of quasi-sovereign tribal entities. . . . [T]he preference is reasonably and directly related to a legitimate, nonracially based goal.[37]

To the extent that race figures in the preferential policies, as in the blood quantum requirement, it is simply a means of determining membership in the tribe; and the preference is based not on race but on the status of the tribe and on membership in it. We will encounter this distinction again in describing the preferential policies of Malaysia.

Comment may be in point here on the stand that Nathan Glazer takes in *Affirmative Discrimination.* He acknowledges that American Indians are " 'enrolled' in an ethnic group [and enjoy] a formally distinct political status defined by birth," but he gives the fact little attention.[38] It is to him simply an exception, an anomaly. Given his focus on domestic American problems, this may be justified. But no one concerned with questions about "affirmative discrimination" over the world can afford to dismiss policies toward the American Indians so lightly. Most other countries face comparable problems, and Americans who want to understand and appraise their policies should be aware of what the United States itself does. Moreover, policies toward the American Indians are as good an indication as any of the fact that the melting pot is not necessarily the solution to the problem of ethnic differences and of the fact that ethnic groups as corporate units sometimes have rights that are in potential conflict with the rights of individuals.

THE NATIVES OF AMERICAN SAMOA

The indigenous peoples under the jurisdiction of the United States also include the natives of American Samoa, and protective measures apply to them. According to the constitution of American Samoa, it shall be the policy of the Government of American Samoa to protect persons of Samoan ancestry against alienation of their lands and the destruction of the Samoan way of life and language contrary to their best interests. Such legislation as may be necessary may be enacted to protect the lands, customs, culture, and traditional family organization of persons of Samoan ancestry, and to encourage business enterprises by such persons.[39]

In accordance with this provision, communal land in Samoa (96 percent of the total) is by law inalienable, and land individually owned by Samoans can be sold only to other Samoans—that is, to persons with 50 percent or more Samoan blood.[40] Thus, as in the Aaland Islands, the effort is to protect the local population against an adulteration of its culture. At the same time, Samoans and non-Samoans are differentially treated, and the question is whether the differentiation is discrimination.

The answer is approximately the same as in the case of the American Indians. The Samoans are an indigenous people—weak and vulnerable. By the standards of the Indigenous and Tribal Populations Convention, special measures to protect them are appropriate, and such measures should not be regarded as discriminatory against non-Samoans whose freedoms and opportunities are thus limited. Even if the differentiation is judged to turn on race it is justified by provisions of the convention on racial discrimination quoted above. The major question is the same as the one raised by policies of a separatist sort toward the Indians—whether such policies must be temporary and transitional or whether they can legitimately be enduring.

THE MAORIS OF NEW ZEALAND

Like the United States in the case of the Indians and the Samoans, New Zealand treats its Maori population differentially. For present purposes, only two aspects of New Zealand's policies need to be noted, and the two are quite different. The first concerns the tendency of New Zealanders to ignore the fact that the Maoris are indigenous and to speak of them in terms of race. The second concerns arrangements in New Zealand for the participation of the Maoris in government and politics.

In the light of what has already been said, the focus on race might be dismissed as of no consequence, for the convention on racial discrimination indicates that special measures designed to promote the equal enjoyment of human rights by a less advanced racial group are not to be considered discriminatory. New Zealand has ratified the convention, doing it after searching scrutiny of its own policies. In connection with ratification it enacted a Race Relations Act (1971) designed to bring its law into full conformity with the requirements of the convention. The act prohibits discrimination in a number of areas, and it provides for affirmative action. It does the latter by specifying that

anything done or omitted which would otherwise constitute a breach [of the various provisions of the act] shall not constitute such a breach if—

a. It is done or omitted in good faith for the purpose of assisting or advancing particular persons or groups of persons or persons of a particular color, race, or ethnic or national origin; and

b. Those groups or persons need or may reasonably be supposed to need assistance or advancement in order to achieve an equal place with other members of the community.

It is arguable that in this book I should go along with the practice of the New Zealanders and treat policy toward the Maoris as a matter of race, in which case the subject would be deferred to a later chapter. I do not do so for several reasons. First, the Maoris are the indigenous people, making it at least as logical to treat them in the present chapter as in a later chapter on race. Second, I am inclined to doubt that race as such is the characteristic that leads to the differential treatment of the Maoris, and think it potentially misleading to do anything that might suggest the contrary. I am inclined to think that the New Zealanders use race as a surrogate for the characteristic with which they are genuinely concerned: the indigenous origin of the Maoris, and more particularly the weakness and vulnerability that this implies. Third, I am wary of discussions focusing on race because of potential implications for the later appraisal of the unquestionably racial policies of South Africa. Even if I were to ignore the indigenous origins of the Indians, the Samoans, the Maoris, the Fijians, and the Malays and were to discuss policies toward them in terms of race, I believe it would be possible to demonstrate that the policies belong in a different category from most of those followed in South Africa. But the contrast will be sharper if the idea is kept at the forefront that policies designed to promote the equal enjoyment of human rights by less advanced peoples are at issue in the one category and that policies designed to maintain white identity are at issue in the other.

New Zealand's arrangements for the participation of Maoris in government and politics are quasi-communal. The law provides for two electoral rolls. Until 1975 they were rolls for Maoris and Europeans, respectively, and neither the Maoris nor the Europeans had a choice about the roll on which to register. An amendment of 1975 speaks not of the European but of the general roll, and permits any descendant of a person of the Maori race to choose the roll on which to register. Others have no choice, being permitted to register only on the general roll. The law also provides for Maori and general electoral districts, and as the formula currently works out, 4 of the 87 districts are Maori districts. (This means that the whole country is divided into 4 Maori districts and also into 83 general districts; in terms of square miles, the Maori districts are thus much larger.) Only those who register as Maoris may vote or be elected in the 4 Maori districts; thus the Maoris are assured of 4 seats. At the same time, any Maoris who choose to register on the general roll may vote and stand for election in the general districts. Four seats give the Maoris representation in rough proportion to their number.[41] Since registration on the Maori roll depends on the free choice of the individual Maori, the imposition of any stigma is avoided. In fact, for electoral purposes, the differential treatment of the Maoris will end whenever they spurn the separate electoral roll and register with the others on the general roll.

The contrast between New Zealand's quasi-communal system and the more common territorial system should be emphasized. In New Zealand's system, the indigenous people (the less advanced people) may set themselves apart for electoral purposes and make sure that they obtain representation in parliament. The principle that public offices are equally open to all citizens gives way to the principle that certain of them are open only to those who voluntarily classify themselves as Maoris. Open competition with rewards based on personal merit is qualified, for competition in the Maori districts is open only to Maoris. Maoris may look to their inherited characteristics, characteristics for which they are not responsible, and see to it that these characteristics are taken into account in connection with the distribution of opportunities and rewards.

The arrangement for the Maoris is obviously benign. It permits them to avoid a situation in which they would be a relatively small minority in many electoral districts, unable to win in any of them. Europeans are denied equal opportunity, but as the counterpart of an effort to advance the Maoris toward the equal enjoyment of human rights. This is justified according to the standards of both the convention on indigenous populations and the convention on racial discrimination. I would argue that it is also justified as a means of avoiding the disaffection and alienation that might sometime ensue (as in Northern Ireland) if the rules of politics kept participation on the part of the Maoris minimal and ineffective.

The arrangement for the Maoris is provided for in law, and the law is open to change. But nothing about the law suggests that it is temporary. There is thus no explicit acknowledgment of the requirement of the indigenous populations convention and the convention on racial discrimination that differential measures shall be temporary and transitional. The apparent assumption is that the objective of assuring representation for the Maoris will remain valid as long as a substantial number of Maoris choose to register on their own separate roll.

If New Zealand's practices were transferred to the United States—if New Mexico, for example, were to establish separate electoral rolls and separate electoral districts for Mexican-Americans—the courts would presumably hold that equal protection was being denied; but the view that prevails within the United States is obviously not the only possible one.

THE FIJIANS

The Fijians comprise a much larger portion of the population of Fiji than is the case with the American Indians and Maoris. They comprise 44 percent of the total, or 46 percent if the Rotumans and other Pacific islanders are counted with them, as they are for electoral purposes. Indians—people whose ancestors lived in India—comprise 50 percent of the total. The figures are given in Table 2.

Differences between the population groups are sharp. Fijians and Indians differ in race, language, religion, and life style; and they differ in level of education, level of advancement, and motivation for Western-style progress. Little intermarriage occurs. The Indians are mainly Hindus, but include some Muslims and a few Christians.

Fiji achieved independence in 1970, having been a British colony since 1874. Britain's policies had been mixed, favoring individualism in some respects and communalism in others. Individualism figured most notably as the basis for immigration policies. In 1874, some immigration from Europe had already occurred, and Europeans (mainly British) had already acquired about 10 percent of the land, including the portion most suitable for raising sugarcane. These Europeans needed field hands, and found Indians more suitable than Fijians. Britain therefore permitted the importation of indentured Indian workers as needed; and it permitted other immigration. Noth-

Table 2
Population of Fiji. 1976 Census

	Number	Per cent
Indians	293,000	50
Fijians	260,000	44
Rotumans	7,000	1.2
Other Pacific Islanders	7,000	1.2
Part-Europeans	10,000	1.7
Europeans	5,000	0.8
Chinese	5,000	0.8
Others	1,000	0.2
Total	588,000	

Source: Keesing's *Contemporary Archives*, November 25, 1977, p. 28681.

ing in an individualistic creed suggested a different course; that is, nothing in an individualistic creed suggested that differences of race, language, religion, or culture should be taken into account in formulating public policy.

But Britain's policies were not entirely individualistic. Britain accepted and confirmed not only the Fijian system of land tenure—a communal system—but also Fijian ownership of about 83 percent of the land of the islands. It reserved this land inalienably for the Fijians; none could be sold.[42] This arrangement concerning the land has survived independence, and is one of the issues in relationships between the various communities.

Britain also provided for communalism in the political sphere. Prior to World War II it established a Legislative Council in which, apart from the official majority (ex officio members), communities as such were represented—on a parity basis despite their disparity in size. The Fijian, Indian, and European communities each had five seats. The British made no official statement identifying the characteristics that led them to distinguish between these communities, but differences of race and culture were obvious. Among other things, Britain saw to it that one of the Indian seats went to a Muslim.[43]

In the 1960s, when Britain arranged for elections in connection with local government, it backed away from communalism and provided for open competition on the basis of a common franchise, but the significance of the fact was qualified by the existence of a separate administration for the Fijian areas. And communalism triumphed in connection with the grant of independence in 1970. It triumphed on the insistence of the indigenous Fijians and against the wishes of the Indians. The Fijians feared the result of unrestricted competition on an individualistic basis, and insisted on special measures relating to participation in politics and government and special protection with respect to their ownership of land.

The special measures relating to participation in politics and government include separate electoral rolls—one for Fijians, one for Indians, and one described as general. Individuals have no choice about the roll on which to register. The constitution specifies that a person shall be regarded as a Fijian if, and shall not be so regarded unless, his father or any of his earlier male progenitors in the male line is or was the child of parents both of whom are or were indigenous inhabitants of Fiji or any island in Melanesia, Micronesia or Polynesia.

And the constitution defines Indian in the same way, *mutatis mutandi.* Discrimination based on sex is obvious. The constitution requires that those Fijians and Indians who register to vote shall do so on their respective rolls, and that all others shall register on the general roll. The others include not only Europeans and Chinese, but also many of mixed European and Fijian ancestry; and they tend to side with the Fijians. The three rolls combine to make a fourth, called the national roll. Britain resisted pressures for additional communal rolls, e.g., one for the Rotumans and one for the Chinese, for it considered such rolls to be "against public policy."[44] It insisted that the Rotumans and other Pacific islanders should go on the same roll with the Fijians, and that the Chinese should go on the same roll with the Europeans. The Europeans and Chinese have economic power disproportionate to their number.

The communal arrangement also includes the allocation of seats in parliament on a quota basis. In the House of Representatives, the Fijian and Indian communities each have 22 members, and the others have 8. Of the 22, 12 in each case are elected by those on the communal roll and 10 by those on the national roll. Of the 8, the corresponding division is 3 and 5. The Senate consists of 22 persons, all appointed by the governor-general on advice from communal sources: 8 on the advice of the Fijian Great Council of Chiefs; 7 on the advice of the prime minister (so far, a Fijian); 6 on the advice of the leader of the opposition (so far, an Indian); and 1 on the advice of the Council of Rotuma. In both the House and the Senate, special majorities are required for the enactment of certain kinds of measures, meaning most notably that the Fijians can block certain kinds of change. For example, a bill that alters any provision of a variety of ordinances having to do with Fijian land, custom, or customary rights may be enacted only if it is supported by not less than three-quarters of the members of the House and by at least six of the Senators appointed on the advice of the Fijian Great Council of Chiefs.

The arrangements in Fiji raise obvious questions about group rights, on the one hand, and the equal treatment of individuals, on the other. What I propose to do is to discuss specific features of the arrangement first and then discuss more general principles. The specific features most open to question are described in the following paragraphs:

1. The constitutional provision making descent the crucial factor in classifying individuals as Fijian, Indian, or other. People are born into a given category and cannot escape it; and certain rights, eligibilities, and opportunities depend on the category in which they find themselves. The tendency in the West is to condemn such practices, though exceptions are to be found—and not only in South Africa. In the United States, for example, as noted above, individuals count as Indian for certain purposes only if they have the requisite amount of Indian blood, and in New Zealand a person whose parents are European cannot register as a Maori. I am inclined to judge such practices in terms of the context in which they are found and in terms of their purpose and effect, and on this basis I see little to suggest condemnation. After all, the cultural differences indicated by birth are sharp and deep, and with respect to participation in politics and government the consequences of classification by birth are of limited significance. It is not a question of conferring special privileges or special burdens. Fijians, Indians, and others are all eligible to vote and to be elected, and to serve in government. Government is representative of them all.

2. The separate electoral rolls, and the allocation of quotas of seats in the House of Representatives. The above comment carries over to this issue. I do not want to defend precisely the 22:22:8 ratio, but I see merit in constitutional guarantees that communities that differ profoundly from each other will each be represented—fairly represented—in government. The relevant considerations are those advanced by Lewis, summarized in Chapter 1 and restated more than once already. In some countries different population groups are concentrated in such

a way that territorially delimited electoral districts assure each group of appropriate representation, but where this is not the case, provision for separate electoral rolls and the quota allocation of seats is quite understandable. The appropriate criticism of Fijian arrangements, as I see it, is not that the constitution provides for this but that it fails to provide formally for the representation of the different communities in the executive and judicial branches of government. If the domination of the legislature by one community is undesirable, the domination of the other branches by that same community is fraught with great danger too. Of course, if the Indians were to gain full domination of all three branches of government, they might be benign, assuring the equal enjoyment of human rights to all, but the general record of majorities (including the majority whites of the United States during the period of slavery and Jim Crow) does not provide a basis for a confident expectation that this would be the case.

3. The composition of the Senate. As noted above, the Senate consists of 22 members appointed by the governor-general according to advice extended by communal leaders. If they all recommend only members of their own communities, the Fijians and the Rotumans, comprising 46 percent of the population, end up with 16 of the 22 seats, or 73 percent. The disproportion is gross, and I would count it as a denial of equal treatment—as discriminatory.

4. The safeguarding of Fijian land ownership. As indicated above, the Fijians have communal ownership of 83 percent of the land. More specifically, a Native Land Trust Board administers 83 percent of the land of the country on behalf of 6,600 communal land-owning units. Most of it is reserved for members of the "Fijian race," but some may be leased to anyone.[45] Constitutional arrangements, especially those relating to the Senate, permit the Fijians to veto change in laws and ordinances relating to the land.

Judgments can readily differ on the justice of the situation. The economic progress of the Indians and others is no doubt impeded. But the situation is not analogous to situations in other countries that have led to land reform. Ownership is not in the hands of a few who enrich themselves by exploiting a peasantry. Rather, the culture and the way of life of the Fijians depend on the arrangement. The focal issue is presumably whether the law should be changed so as to eliminate centralized administration of the Fijian land and to permit the various Fijian land-owning units to sell or lease as they please. The potential consequences are obvious. If emphasis is placed on the right of the Fijians to preserve their culture and if it is granted that preserving a culture is more a community than an individual enterprise, the judgment might well be that continued centralized Fijian control is essential. It is an effective means to a legitimate end.

The above discussion of the specific features of the arrangements in Fiji that are most open to question involves obvious appeals to general principles. These principles are individualistic, on the one hand, and communal, on the other. Thoroughgoing individualism leads to adverse judgments. Such individualism holds that only individual persons and sovereign states have rights, or negatively, that peoples or culture groups within the state do not have rights. It further holds that so long as individuals enjoy the equal protection of the laws, open competition should be the rule, with individuals winning on the basis of whatever personal qualities turn out to count for most in the struggle. If individuals lacking these qualities suffer, and if indigenous or other recognizable culture groups or communities are destroyed, the outcome should be accepted as an unavoidable concomitant of progress.

The individualist line is reinforced by the argument that the fortunes of the Indians in Fiji should in no way be prejudiced by their alien origin or ancestry. They were allowed to immigrate—and in most cases were encouraged and helped to immigrate—as individuals, and they have made Fiji their permanent home and the object of their loyalty. Even if it be granted for the sake of argument that first-generation immigrants have a special obligation to adjust and adapt to the new environment that they have chosen, and should not make waves, the argument becomes irrevelant to succeeding generations, who are native born like the others. According to this argument, no valid basis exists for taking communal or racial or other differences into account in connection with political participation and representation. And the argument can be extended by deploring the divisiveness of communalism and by expressing the hope or conviction that, given free choice, individuals will not regularly line up so as to pit community against community, or race against race, but will at least to some extent divide along other lines, promoting national integration.

The individualist line can also be reinforced by rejecting an assumption that I make above—that the Fijian community depends for its survival on special measures of protection. The argument is that, though the Fijian community is less advanced, the disparities are not extreme, and that, in any event, the Fijians are sufficiently numerous that they do not need to be classified as weak and vulnerable. The argument further is that the Indians are so divided among themselves as to give the Fijians a considerable measure of safety.

The individualist line of argument—the melting pot line— has been dominant in the United States. Those taking it in the United States tend either to forget about the Indians or to believe that the Indians, for their own good, should be like us. And it seems probable that few who take the melting pot line have any idea that Samoans come under the jurisdiction of the United States; in any case, it would not be surprising if Americans dedicated to individualism within the 50 states would grant an exception to a small group on a relatively remote Pacific island. The issue is ordinarily considered in the United States not in terms of indigenous peoples but in terms of individuals who have immigrated into the country, whether voluntarily or involuntarily: the ethnics of European or Oriental extraction, the Puerto Ricans, the Mexican-Americans, and the blacks; and the dominant thought is that these persons should be integrated, if not assimilated, into the national community, little or no attention being paid to racial or cultural differences that distinguish them. As we have seen in Chapter 2, this statement needs to be qualified with respect to language, but in the main it holds.

In Fiji, however, no national community exists. There is no mainstream for individuals to enter. There are instead quite different communities with different cultures and different values. And policies that ignore the differences seem likely to lead the Fijians to about the same fate that the American Indians have suffered, except that in Fiji there presumably would be no genocide.

It is worth recalling that both the convention on indigenous populations and the convention on racial discrimination reject the thorough-going individualistic approach to cultural and racial differences. It is also worth noting that anti-communalism may itself be a form of communalism, just as anti-racism may be a form of racism. Fairness to the Indian community of Fiji requires an acknowledgment of the fact that it opposed communalism even when it was in a minority; but opposition to communalism is surely encouraged by the prospect that thorough-going individualism would be to the advantage of the Indian community. In the same way, blacks in South Africa can oppose the communalism of the whites and champion the slogan of one person, one vote and majority rule, for they can be sure that this will lead to black control.

Communalism reverses the emphasis that individualism connotes. Communalism stresses the importance of the community. According to the communal view, the community is a kind of corporate entity, with a right to protect precious features of communal life. The community has the right to decide what kinds of behavior are acceptable, without any pretence that this right depends on unanimous consent, whether given now or in the past. The community is the central factor in socializing individuals and shaping their values, attitudes, and personalities, giving meaning to their lives. It is the framework within which culture develops and is sustained—language, religion, fundamental beliefs, art, literature, knowledge, scientific and technological progress. The really self-made man is a myth, an impossibility. Without the community individuals would not develop human qualities. Without the multiple benefits that come from association with others, without the institutions and traditions that the community has developed, without both the limitations and the opportunities that membership in a community implies, the individual would be lost, rootless, incapable of significant accomplishment, and perhaps

a danger to others. True, communalism reflects social divisions
and has often seemed to accentuate them. The very word communal has come to be associated with strife. Harmonious cooperation among communities is a problem, just as it is among
sovereign states, but the destruction of the lesser communities
of a country, and the accompanying cultures, is scarcely the
desirable way of seeking to solve the problem.

The communal argument does not necessarily mean that
every aspect of the communal arrangement in Fiji should be
maintained. Whether seats in the House should be allocated
on precisely the 22:22:8 ratio is open to argument. Perhaps the
Indians should have one or two more seats and those on the
general roll one or two less; or perhaps the quotas, instead of
being fixed numerically, should be made proportionate to population and thus subject to adjustment after each census; or
perhaps they should be made proportionate to the votes cast.
Or recommendations that a Royal Commission made in 1975
might be implemented. Those recommendations are that the
Fijian and Indian communities should each be guaranteed not
22 but 12 seats in the House, that those on the general roll
should be guaranteed not 8 but 3, that an additional seat should
be created for Rotuma, but that no other House seats should
be reserved. Instead, those on the national roll (that is, all
voters) would fill other seats as they choose, each voter having
a single transferable vote and each party securing seats in
proportion to its electoral support. The role of communal or
racial concerns in filling these other seats (a total of 25 out of
53) would thus depend on the choice of individual voters. The
recommendations look sensible, and if they were implemented
they would provide evidence of the consequences of a reduction
in the formal emphasis on communal differences. It should be
noted, however, that the Commission did not recommend the
complete abandonment of communal differentiation. Moreover,
since its mandate related only to the House, it could assume
that the allocation of seats in the Senate would remain un-
changed and that this would continue to give protection to the
Fijians. It is the grossly disproportionate representation of the
Fijians in the Senate that seems to me to be most vulnerable
to criticism.[46]

When Fiji was still a British colony, but when arrangements like those included in the constitution were already in effect, the General Assembly adopted resolutions that were critical. It noted that the Fiji electoral system was "not based on generally accepted democratic principles," and it invited Britain to work out "a new constitution providing for free elections conducted on the principle of 'one man [*sic*!], one vote'...." It did not speak of majority rule, but called for "the creation of representative institutions," and recommended efforts "to achieve the political, economic, and social integration of the various communities."[47] Later it held that the constitutional changes Britain was considering "would stand in the way of the political, economic, and social integration of the people as a whole," and it requested Britain "to repeal all discriminatory laws...."[48] The next year it asked for "the abolishing of all discriminatory measures so as to foster communal harmony and national unity...."[49] Various speakers accused Britain of a divide and rule strategy.[50] Similarly, an independent scholar (of Indian extraction) speaks of the "blatantly discriminatory" arrangements in Fiji and of the constitution that "establishes minority rule."[51]

As is perhaps already clear, I do not accept these judgments, at least not on a general and wholesale basis. Some specific aspects of the arrangements in Fiji should no doubt be changed, but special measures to protect the Fijian community and culture seem to me to be justifiable.

While Fiji was still a colony, Britain acted in its behalf in ratifying the convention on the elimination of racial discrimination, but attached reservations. Since Fiji has become independent, it has confirmed its acceptance of the obligations of the convention, but has also renewed and reworded the reservations. As might be expected, the reservations cover the areas in which Fijian practices raise issues. Fiji reserves the right not to implement provisions of the convention that go counter to Fijian law concerning elections, concerning land ownership and land tenure, and concerning the school system.[52] This seems to imply an admission that various provisions of Fijian law violate the requirements of the convention, and perhaps they do in some respects. But in the main Fiji could defend its prac-

tices with the argument that indigenous and less advanced
people are entitled to special measures to promote their equal
enjoyment of human rights, and with the argument that all
peoples are entitled to preserve their culture.

CONCLUSION

In many countries, indigenous populations are treated differentially on a communal basis, which means that the principles associated with individualism are not applied. The
emphasis is not so much on the rights of individuals as on the
rights of communities. In the United States the fact has received little attention, despite its application to policies relating to the American Indians and the American Samoans. It is
possible to treat the special measures for the Indians and Samoans as an exception, and to assume that the rules of individualism remain unchallenged and unaffected.

It is much more difficult to dismiss the treatment of the
indigenous as an exception, and thus without any intellectual
significance or consequence, when the situations and practices
of other countries are considered. Even if in other countries
the indigenous were always as small a portion of the total
population as they are in the United States, the fact that so
many other countries are involved should give pause. An exception that has to be made in a considerable portion of the
countries of the world takes on more importance than an exception that is rare. Further, in some instances, most notably
in Fiji and Malaysia (to be discussed in the next chapter) the
indigenous population comprises such a large portion of the
total that it is simply not sensible to say that the prevailing
philosophy is individualist and that the special measures classify as exceptions. To be sure, the rights of individuals are
everywhere recognized (sometimes more in theory than in practice); but it is important to acknowledge that in the United
States and in a great many other countries the rights of indigenous groups are recognized too. This means that individuals are differentially treated depending on their membership,
and the requirement of equal and nondiscriminatory treatment

is interpreted accordingly. In the countries with large indigenous populations, the fact of group rights (communal rights) takes its place in importance side by side with the fact of individual rights.

5

The Bumiputra: *Malaysia*

This chapter, like the preceding one, is on the problem of the conflict between the human rights of individuals and the claims of indigenous peoples. The indigenous peoples dealt with in the two chapters differ in their level of advancement and in the justifiability of their claims for special measures for their benefit. The case for special measures, and thus the case for the view that differentiation and even preferential treatment may be legitimate and not discriminatory, is especially strong in the case of the American Indians, the Samoans, and the Maoris. The case is still good, though relatively weaker, in the case of the Fijians. Questions about Malaysia's policies on behalf of the Malays are more difficult.

The composition of the population of Malaysia is given in Table 3. The Malays and Chinese (47 percent of the total, and 34 percent, respectively) are found in the peninsular states and in the Borneo states of Sabah and Sarawak (East Malaysia). The Indians are mainly on the peninsula. The Dayaks and Kadazans live in the Borneo states, and might well be subdivided into a number of tribes or peoples.

Once more a comment is in place on the question whether the Malays should be conceived as an indigenous people—the *bumiputra*—or in terms of race. I choose to treat them as indigenous. The basic justification is that, though racial differences are obvious, the Malays (and the Dayaks, Kadazans, and other natives) count as indigenous according to the definition

Table 3
Population of Malaysia, 1976

	Number	Per cent
Malays	5,838,000	47
Chinese	4,167,000	34
Indians and Pakistanis	1,083,000	9
Dayaks	436,000	4
Kadazans	224,000	2
Other indigenous	421,000	3
Others	234,000	2
Total	12,403,000	

Source: Malaysia. Ministry of Information. *Malaysia 1977. Official Year Book.* Vol. 17. Kuala Lumpur, 1979. Pp. 23-24.

in the convention on indigenous and tribal populations. They were already in place when the Chinese and Indians came as immigrants. The argument that they need special measures for their protection and advancement is weakened by the fact that they are so numerous; nevertheless, they are in fact less advanced than the Chinese and Indians. They are roughly comparable to the Fijians in that in general they are less well educated, less skilled, less motivated to obtain education and skills, and more inclined to forgo work on behalf of increased leisure. The Chinese and Indians have long been in the lead in the economic and commercial life of the country and in the professions.

The case for considering the Malays in terms of indigeneity rather than in terms of race is strengthened somewhat by the definition of *Malay* included in the constitution (Article 160). It says that a Malay is "a person who professes the religion of Islam, habitually speaks the Malay language, [and] conforms to Malay custom...." It goes on to specify that to be accepted as a Malay one must also have been born before independence in the Federation or in Singapore, or must have at least one parent who was so born or who was on independence day domiciled there or who is descended from such a person. This latter provision is designed to keep at a minimum the number of immigrants, or the number with immigrant ancestry, who can qualify as Malay, and might or might not be considered a racial qualification. Over time, some Indonesians, some Arabs, and some Muslims from India have come to be accepted as Malays, which tends to indicate that race is not crucial; but Chinese are scarcely ever accepted as Malay even if they convert to Islam, which tends to indicate the opposite.[1] The common practice of Malays and non-Malays alike is to identify the different communities in Malaysia in terms of race—or simply to speak of the Malays, Chinese, and so on, and to leave it to the reader to decide what the relative emphasis should be on the different characteristics that distinguish them. These different characteristics obviously include religion and language as well as social customs and culture. Malaysia has not ratified the International Convention on the Elimination of All Forms of Racial Discrimination, which may or may not suggest a fear that policies pursued do not fully meet the standards prescribed.

Given the similarities between Malaysia and Fiji, essentially the same considerations and arguments concerning equal treatment are relevant. Nevertheless, Malaysian circumstances and policies give rise to distinctive questions. Those taken up here will include the *bumiputra* doctrine, the territorial limits of the state, elections and the composition of the parliament and government, and special rights in connection with public employment. A verbal formula that is much used in Malaysia relates to these questions. It comes from the Federation of Malaya Agreement of 1948. As included in the constitution, it speaks of "the special position of the Malays and the natives of any of the states of Sabah and Sarawak and the legitimate interests of the other communities...." The reference to Sabah and Sarawak was inserted after these states were added to Malaya and it became Malaysia. The key notion is that some elements of the population (all indigenous) have a "special position," whereas other elements have "legitimate interests."

THE *BUMIPUTRA* DOCTRINE

I have not seen a succinct statement of the *bumiputra* doctrine. The term translates roughly as "sons of the soil," and the reference is to the indigenous inhabitants as opposed to immigrants and their descendants. Of course, the Malays themselves were once immigrants, and the population of the country still includes descendants of those who were indigenous when the Malays arrived. Nevertheless, when the contrast is with the Chinese and Indians, the Malays are the *bumiputra*, and the intimation is that the country really belongs to them, the others being outsiders if not intruders. Thus the "special position" of the Malays. The tendency to regard others as outsiders is accentuated by the fact that a high proportion of the Chinese, when they first arrived in Malaya, viewed themselves as short-term residents, come to improve their fortunes and then return to their native land.

British policies in the Malay states reflected a degree of acceptance of the *bumiputra* doctrine. As in Fiji, and in conformity with the earlier policies of the Malay states themselves, the British permitted the immigration of Chinese and others. At the same time they sought to ward off some of the likely political consequences of the immigration. They did this in the main by laying it down that "no pains should be spared to safeguard the position and dignity of the Malay Rulers."[2] That is, they maintained indirect, non-democratic rule. One of the reasons was that this would provide

the greatest safeguard against the political submersion of the Malays which would result from the development of popular government on western lines. For, in such a government the Malays would be hopelessly outnumbered by the other races owing to the great influx of immigrants that has taken place into Malaya during the last few years.[3]

Actually, the Malays were "hopelessly outnumbered" only in some local (mainly urban) areas. In any event, the statement illustrates that the very choice of a form of government may serve a communal (or a racial) purpose. Of course, the safeguarding of the position of the Malay rulers meant a denial of democratic control to the Malay rank and file as well as to the Chinese and Indians, but at least in a symbolic sense the *bumiputra* doctrine prevailed.

The issue continues. Having been maintained in office during the period of British protection, the Malay rulers necessarily figured in the negotiations leading to the grant of independence in 1957. And the negotiations produced a constitution that continues the rulers in power—on a hereditary basis; they serve in nine of the thirteen states, the remaining four being under governors. The Conference of Rulers (which for this purpose does not include the governors) elects the king (Yang di Pertuan Agong) from among its own members for a term of five years; and the Conference has certain other powers. The king in turn has various powers, including the power to appoint a majority of the members of the Senate. He is free to appoint citizens from the Chinese and Indian communities, but his position and prerogatives nevertheless reinforce the "special position" of the Malays—even if some Malays join the Chinese and Indians in resenting the non-democratic features of the arrangement.

Judgment on the question whether the arrangement violates the rule of equal treatment is easy: it does. In making and considering the judgment, however, we should not limit our view to Malaysia. Hereditary succession is the rule in some other countries too. Wherever it exists, even in a homogeneous society, it is non-egalitarian, differentiating among individuals on the basis of birth. In a heterogeneous society it is likely to be invidiously discriminatory in that it gives special status to the group from which the privileged family comes. In Britain it gives special status to whites and to members of the Church of England. It is no more likely that a West Indian or a Pakistani citizen of Britain, or a Catholic, will succeed to the throne at Westminster than that a Chinese or an Indian will become the ruler of a Malay state. Largely because of the non-egalitarian and discriminatory features of hereditary succession, revolutions and other developments have in some countries brought it to an end, and in others (again with Britain as an example) the powers of hereditary rulers have been sharply curtailed. The king in Malaysia has relatively greater powers than the king or queen does in Britain, but the difference is not extreme.

The *bumiputra* doctrine is applied also at the state level. The rulers (sultans) are state officials. In the nine states having a sultan, according to Gordon Means, the chief minister must also be a Malay, although six of the nine permit exceptions to this rule. Six states also require that the chief administrative officer be a Malay, and six require that members of state councils associated with the monarchy be Malays. In Sabah and Sarawak, the tendency is to insist that one of the two top positions go to a Malay.[4] And the application of the doctrine extends to the local level. According to Alvin Rabushka, the Malays

have systematically sought to discriminate against non-Malays (Chinese and Indians) in local government elections by using a variety of techniques including suspension of municipal councils controlled by non-Malay political parties, federal and state inquiries into municipal council practices, and the outright cancellation of municipal elections in selected communities.[5]

Note that Rabushka describes what happens as discrimination, which implies a judgment. And the judgment may be justified, for the kinds of actions that he describes seem arbitrary. But it should not be taken for granted that immigrants (or the children of immigrants) should be allowed to push the *bumiputra* aside. That is what happened to the American Indians and to the blacks of Rhodesia and South Africa. The Malays are said to fear that they may be "reduced to the status of Red Indians striving to live in the wastelands of America."[6] The fear may be exaggerated, but it should not be dismissed.

Some kinds of special measures on behalf of the Malays seem to me to be justified. The *bumiputra* doctrine, however, is questionable as a basis for them, for as between native born citizens it is not at all clear that those whose ancestors got there first are morally entitled to a special position. Two other bases for communally-minded policies are less open to question. One is that the Malays are weaker (despite their number) and less advanced, and thus should have the benefit of special measures to promote their equal enjoyment of human rights. This basis for differentiation would remain legitimate for as long as the special need exists. The second basis for communally-minded policies is the right of a people to self-determination, and more particularly its right to preserve its culture; and this right should operate not only for the benefit of the Malays but also for the benefit of the Chinese, Indians, and others.

The *bumiputra* doctrine is relevant also to policies concerning the granting of citizenship. After all, the "special position" of the sons of the soil can be kept most secure by denying citizenship to others or, if that is impossible, by granting citizenship on a strictly limited basis. The Malays made concessions on the issue in the negotiations leading to independence in 1957, and the new constitution provided for *jus soli*, that is, for the automatic acquisition of citizenship (with minor exceptions) by anyone born in the country thereafter. The constitution did not make the rule retroactive, out of fear of the possible consequences if large numbers of additional Chinese became citizens forthwith. Instead, it fixed conditions under which those born previously in Malaysia or elsewhere might acquire citizenship by registration or naturalization. In 1962 the constitution was amended so as to make the acquisition of citizenship by non-Malays somewhat more difficult. So far as *jus soli* is concerned, the qualifier was added that at the time of the birth at least one parent must be either a citizen or a permanent resident.

The passage of time is ameliorating the situation, for immigration has declined and the portion of Chinese and Indians who qualify for citizenship at birth is increasing. Leaving aside questions pertaining to refugees and those seeking asylum, no human right is violated if a country refuses to accept immigrants, but those allowed to enter surely have a moral claim not to be kept in second class status.

The *bumiputra* doctrine relates also to the question of the appropriate boundaries of the state, but it is best to treat that question under its own heading.

THE TERRITORIAL LIMITS OF THE STATE

Questions concerning the territorial limits of Malaya arose because history did little to indicate where the boundary lines should be. Historically, what is now Malaysia was divided into a number of political entities, and it remained divided during most of the period of British hegemony. Singapore, Penang, and Malacca were separate colonies, and the nine states of the peninsula were separate protectorates. Brunei, Sabah, and Sarawak were far away on Borneo, and had predominantly non-Malay populations. Immigration into these various entities began before the arrival of the British, and the British permitted it to continue, with results already given in Table 3. The Chinese came to constitute an especially high proportion of the population of Singapore, and had it been included in Malaya, they would have been numerous enough to dominate the political life of the country, just as they already dominated its economic life. Largely for communal reasons, therefore, Singapore was excluded.[7] And later when Singapore was briefly included, it was on the basis of a set of terms inspired by communal considerations: Sabah and Sarawak were also included so as to restrict the relative increase in Chinese power; they were given a disproportionately large number of seats in the House of Representatives, and Singapore a disproportionately small number; and citizens of Singapore who moved to other parts of the country did not necessarily retain full rights of political participation.[8] Even so, the admission of Singapore (involving a change in the name of the country from Malaya to Malaysia) accentuated communal strains and tensions, especially when political leaders in Singapore began agitating for a Malaysian rather than a Malay Malaysia; and in fairly short order (after two years) Singapore was expelled.

Theoretically, communal considerations might in the future induce support for other decisions on the territorial limits of the state. If the Malays considered themselves seriously threatened by their Chinese compatriots, they could seek a merger with Indonesia, with which they have both a religious and a linguistic affinity. And they might go still farther and support the creation of Maphilindo—a merger of Malaysia, the Philippines, and Indonesia. In either event, the Chinese would be swamped in a much larger country, and implicitly they would be threatened with the same gross harassment and persecution that the Chinese minority in Indonesia has suffered.[9]

I mention these matters mainly to illustrate some anomalies in prevailing thought about the legitimacy of adjusting political arrangements to communal differences. Everyone agrees, I assume, that the exclusion of Singapore from Malaya/Malaysia did not violate any moral or legal imperative. Neither the Chinese of Singapore nor the Chinese of the peninsula nor anyone else had a right to expect that Singapore would be included. This means, however, that gerrymandering of a sort is acceptable in fixing the boundary lines of the state, though it may deny equal protection if it occurs within the state. Of course, we are accustomed to the idea that the boundaries of the state should be adjusted to the boundaries of a nation, but that is not what went on in Malaya, for Malaya was not a nation. What went on was the drawing of boundary lines (and the making of other arrangements) so as to give the Malays substantial assurance that they would not be swamped and dominated by the Chinese. Communal considerations prevailed.

Another anomaly might be noted as well. It exists because of the fact that the comparisons involved in questions about discrimination relate to the treatment of persons within the same country. An Iranian child whose schooling is not as good as that of an American child is not thought of as a victim of discrimination. According to the same logic, it would be theoretically possible for a Singaporean to suffer discrimination in comparison with a person on the peninsula if Singapore were a part of Malaysia; but with Singapore excluded, the comparison is not considered relevant, and precisely the same kinds of treatment are not discriminatory.

Finally, it is interesting to observe that prevailing liberal, individualistic thought finds it acceptable that the people of Singapore are a corporate entity and count as one when they comprise a sovereign state, but not when they are a part of a larger state; when they are included in a larger state, they are ordinarily thought of as an aggregation of persons who count in proportion to their number. By the same token (if a slight digression be permitted) the Tamils of Ceylon could be a group with rights until the British united them with the Sinhalese in one political entity. Now that they are parts of that one political entity, Sri Lanka, those inspired by liberal individualism necessarily resist the thought that they retain, or should enjoy, corporate rights.

ELECTIONS AND THE COMPOSITION OF THE PARLIAMENT AND GOVERNMENT

Communalism figures prominently in Malaysian elections and in determining the composition of the parliament and gov-

120 Human Rights, Ethnicity, and Discrimination

ernment. Its role reflects freely made choices, not provided for by law. Voters register on a common electoral roll, and are free to organize and contest elections, whether on a communal or a non-communal basis. Except for the arrangements concerning the Malay rulers and the king, described above, the constitution does not assign political offices communally. But the political parties are communal, though a few seek not to be; and dominant among them is the United Malay National Organization (UMNO). For long it joined in an Alliance with the Malayan Chinese Association (MCA), and the Malayan Indian Congress (MIC); and then in 1974 it organized a still broader alliance, the National Front. The Front, like the Alliance before it, always wins the elections and thus controls parliament and the formation of the cabinets. UMNO is willing to concede some cabinet posts to persons from other parties, and in general it is considerate enough of the Chinese and Indians that many of them are willing to give it support in order to keep more extreme Malays at bay; but UMNO always claims the prime ministry and ultimate control for itself.

The constitution provides for a bicameral national legislature. The Senate consists of two members for each state, elected by the state legislative assemblies, and 32 others appointed (as already indicated) by the king. The constitution names various types of persons whom the king is to appoint, including those "representative of racial minorities or...capable of representing the interests of the aborigines." This is a type of affirmative action, a special measure designed to give the minorities and the aborigines assurance that their interests and rights will be considered. It is no more discriminatory than when the president of the United States takes race or religion or sex into account in making appointments to the Supreme Court.

The House of Representatives consists of 154 members elected by popular vote, seats being allocated by states. Especially in the light of the movement of population and limitations on the granting of citizenship, the allocation to the various states has always given the Malays more seats, and the Chinese fewer, than their numbers suggest. Moreover, there is deliberate communal "malapportionment." A 1962 amendment to the constitution abandoned the equal population principle that had hitherto prevailed and specified that "weightage for area" might occur, with rural constituencies containing "as little as one half the electors" of urban constituencies. Since the Malays are predominantly rural and the Chinese and Indians predominantly urban, the effect of this was to accentuate the advantage of the Malays. For the 1964 elections, two of the 104 constituencies included fewer than 15,000 voters, and 24 included more than 30,000. A 1973 amendment left the idea of "weightage for area" intact, but repealed the explicit statement about the possible discrepancy between rural and urban constituencies, leaving judgment in the matter to those drawing the boundary lines.[10]

The question is whether, in giving "weightage for area" and thus in giving the Malays disproportionate representation, Malaysia should be said to engage in discrimination. By claiming that the weightage is "for area" rather than for Malays, the government seems implicitly to admit that the case for what it is doing is not strong. Whether it can be justified in terms of the *bumiputra* doctrine, or as a way of giving special protection to a weak element of the population, is doubtful.

In deviating from the equal population principle, Malaysia has much company. Few states are as strict as the United States in upholding that principle, and its respect for the principle is a development of the 1960s and 1970s.

THE OFFICIAL LANGUAGE AND THE OFFICIAL RELIGION

In Chapters 2 and 3 I have already taken up questions of equality and discrimination relating to language and religion, but chose then to say little about Malaysia. A note should thus be added here.

The constitution makes Malay the national language, and the law specifies that the national language is the sole official language. At the same time, the law permits "translations of official documents or communications in the language of any other community of the Federation...for such purposes as may be deemed necessary in the public interest." And the law is that the king "may permit the continued use of the English language for such official purposes as may be deemed fit."[11]

Obviously these terms are not onerous. Even the practical significance of naming Malay as the official language is not clear, for the other languages may still be used for official purposes. At the very least, however, the naming of Malay has a symbolic significance. It gives the Malays a special source of satisfaction and pride: their language has a status, and thus inferentially an importance and worth, that Chinese and Tamil lack. A practical advantage is added insofar as Malay is actually used, for this means that Malays can operate in their mother tongue while others have the burden of learning and using a foreign tongue. It is thus bound to be the case that the Chinese and the Indians, in comparison with the Malays, face a linguistic handicap in pursuing political and governmental careers. Moreover, even if the language policy actually followed is "super-liberal," the "super-liberalism" is not assured either by the law or the constitution. The provisions of these instruments give encouragement to those who want Malay to be used more, if not exclusively, whereas the protections for other languages lie in the attitude of the king, who is a Malay, and others who are likely to be Malays.[12]

So far, the Malays have seen fit to permit the widespread use of English for official purposes, which reduces their relative advantage in that it means that they too have the burden of learning and using a foreign language. The use of English gives the advantage to all who know it, regardless of communal identity. At the same time, it puts all others at a disadvantage. The fact illustrates how difficult it is to get away from discrimination where different languages are concerned.

The special status of Malay has about it a suggestion of the *bumiputra* doctrine. But the justification commonly advanced is not in its terms but rather in terms of the need to weld the various communities into one nation and the need for a common language for the purpose. The justification is doubtful. One could as well argue that the greater the insistence on the use of Malay, the greater the discrimination against the Chinese and Indians, and the greater the resentments caused. Conversely, the more "liberal" the language policy (that is, the greater the use of English, Chinese, and Tamil), the more the official justification is undermined. A number of other countries have found it possible to build or maintain a sense of nationhood while giving official status to two or more languages. And in doing so, some cite the very reason advanced in Malaysia to justify the selection of only one: that equality of status for the languages of different groups is essential to harmony within the state, if not to the continued unity of the state. This is the judgment in Belgium, Canada, and Switzerland. Singapore gives official status to four languages. This is not to say that government must operate in any language that a citizen chooses to speak. The United Nations itself does not give equal status to the languages of all members, and thus by its own practice lends sanction to the view that differentiation as to language is sometimes justifiable. But when a minority comprises a third of the population of the country, as the Chinese do, the case for giving official status to its language is powerful. And even the Indians (9 percent of the population in 1970) can reasonably claim recognition for their language in some connections.

In addition to making Malay the national language, the constitution, as noted in Chapter 3, makes Islam the national religion, and makes the king the head of the religion. Further, in various ways the law gives special status and protection to Islam. Other religions "may be practiced in peace and harmony," but they are nevertheless secondary. The arrangement is obviously discriminatory, just as like arrangements in many other countries are discriminatory. A substantial portion of the members of the United Nations, who are required by the Charter to promote human rights without distinction as to religion, actually do not observe the requirement—at least if it is interpreted to mean what the words plainly seem to say. In Malaysia, the matter has not been a serious issue, though reports from Sabah indicate that governmental leaders are using material pressures to induce people to convert to Islam.[13] In any event, a contradiction exists between domestic practices and the international requirement.

In the case of the Malays, as already noted, race and religion are intertwined. Only a person who professes the religion of Islam may be a Malay. If a Malay renounces Islam, he thereby renounces his status as a Malay. He thus ceases to be entitled to the benefits of any of the special measures adopted for the protection and advancement of the Malays.[14]

SPECIAL RIGHTS

The fact is noted above that the constitution speaks of the "special position" of the Malays and the natives of Sabah and Sarawak, and of the "legitimate interests" of the other communities. I should now add that the constitution requires the king to safeguard the "special position." He must reserve for Malays and for the natives of Sabah and Sarawak a reasonable proportion of: (a) positions in the federal public service; (b) scholarships and like benefits; and (c) licenses for those businesses that can be taken up only on the basis of licenses.

Prior to independence, Britain had already established the principle of preferential hiring for Malays in the public service. In fact, until 1952, Asians other than Malays were simply not eligible for posts in the elite Malayan Civil Service, though they already outnumbered the Malays in the lower ranking civil service positions. Once independence was achieved, the king laid it down that four out of every five new recruits into the Malayan Civil Service, and three out of every four new recruits into several of the lower ranking services must be Malays.[15] The result was that by 1968 the Malays comprised more than 85 percent of the Malaysian Civil Service.[16]

As in the case of Fiji, a distinction must be made between the principle of adopting ratios and the precise ratios adopted. I do not argue that the precise ratios are justifiable. Eighty-five percent of the posts for a community that comprises 47 percent of the population looks indefensibly high. The disproportion is not so great in the lesser services. Regardless of the precise ratios, however, there are many precedents for the principle, as noted especially in Chapter 2. The United Nations itself follows it in allocating posts in the Secretariat to member states, and both Belgium and Switzerland follow it with respect to the language groups into which their populations divide. As African states received independence, many of them set about "Africanizing" their civil services.

Tanganyika provides one of the most interesting illustrations. At the time it became independent, few citizens of African ancestry, but more citizens of Indian ancestry, had the educational and other qualifications for positions in the upper levels of the civil service. Had appointments been made according to merit on the basis of open competition, the Indian community would have been grossly overrepresented; and in the long run the support of blacks for the regime would have been jeopardized. The solution was to recruit blacks preferentially when qualified applicants were available, and to pass over qualified Indian citizens in favor of Europeans. The Europeans were to serve until blacks received the necessary training. Nyerere himself approved racial differentiation in the interest of Africanizing the civil service. Even after he endorsed "complete equality of opportunity for all Tanganyika citizens" and prohibited discrimination on grounds of race, tribe, color, sex, creed, or religion, he added a proviso that "temporarily this shall not preclude the Government, or any other appropriate authorities, from taking steps to correct any imbalance which results from past discrimination on any of these grounds."[17] Kenya followed somewhat similar policies.[18]

Essentially the same principle is accepted in American politics in both formal and informal ways. Formally, federal courts have been ordering ratio-hiring, especially in connection with municipal police and fire departments, to bring about greater minority representation. And informally presidents of the United States and many others who make appointments or who help make up slates of candidates seek some kind of "balance"; that is, they depart from the strict rule of individual merit and seek what they regard as appropriate representation for racial and ethnic groups, and for women.

Whatever the judgment of the ratios of representation adopted in specific cases, the principle involved is easily defensible on several grounds. The most obvious grounds have already been cited several times: the right of weaker and less advanced indigenous peoples to special measures designed to promote their equal enjoyment of human rights, and the right of every people to preserve its culture. Both of these rights necessarily raise the question whether representation in government and in the public service should be provided for, and in some cases the answer is surely in the affirmative. Those communities that come up to some minimum size and that have reached a certain level of civilization should surely be represented if they so desire. A pragmatic consideration reinforces concern for their rights in this connection: those who see that their own kind are playing an appropriate role in government are more likely to be supportive than those who believe that government is in the hands of an alien group.

Special rights for the Malays also include the reservation of more than four million acres of land for them, creating a situation analogous to the one existing in the Aaland Islands, in Fiji, and in American Samoa: some citizens are eligible to buy the reserved land, and others are not.

COMMUNAL RIOTS AND ADDED GUARANTEES

Political arrangements in Malaysia reflect a "constitutional contract among communal groups," developed in the period leading up to independence. The contract was not negotiated and signed as one document, but was developed in a series of bargains and understandings. It is described implicitly above. On the one hand, it conceded political preeminence to the Malays and the right of Malays, as the less advanced people, to special measures designed to promote their advancement. It included the acceptance of Malay as the national language and of Islam as the official religion. On the other hand, the contract assured the Chinese and Indians that their economic and business interests would be respected, and it assured them of a right to participate in politics and government, even if as junior partners. It eased the requirements for obtaining citizenship, and thus enhanced Chinese and Indian voting strength; and it gave the Chinese and Indians freedom to preserve their own languages and religions, even if without the governmental support enjoyed by Malay and Islam.[19]

The contract was expedient in providing a basis for stable communal relationships for a number of years. But it gave the Malays some advantages they had no right to expect, and forced the Chinese and Indians to make concessions in order to be assured of the kind of treatment to which they were entitled in any event. I have in mind especially the concessions of the Chinese concerning language.

The contract continues to be observed, but through the years it has been challenged. Some Malays challenge it. They start with the assumption (as asserted by a political leader who later became prime minister) that "Malaya has always been, and still is, their land.... [T]he Malays are the rightful owners of Malaya...."[20] This outlook leads easily to the view that the Malays have already conceded too much to the Chinese and Indians and that the "special position" of the Malays should be made special in a fuller and more rigorous sense. Moreover the terms of the constitutional contract were such that in the economic realm the Chinese and Indians could promptly get what was due them whereas advancement for the Malays was slow in coming; and many Malays developed resentments over this.

It should be noted that neither the Malays who support the contract nor those who challenge it are ever accused of racism in the sense of attitudes of racial superiority. Even the *bumiputra* doctrine rests not on a claim of superiority but on chronological priority. "The motive behind preferential treatment is not to put the Malays in a superior position, but to bring them up to the level of the non-Malays."[21]

The Chinese and Indians are more divided about the contract than are the Malays. Their parties within the National Front are clearly subordinate to the UMNO, and crises have occurred between them and the Malays—for example, over the number of seats in the House to be allocated to each community.[22] And the Malayan Chinese Association proved unable to retain the united support of the Chinese community, the main charge being that its leaders sold out the interests of the Chinese in general in an effort to buy protection for the economic and business interests of the Chinese upper class. Further, some racism exists on the Chinese side. For example, Karl von Vorys speaks of the Chinese tradition that "only Chinese could be civilized. Others were not only different, they were plainly inferior."[23]

Discontent with the contract led in 1969 to communal riots in Kuala Lumpur, which induced the government to declare an emergency, as it was entitled to do under the constitution. Power was then concentrated (for what turned out to be a two year period) in a National Operations Council (NOC), and the NOC took measures designed to reduce the possibility that riots would recur. It formulated a national ideology (*Rukunegara*); it made legal and constitutional changes; and it set out in a more determined way to advance the Malays toward social and economic equality with the Chinese and Indians.

The national ideology, as might be expected, consists of the principles reflected in the constitutional contract and the constitution itself.[24] The legal and constitutional changes relate to sedition. The NOC strengthened the already-existing Sedition Ordinance, prohibiting as seditious any questioning of the constitutional provisions most at issue, that is, the provisions relating to citizenship, to the national language, to the special position of the Malays, and to the sovereignty and powers of the rulers.[25] Speech "intended to be a criticism of Government policy or administration" with a view to obtaining change or reform is permissible; but speech that "has the tendency of stirring up hatred, contempt or disaffection against the Government" is banned.[26] After the emergency, the constitution itself was amended to authorize the legislation on sedition.[27] The line between permissible criticism and sedition is unclear, but an effort to safeguard the "special position" of the Malays is obvious.

The goal of advancing the Malays toward social and economic equality is pursued through a New Economic Policy, which according to the official statement seeks " 'to restructure Malaysian society so that the identification of race with economic function and geographical location is reduced and eventually eliminated.' "[28] The more specific goals are:

(a) to bring the balance of employment in the various sectors of the economy and by occupational level into line with that of the racial composition of the population, and (b) to ensure the creation of a commercial and industrial community among the *bumiputra* so that within one generation they will own and manage at least 30 per cent of the total commercial and industrial activity in the country (the same proportion as foreign investors) across all categories and scales of operation.[29]

These objectives are being pursued by various means, including an emphasis on the preferential admission of Malays into institutions of higher learning and the organization of QUANGOs (Quasi Non-Governmental Organizations) to promote Malay participation in, and ownership of, business enterprises. Preferential admissions mean relative disadvantage for the Chinese and the Indians, promoting disaffection among them. Efforts to expand the role of Malays in economic life also involve costs for the Chinese and Indians, but here the impact is more diffuse. Gains for the *bumiputra* can be obtained in part by reducing the role of foreign investors and foreign concerns, without much effect on the Chinese and Indians. And the gains can be obtained in part not by taking anything away from the Chinese and Indians but by directing the benefits of the growth of the Malaysian economy (and the growth has been substantial) disproportionately toward the Malays. Nevertheless, Malaysian practices raise serious questions concerning discrimination.

CONCLUSIONS

The treatment of the indigenous described in this chapter and the preceding one raises obvious questions about discrimination. In country after country governments find it desirable to treat indigenous communities on a differential basis, and to treat individuals differently depending on the community to which they belong. Two main considerations justify the practice and suggest that—in many cases at least—the differential treatment should not be considered discriminatory.

One consideration is that, as a rule, indigenous people are less advanced and weaker than people in the dominant community and are unable to protect and promote their own interests in open, individualistic, and competitive relationships with outsiders. In the absence of special measures for their protection, they have often been the victims of despoliation and oppression, and sometimes even of genocide. If they are accepted as human beings of equal worth, entitled to the equal enjoyment of human rights, the implication is that differential treatment is necessary and justifiable.

The second consideration is based on the central implication of the very idea of indigeneity: that the indigenous people are a people apart, distinct from those in the dominant community. Their preferences concerning their own way of life are entitled to respect, and if they want to maintain their distinctiveness, appropriate arrangements should be made to enable them to do so. This is an aspect of the right of peoples to self-determination, including their right to maintain their culture.

Problems of various sorts arise. The right to self-determination is not absolute and unconditional, for it needs to be interpreted with due respect for the rights and compelling interests of others. This need, as well as concern for the well-being of the indigenous themselves, usually means that they should not have the status of separate, sovereign states, but a number of kinds of special measures of a political sort (for example, autonomy, guaranteed representation) are surely justifiable to make neglect and oppression less serious or less likely. Particularly in connection with small and weak groups, the question is whether any measures that are reasonably adjusted to their size have a chance of being adequate.

Other problems arise because levels of advancement, and the numbers of people in the different groups, are sometimes not very far apart. As Malaysia illlustrates, those counted as indigenous are sometimes more numerous than the others, and many who count as indigenous may be relatively advanced. Special measures that are protective and thus justifiable in one circumstance become questionable at best in another. Special measures become indefensible when, instead of promoting the equal enjoyment of human rights, they confer privilege or accentuate advantage.

Still another problem arises when the claims of the indigenous are based on the fact that they got there first. Such claims may be good vis-à-vis actual immigrants, but surely they lose their force vis-à-vis native-born descendants to whom the new country is home and who make it the object of their loyalty.

6

Race: The United States

Nathan Glazer, at the beginning of his book on *Affirmative Discrimination*, speaks of three decisions that developed in American history, culminating in "the consensus of the middle 1960s" and marking "a distinctive American orientation to ethnic difference and diversity."[1] The first decision was that there would be no discrimination among potential immigrants, and that immigrants could become equal citizens, with no group subordinate to another. The second was that "no separate ethnic group was to be allowed to establish an independent polity in the United States. This was to be a . . . nation of free individuals, not a nation of politically defined ethnic groups." And the third was that "no group . . . would be required to give up its group character and distinctiveness as the price of full entry into the American society." Then in the very last sentence of the same book Glazer appeals for the reestablishment of a "simple and clear understanding, that rights attach to the individual, not the group, and that public policy must be exercised without distinction of race, color, or national origin."

Much can be said, of course, in support of Glazer's view. America has prided itself on its individualism. The ringing statements of the Declaration of Independence are individualistic: all men are created equal, and endowed by their creator with certain inalienable rights. The constitution is individualistic, among its hallmarks being the freedom of the individual and his/her right to equal and nondiscriminatory treatment.

We have chosen to think of the United States as the land of opportunity, where (in Horatio Alger fashion) the future is open to those, even the lowliest, who demonstrate distinctive merit.

At the same time, American history has other aspects. During most of it, a high proportion of the whites have insisted in practice (whatever the rhetoric) on distinctions of various sorts. They have insisted on distinctions as to race, for example. As a group, whites arrogated to themselves the right to rule, denying blacks any share of political power even after slavery ended. Moreover, whites insisted on preferential treatment in connection with schooling. In much of the country they insisted on segregation by race, and as a rule provided better schools for themselves than for blacks. Whites in control of institutions of higher education, including those offering professional training, gave preference to other whites in connection with admissions, perhaps excluding blacks altogether. Whites also insisted on preferential treatment in certain kinds of jobs, reserving some kinds for themselves alone. It was not that individual white and black persons were considered on their merits, with the judgment always going in favor of the white. People were simply classified as white or black, and had opportunities accordingly. Moreover, whites insisted on comparable advantages vis-à-vis Hispanics and Orientals.

Further, the ruling whites made distinctions on grounds in addition to race. As we noted in Chapter 2, those who spoke English (in many of the states) insisted on their primacy over those who did not, even denying others the vote. And those who were Protestant Christians insisted on occupying a special position in government, if only by refusing to vote for Catholics or Jews. Finally, we should recall that the whites have classified the Indians as domestic dependent nations or as a people apart, possessing separate polities, and that the whites have put the natives of American Samoa under a special regime designed to enable them to preserve their culture. Thus the American record, as distinct from the rhetoric, does not suggest a "simple and clear understanding, that rights attach to the individual, not the group . . . ," and an appeal to "reestablish" that understanding seems strange.

Glazer is correct, of course, that the dominant American myth has been and is individualistic. Moreover, the United States has perhaps practiced individualism, especially since the 1950s, more than a number of other societies that are ethnically and racially divided. Furthermore, the prevailing commitment is so much to individualism, and to the idea of the melting pot, that it would be quixotic to argue for communalism. Nevertheless, our individualism is not pure, and cannot be. And a tenable conception of the requirements of equal and nondiscriminatory treatment calls for an awareness of respects in which group rights, or something closely akin to them, need to be taken into account. In this chapter we will seek the necessary awareness not by looking back into American history, but by examining contemporary issues in three areas—issues relating to the public schools, to black participation in politics and government, and to preferential treatment. The question is what kinds of differentiation based on race are justifiable and what kinds should be classified as discrimination.

RACIAL INTEGRATION IN THE SCHOOLS

We have already noted that Unesco's Convention Against Discrimination in Education accepts the "separate but equal" doctrine when differentiation is based on sex, language, or religion, but not when it is based on race. Considered in the abstract, no good reason appears for differentiating between race and the other characteristics. A consciousness of kind, a sense of separate identity, a desire to preserve a distinctive culture, is at least as likely to be associated with race as with sex, language, or religion. The main difference presumably lies in the association between race and slavery, between race and colonial subjection, and between race and ideas of inferiority and superiority. Slavery, colonial subjection, and imputations of inferiority are now almost universally condemned, even by whites who were once largely responsible for them. Further, though separate treatment is often unequal when based on sex, language, or religion, it has been unequal so regularly and so notoriously when based on race that few can any longer regard the "but equal" part of the doctrine as credible. The result is a widespread and special sensitivity to the use of race as a basis for differentiation. At the same time, race and the cultural differences associated with it have figured so prominently in human relationships, and remain so prominent, that they are difficult to ignore. They identify both individuals and collectivities and affect relationships among them.

The *Brown* decision of 1954 is of course the basic one in connection with race and the public schools. The decision was based on the rule of the fourteenth amendment that no person is to be denied the equal protection of the laws. Linda Brown was the person in question. At the same time, the decision focused on segregation as such, not on shortcomings distinctive to the treatment of Linda Brown, and thus not on shortcomings that might be corrected without integration. The Court ruled that "separate educational facilities are inherently unequal." In the field of education, it said, "the doctrine of 'separate but equal' has no place."

[T]o separate [black children] from others of similar age and qualifications solely because of their race generates a feeling of inferiority as to their status in the community that may affect their hearts and minds in a way unlikely ever to be undone.[2]

The judgment can properly be interpreted as individualistic even if it applied to all black children as a class. Moreover, the decision was also individualistic in another sense: it denied a group right to the whites—a right to maintain separate schools for themselves.

Later decisions have tended implicitly to switch the emphasis to the group. One of these decisions ruled out freedom of individual choice of the school to attend,[3] and others ruled out reliance on the neighborhood school principle.[4] Simply the termination of any effort to enforce segregation against individuals was not enough. Affirmative programs had to be adopted to bring about integration, and judgments about what constituted integration had to be based on the relative size of population groups. Thus in *Swann* the Supreme Court agreed that school authorities were justified in concluding that "each school should have a prescribed ratio of Negro to white students reflecting the proportion for the district as a whole." But at the same time the Court obviously wished to safeguard an individualistic approach to the problem, denying that "any particular degree of racial balance or mixing" was a "substantive constitutional right." Mathematical ratios, it said, were to be "no more than a starting point in the process of shaping a remedy." To have made a "mathematical ratio" a constitutional right might have been interpreted as an acceptance of the view that racial communities had rights as collective entities, and this is an interpretation that the courts did not want to encourage. Nevertheless, the use of mathematical ratios continues.[5]

The need to take groups into account as collective entities shows up even more sharply in connection with the treatment of Mexican-Americans. If Mexican-Americans were not legally recognized as a distinct group but were instead lumped in with whites, it would be difficult to prove discrimination against them. Their names could be omitted from jury lists, but this would not distinguish them, for the names of many whites are omitted. Mexican-Americans could be assigned to separate schools, but in the absence of a black community it is not regarded as discriminatory to assign different groups of whites to different schools. Or Mexican-Americans could be used to accomplish "integration": they could be intermixed with blacks, while Anglos retained their own separate schools.

To have a basis for preventing such treatment, the courts have found it necessary to go beyond individualism and race and to adopt the concept of the "identifiable" or "cognizable" group.[6] Given this concept, and given the judgment that Mexican-Americans are identifiable as a group, statistical measures can then be employed to determine whether discrimination is occurring.

The recognition that one or more groups have rights is a necessary implication. At the very least, a right is claimed for the public as a whole—for the population for which the government speaks; it has a right to see to it that integration occurs, and to this end to treat persons not as individuals but as members of the cognizable minority. The cognizable minority is to be represented in the various schools in a prescribed proportion. This is in accordance with the idea of a "compelling public interest," which I will mention in another context below. The "compelling public interest" (in other words, the right of the public) overrides any conflicting private rights. In addition the integration cases implicitly involve a recognition that the cognizable minorities as such have rights. The courts do not say that on the basis of the equal protection clause a specific child has a right to attend a specific school; rather, they say that the right to equal protection is satisfied when the minority as a whole is appropriately represented in the different schools.[7]

The integration of the schools involves other problems that ought to be acknowledged even if they are not discussed. Two attend the principles already described. The pursuit of mathematical ratios is not simply a matter of counting, for decisions must also be made concerning the boundary lines within which to count. It is easy to decide to ignore, or to require change in, boundaries deliberately drawn with a segregative intent; and it is easy to accept boundaries that are untainted by racial prejudice or effects. Between these extremes, however, are many boundaries that are open to question, perhaps because they were drawn with some degree of segregative intent or perhaps because changes have unintentionally given them segregative effects, as when whites and blacks have moved back and forth. The problem of boundaries is especially difficult in metropolitan areas where the central city has become largely black and the surrounding suburbs are largely white.[8]

The second problem attending the principles already described is that of busing. Rejection of the principle of the neighborhood school and adoption of statistical tests of integration make busing necessary. Now, busing is not new. It was also employed to enable the whites to have their own separate schools, and sometimes it is necessary for entirely non-racial reasons. But the use of it to make sure that the various communities are appropriately represented in each school has aroused great controversy.

Another problem is of a broader sort, relating to the fundamental principles of *Brown* and of many subsequent cases. The problem is presented in its most extreme form by the black separatists, who argue for decentralization and community control. They want schools that are predominantly or exclusively black, with black superintendents, black principals, and black teachers, so as to provide a basis for black pride and racial solidarity. Integration, if it comes, should come later when black progress will permit blacks to deal on more nearly even terms with whites. In less extreme form, the problem is presented by those who believe that the courts were wrong to rule out freedom of choice and the principle of the neighborhood school. Those who endorse one or the other of these options are willing to accept any racial distribution that follows in the schools; and they may add that the important consideration is the quality of the education provided and not the racial composition of the student body and teaching staff.

The constitution undoubtedly forbids legally enforced black separatism, just as it forbids white separatism.[9] The problem about freedom of choice and the neighborhood school principle is that they would presumably involve no effort on the part of government to undo the effects of previous illegal policies. And in communities that remained under white political control, separate black schools might or might not get adequate tax support.

PARTICIPATION IN GOVERNMENT

Significant change has occurred in the treatment of blacks in connection with politics and government, just as it has in connection with education. Court decisions and federal laws have finally given substantial effect to the amendments adopted after the Civil War. In general, and with no challenge in principle, blacks now have the vote and are eligible to serve in public office.[10]

Serious issues of principle remain, however, over the question of the "dilution" or "debasement" of the black vote. These are the words used in the federal courts, including the Supreme Court, but they are transferred from another context and are not apt. The other context is malapportionment as between electoral districts that are geographically delimited. In that context the courts faced gross departures from the equal population principle, one district including, say, 10,000 persons and another 100,000, with each entitled to one representative.

In that case, votes in the more populous district were said to be "diluted," having less weight or value or efficacy than votes in the smaller district. But the "dilution" of the black vote does not relate to malapportionment or to any problem that can sensibly be discussed in an individualistic framework. It is not a question of the weight or value of the individual vote, for the "diluted" black vote counts as much as the "undiluted" white vote. The question concerns the voting power of communities as collectivities. It is a communal matter, not an individual matter. The assumption is that race counts, that members of each race tend to vote for their own kind. The communal nature of the issue is so plain that it shows up in the language employed, but given the individualistic provisions of the constitution and the prevailing individualistic outlook, a full switch to the language of communalism does not occur.

"Dilution" is illustrated by racial gerrymandering, which is accomplished by various methods. Sometimes the method is to draw the lines of electoral districts in such a way as to disperse the blacks and make the whites a majority in every district. Sometimes it is to draw the lines so as to concentrate the blacks in the fewest possible number of districts, conceding black control over them while assuring white control over the rest. In a few instances, whites have changed the boundary lines of a city, disgorging or annexing territory, thus reducing the number of black voters or increasing the number of white voters. And, whether or not at-large elections are an indication of gerrymandering, they may produce the same effect. In some instances, when whites feared that one or more blacks might win in single-member districts or ward elections, they have shifted to multi-member or at-large elections, hoping thereby to swamp the black vote. And in other instances the problem is made more difficult by the fact that at-large elections have come to have racial effects even if they were first adopted for entirely non-racial reasons.

It is important to emphasize that racially influenced voting underlies the problem of the "dilution" of the black vote and the possibility of racial gerrymandering. If the rule of the equal protection of the laws could have a counterpart that would preclude racial discrimination in voting, racial gerrymandering could not occur. But no such counterpart exists. Discrimination can be outlawed in many areas. It can be outlawed in connection with public and private policies relating to employment, promotion, and pay. It can be outlawed in connection with access to public facilities and amenities. It can even be restricted in connection with the votes of members of legislative bodies, for measures that are racist can be nullified in the courts. But discrimination cannot be outlawed in free and secret elections. Behind the curtain in the polling booth, whites can vote for whites, and blacks can vote for blacks, for purely racist reasons. Thus whenever those of either race have the votes, they can exclude members of the other race from office.

Although what the individual does in the secrecy of the polling booth is beyond legal control, racial gerrymandering is open to attack in the courts, and the attacks force the judges to take some kind of notice of groups even while attempting to maintain an individualistic stance. The first judicial opinion on the matter spoke of the "debasement" of the votes of the blacks as if the value of the individual votes had been reduced, but it also said that a "dilution of Negro voting power" had occurred, as if this had happened to the black community.[11] A later judgment included the statement that "any plan of apportionment, to be constitutionally acceptable . . . must not be so designed as to dilute the voting strength of any *person or group*."[12] A judgment relating to the city council of Chicago refers unabashedly to groups.

There is no principle which requires a minority racial or ethnic group to have any particular voting strength reflected in the council. The principle is that such strength must not be purposefully minimized on account of their race or ethnic origin. . . . The gerrymander . . . does not directly or necessarily affect the individual right to vote. It is aimed at groups of citizens and is intended to diminish the likelihood that their candidate will be elected.[13]

As in cases relating to the integration of the schools, the courts began speaking of "identifiable minorities" and "cognizable groups," sometimes referring back to a much earlier statement by a justice of the Supreme Court that evidence of "prejudice against discrete and insular minorities" might call for especially searching judicial inquiry.[14] On one occasion a dissenting justice of the Supreme Court abandoned individualism altogether, saying that the requirements of the Voting Rights Act of 1965 are "not satisfied unless, to the extent practicable, the new electoral districts [in New Orleans] afford the Negro minority the opportunity to achieve representation roughly proportional to the Negro population of the community."[15]

One case of alleged racial gerrymandering led to two especially interesting problems. The case involved reapportionment affecting a number of electoral districts in the New York metropolitan area with a mixed population—white, black, and Puerto Rican. In accordance with a requirement of the Voting Rights Act of 1965, the officials responsible for re-drawing the boundary lines submitted their plan to the attorney-general in Washington, who needed to be satisfied that the plan did not have the purpose and would not have the effect of denying or abridging the right to vote on account of race or color. In most of the districts in question the blacks and Puerto Ricans combined were to have majorities of over 70 percent, but in two these majorities were to be below 65 percent.

To get the full import of what the attorney-general did, it is important to recall the judicial view cited above that no affirmative obligation exists to delimit districts so that the voting strength of various groups is accurately reflected; rather, the obligation is a negative one—not to delimit districts so as to minimize or cancel out the voting strength of a group. The distinction is tenuous. What the attorney-general did was to take the stand that the plan over-concentrated blacks and Puerto Ricans in some districts and fragmented or diffused them in others.[16] He assumed that they would register and vote in lower proportion than voters from other ethnic communities, and that anything less than a "substantial majority" for them would be evidence of racial gerrymandering. He conveyed the impression that a majority of less than 65 percent would not be substantial enough to be approved. Thus the plan was revised to give the blacks and Puerto Ricans a "viable majority" and a "realistic opportunity to elect a candidate of their choice."[17] In other words, where the blacks and Puerto Ricans were relatively numerous, the way to prove that their vote was not being minimized was to make arrangements designed to enable them to win. The requirement was suggestive of proportional representation.

The arrangements that were made led to a second problem, concerning the criteria for saying that a group is identifiable or cognizable. In order to get at least a 65 percent majority for the blacks and Puerto Ricans, a community of Hasidic Jews was split between two electoral districts; and the Hasidic Jews objected. They did not explicitly claim that they had a right as a community to be treated as a unit, although it is reasonable to infer this claim from some of the statements made. For example, the brief presented on their behalf spoke of them, after referring to the blacks, as "another ethnic group that deserves equal sympathy and at least as much in the way of affirmative action to cure society's inequities."[18] And an assumption that the Jewish community should be thought of as one whole underlay the claim that the electoral arrangement being protested halved the efficacy of the Jewish vote. The explicit argument was that the drawing of electoral boundary lines on the basis of race was unconstitutional; it was unconstitutional (violating the fourteenth and fifteenth amendments) in the absence of a finding that it was necessary in order to correct past discrimination.

The Supreme Court rejected the argument, affirming the judgments of lower courts. It held that the Voting Rights Act of 1965 established an acceptable basis for taking race into account in some kinds of circumstances so as to prevent racial gerrymandering, and (more to the point here) it simply assumed, tacitly and without argument, that the Hasidic Jews are to be treated as whites and not acknowledged as a cognizable group. It held that the reapportionment plan "did not minimize or cancel out white voting strength [and that] as long as whites . . . , as a group, were provided with fair representation, we cannot conclude that there was a cognizable discrimination against whites. . . . "[19] Justice Brennan, concurring in part, spoke of "the impression of unfairness . . . when a coherent group like the Hasidim disproportionately bears the adverse consequences of a race assignment policy,"[20] but he noted that "they do not press any legal claim to a group voice. . . . "[21] Chief Justice Burger, dissenting, took the view that "petitioners certainly have no constitutional right to remain unified within a single political district, [but] they do have, in my view, the constitutional right not to be carved up so as to create a voting bloc composed of some other ethnic or racial group. . . . "[22] His main contention, however, was that the "drawing of political boundary lines with the sole, explicit objective of reaching a predetermined racial result cannot ordinarily be squared with the Constitution."[23]

For present purposes, the chief significance of the decision is that it threw into question the criteria for determining which groups are "identifiable" or "cognizable." The courts have never spelled the criteria out. In 1954 the Supreme Court spoke of "easily identifiable groups, which have at times required the aid of the courts in securing equal treatment under the laws." It held that "whether such a group exists within a community is a question of fact," and that "one method by which this [fact] may be demonstrated is by showing the attitude of the community." It went on to cite evidence that Mexican-Americans were in fact treated as a separate class, and so, in effect, it held that they were cognizable.[24] Later a district court treated the Navajos as a cognizable group.[25] And it goes without saying that the courts have treated the blacks as cognizable. But the Hasidic Jews of Williamsburgh were not cognizable, and the reason is not entirely clear. Perhaps it is because they did not explicitly claim a right to be treated as a group. Perhaps it is because they had not been the victims of discriminatory governmental actions. Perhaps it is because of a belief that for practical reasons the number of groups treated as cognizable must be kept small. In earlier cases the federal district court in New York had taken the view that "pleas for separate community recognition" must be rejected. It said that, though there might be twenty or more identifiable communities in Brooklyn, "even Brooklyn's large population will not support twenty community congressmen. Of necessity, there must be lines which divide."[26] Thus the individualism of American law and practice is maintained, but problems arise about groups, and anomalies exist in the handling of those problems.

As indicated above, the provisions of the Voting Rights Act of 1965 relating to changes in electoral arrangements require that the changes shall not have the purpose or the effect of denying or abridging the vote on account of race. Where the issue of "dilution" arises on a constitutional rather than a statutory basis, however, the prevailing view is that only intent counts, not effect. That view is questionable. The governing precedent relates to a different context, where the question concerned a test administered to potential recruits for a police force. The test screened out blacks in higher proportion than whites, and blacks went to court claiming that the differential impact of the test made it discriminatory, even though no one intended that it should be; and precedents gave some basis for the argument. In a number of cases, the courts of appeals had held that "the substantially disproportionate racial impact of a statute or official practice . . . suffices to prove racial discrimination violating the Equal Protection Clause," absent some special justification. But the Supreme Court, whose words I have just quoted, took a contrary stand. It reaffirmed "the basic equal protection principle [adhered to in desegregation cases] that the invidious quality of a law claimed to be racially discriminatory must ultimately be traced to a racially discriminatory purpose."[27]

The principle is no doubt sound in some connections. The equal protection clause is vague, and seems especially so in the light of the fact that many kinds of laws and practices have differential impact on different persons and groups, including racial groups. A supplementary standard of some kind is essential to its interpretation, and intent is one of the possibilities. But a precedent fixed in connection with the impact of a test used in recruitment is not necessarily relevant to voting. The expectation is that tests will differentiate, but no such expectation attends electoral arrangements. No one has a right to pass a test, but blacks and others do have a right to vote regardless of color, and accompanying arrangements should do nothing to reduce the efficacy of their votes.

Questions about the "dilution" of the vote of black communities, and about the roles of intent and impact, have come before the courts in cases concerning at-large elections in Mobile, Alabama, and Burke County, Georgia. In both Mobile and Burke County the blacks comprise a substantial portion of the population—35 percent in Mobile and 54 percent in Burke County. Nevertheless, up to the time of the suits no black had been elected to office. In Burke County part of the explanation is the failure of the blacks to register and vote up to their potential; but, given the fact that the blacks who went to the polls were a minority, their exclusion from public office is traceable to at-large elections, coupled with racially polarized voting: whites, voting as a bloc, always elected the white slate of candidates.

In both cases the lower federal courts ruled in favor of the black community, but in the first case the Supreme Court reversed the judgment and allowed Mobile to retain its at-large system.[28] The nine justices split badly on the issue, four joining in one opinion and the other five all writing separate opinions. The four agreed that differential impact on a racial basis is not itself enough to indicate a violation of either the fourteenth or the fifteenth amendment—that "an illicit purpose must be proved before a constitutional violation can be found."[29] Moreover, these four held Mobile not guilty of an illicit purpose. It had adopted its at-large system in 1911 when blacks did not vote at all.

The five other opinions went along different lines that are not all relevant for present purposes. Four justices found Mobile guilty of an illicit purpose not in originally adopting the at-large system but in maintaining it, though two of the four denied that intent should be the governing consideration. Two held that a discriminatory impact is sufficient regardless of intent. One of these last two quoted and obviously approved the statement that

where what is denied is something to which the complainant has a substantive consitutional right—either because it is granted by the terms of the Constitution or because it is essential to the effective functioning of a democratic government—*the reasons it was denied are irrelevant.*[30]

The Burke County case came later and turned out differently. The Circuit Court, ruling in favor of the black community, treated it sometimes as an entity and sometimes as an aggregation of individuals.[31] It perforce accepted the rule that purpose or intent is the controlling consideration, but it followed the example of four of the justices of the Supreme Court in the Mobile case in focusing on the intent of the whites not in adopting the at-large system but in maintaining it. Moreover, as in earlier cases, the court was unwilling to take the view that the requirements of the fourteenth and fifteenth amendments were necessarily satisfied by arrangements that merely permitted the blacks to vote as so many individuals. It talked not simply of voting but of "effective participation in the electoral process" and of "access to the political process" by the identifiable group. "Effective participation," it held, means "that the system of government . . . must serve the interests of all the people; at least to the extent that one group's interests are not invidiously discriminated against." "A racially definable group," the court held, could challenge an electoral system on dilution grounds by showing that it invidiously operates to the detriment of "their" interests. And it ruled that the black community of Burke County had done precisely that. The white county commissioners, it said, "have demonstrated such insensitivity to the legitimate rights of the county's black residents that it can only be explained as a conscious and willful effort on their part to maintain the invidious vestiges of discrimination."[32] The remedy prescribed is that the county commissioners be elected from single-member districts.

In this case, the judgment of the Circuit Court carried the day. Six of the justices of the Supreme Court agreed that the judgment was not "clearly erroneous" and that it should therefore be affirmed.[33]

Ample evidence exists that, in general, at-large elections in the United States are to the advantage of the whites, and that their abandonment in favor of elections in single-member districts increases the representation of minorities.[34] These cases suggest a disjunction between the problem and the solution. The problem is that individualism and "majority rule" give the whites monopoly control over government, permitting them to use government to advance their own interests and to neglect the interests of the blacks. What is formally an individualistic system turns out to be communal. But the American tradition does not permit a frankly communal solution. It does not permit separate voting rolls for whites and blacks, for example, with each community assured a quota of governmental posts. Instead the solution, based on individualistic premises, is to outlaw gerrymandering and to shift from multi- to single-member districts in the hope that the blacks will be sufficiently concentrated in one or more of the new districts to enable them to gain representation. A communal purpose—an opportunity for effective participation by the blacks—is pursued in noncommunal, indirect ways.

Where blacks are geographically concentrated, the indirect approach to the problem may alleviate it. The fact that they have been forced into ghettos may in this respect be advantageous to them. But what of situations where blacks are so dispersed geographically that they are a minority in every conceivable electoral district? No one clear answer stands out. On the one hand, the argument can be that the only constitutional entitlement of the blacks is the vote, and not necessarily representation, let alone proportional representation. Many other minorities also lack enough votes to get representation. And, like others, blacks have the opportunity—at least in some electoral districts—to use their voting power in bargaining with candidates and parties so as to obtain consideration for their interests.

On the other hand, the argument can be that the general underrepresentation of a sizable, self-conscious element in the population is undesirable, for despite efforts at bargaining, their interests are likely to be relatively neglected if not ignored, especially when a racial bias operates against them, and this is likely to produce or accentuate alienation. Further, blacks who despair of obtaining equal justice through legal political processes will be tempted to resort to other means—perhaps to rioting and even to terrorism. Moreover, as the experience of Northern Ireland attests, more or less proportional representation may not alone be enough to give assurances against such a development. The Catholics in Northern Ireland have always had representation in the Stormont, but have always been a minority and have been excluded from offices in the executive branch of the government, with consequences that are well known. In the long run, then, both roughly proportional representation in legislative bodies and something like it in the executive branch may be both necessary and wise as a means of producing the sense of justice on which so much depends. Recall that in Belgium the constitution requires that, with the possible exception of the prime ministry, the cabinet be divided half and half between French- and Dutch-speaking ministers; and Belgium insists on parity between the two main language communities in recruiting personnel for the civil service.

The issue posed here is fundamental, deserving the most serious consideration. It is not enough to take cover behind the constitution and to say that it is individualistic and does not provide for the proportional representation of groups. The first task is to develop an intellectually and morally defensible position and then face the constitutional problem. Depending on what the position is, the problem may or may not be difficult.

Adequate basis exists in the constitutional tradition for saying that the black community is "cognizable" and that electoral arrangements that lead to the gross underrepresentation of that community amount to an "abridgement" or "dilution" of the black vote. In other words, it is possible, within the constitutional tradition, to adjust electoral arrangements, including the boundaries of electoral districts, with the deliberate aim of enabling blacks to go in the direction of proportional representation; and, as I see it, this should be done.

A supplementary step would depart from the constitutional tradition, but deserves to be debated nevertheless: where territorially delimited electoral districts leave sizeable black communities without representation, it would be possible to shift to communal arrangements. "Majority rule" could be retained, but the majority would be found within each racial community rather than within the population of a geographic area; or those elected might be required to gain some minimum degree of support, perhaps plurality support, within each of the racial communities.

Finally, it is worth pointing out—for the sake of an argument that I do not want to pursue here—that "majority rule" is itself not sacred. When people vote, they prescribe, and not simply for themselves but also for others. It is sensible and defensible to hold that human beings should be free and equal in making decisions concerning their own lives—that none should be subordinate to others in this respect. But it is not at all obvious that all persons are equally capable of making appropriate prescriptions for others, or for society as a whole; and the counterpart is that it is not at all obvious why the minority should submit and obey. In this context "majority rule" is arbitrary, and the problem is more acute when the majority is white with a racist record and the minority is black.

Strict individualism in connection with political representation is both impossible and undesirable. Even in the country of the melting pot, it must be limited and supplemented. As long as people's attitudes and behavior are influenced in any significant degree by racial differences, weaker racial groups need special measures for their protection and advancement. To refuse to adopt such measures and instead to profess complete individualism is to concede dominance and privilege to the strongest and most advanced group, especially if that group is itself in any degree racist.[35]

PREFERENTIAL TREATMENT: THE RECORD

Questions concerning preferential treatment are more difficult to deal with than questions concerning either segregation or racial gerrymandering. The case for holding that segregation and racial gerrymandering are unconstitutional and immoral is straightforward and strong; and it is possible to eliminate them without denying equal treatment to anyone. No one has a constitutional right to a segregated school or to biased electoral arrangements. But preferential treatment for blacks (or for members of any minority) is in a different category. By definition it means unequal treatment. When a black gets preferential treatment, a white is denied equal treatment. This can readily be accepted as a matter of just desert if the white denied has discriminated against the black preferred, but the situation is rarely that direct and simple. In practice, preferential treatment is often given to blacks whether or not they have personally suffered specific acts of discrimination; and by the same token unequal and adverse treatment is imposed on whites whether or not they have personally done any wrong. Thus it is easy to conclude that sometimes preference goes to the undeserving at the expense of the innocent.

This theme is developed by a number of persons who have analyzed the problem, among them Alan H. Goldman and Carl Cohen.[36] And some innocent whites, drawing this conclusion in their own cases, have gone into the courts claiming that they have been discriminated against because of race. The most prominent names in this connection are DeFunis, Bakke, and Weber.

The problem of preferential treatment based on race is all the more difficult because, in addition to the equal protection clause, the Civil Rights Act of 1964 is also involved. It forbids racial discrimination in any program or activity receiving federal funds (Title VI) or by employers, employment agencies, trade unions, or those offering apprenticeships or training programs (Title VII). Moreover, the language of Titles VI and VII is plain. Literally read, it rules out any racial discrimination whatsoever, whether directed against blacks, whites, or members of any other race. Title VII includes a few qualifications, but none of them suggests that whites may be denied equal treatment so that blacks may get preferential treatment. One of the qualifications permits the preferential treatment of Indians in connection with employment on or near reservations. Another permits religious institutions to take religion into account in their employment policies. Still another permits race to be taken into account when it is a bona fide occupational qualification. The very fact that Congress included these qualifications tends to strengthen the view that it did not have in mind anything comparable that might permit the preferential treatment of blacks at the expense of whites. Congress even specified that nothing in Title VII shall be taken to require the preferential treatment of any individual or group in the interest of "balance" in the work force. Strictly read and literally construed, Titles VI and VII look clear and conclusive.

Actually, according to the courts, neither the equal protection clause nor the Civil Rights Act of 1964 is as decisive as their words suggest. The courts are themselves ordering preferential hiring in some cases and are permitting it in others, and I take their rulings to be legally decisive. Further, though I am impressed by the case for the view that preferential treatment based on race is immoral and socially undesirable, my argument goes in the other direction.

First on the attitude of the courts. Their view is that in enacting Titles VI and VII the intent of Congress was not as extreme as the words suggest. With respect to Title VI, a majority on the Supreme Court holds that the intent was "to give the Executive Branch of the Government clear authority to terminate federal funding of private programs that use race as a means of disadvantaging minorities in a manner that would be prohibited by the Constitution if engaged in by government."[37] This means that Title VI should be interpreted as an authorization for the president to insist that agencies receiving federal funds observe the same restrictions as those imposed on government by the equal protection clause. Thus the question is what these restrictions are. With respect to Title VII approximately the same interpretation prevails. A majority on the Supreme Court refuses to interpret it strictly and literally, holding that this would "bring about an end completely at variance with the purpose of the statute."

It would be ironic indeed if a law triggered by a Nation's concern over centuries of racial injustice and intended to improve the lot of those who had "been excluded from the American dream for so long" . . . constituted the first legislative prohibition of all voluntary, private, race-conscious efforts to abolish traditional patterns of racial segregation and hierarchy.[38]

The implication again is that Title VII should be interpreted in accordance with the model provided by the interpretation of the equal protection clause.

That model does not require that everyone be treated alike. It permits classification and differential treatment, provided certain conditions are met—conditions fixed as part of what is called the reasonable classification or the antidiscrimination principle.[39] The central requirement of this principle is that classification be reasonable, or, negatively, that it not be unreasonable, arbitrary, capricious, unfair, or invidious. It must be related rationally and in substantial degree to the purpose that is being pursued, and the purpose itself must be a legitimate governmental purpose.

Under these principles a great deal of differential treatment occurs. The progressive income tax is illustrative. So is the fact that when government wishes, it imposes compulsory military service on some while exempting others. So is the preferential hiring of Indians in the Bureau of Indian Affairs and by federal contractors who have jobs to offer on or near reservations. Moreover, just as the government finds classification and differentiation acceptable and desirable in pursuing its own legitimate purposes, so it extends the principle into some areas of private activity, as when it permits religious organizations to take into account the religion of persons whom they contemplate hiring. What is done may or may not be entirely just and fair. One of the purposes of insisting on the right of everyone to participate in government is to give them an opportunity to defend and advance their rights and interests in what is inevitably, if only in part, a competitive struggle with others. But the equal protection clause does not give any assurance that the balance of benefits and burdens will come out the same for everyone. As the Supreme Court once said,

special burdens are often necessary for general benefits. . . . Regulations for these purposes may press with more or less weight upon one than upon another, but they are designed, not to impose unequal or unnecessary restrictions upon any one, but to promote with as little inconvenience as possible, the general good.[40]

As a legal issue, preferential treatment based on race must be considered in this light. By almost universal consent, the equal protection clause does not rule out all classification based on race any more than it rules out all classification based on income or age or sex or geographic location or personal merit. But given the shameful record of the past with respect to race, the courts say that classification based on it is suspect and must be subjected to strict scrutiny. They thus throw the burden of proof onto any governmental unit or agency that wants

to classify by race. They want to be satisfied that the classification (and the accompanying differential treatment) is necessary to serve a public interest that is compelling.

Viewed in this light the prohibition against discriminatory legislation
is a demand for purity of motive. It erects a constitutional barrier
against legislative motives of hate, prejudice, vengeance, hostility, or,
alternatively, of favoritism, and partiality. The imposition of special
burdens, the granting of special benefits, must always be justified.
They can only be justified as being directed at the elimination of some
social evil, the achievement of some public good.[41]

In addition, and quite compatibly with the equal protection
clause, courts considering questions of preferential treatment
tend to appeal to their power to sit as courts of equity and thus
to render decisions that, insofar as possible, provide remedies
for past wrongs. A court of equity "has wide power and discretion to fashion its decree not only to prohibit present discrimination but to eradicate the effects of past discriminatory
practices."[42] It can require an employer to "eliminate the present effects of past discrimination."[43] It can seek to prevent the
effects of past discrimination from being carried into the future,
for that would continue the discrimination. Thus a basis exists
for compensatory action: people who have been classified by
race for purposes of adverse discrimination in the past can now
be classified by race for purposes of preferential treatment in
the future.

Consideration of these principles will be promoted by focusing on concrete cases. One relevant case arose out of a complaint that the City of San Francisco discriminated against
minorities in recruiting members of its police force. Finding
the complaint well-founded, the Court proceeded as a court of
equity. It claimed "the authority to construct an equitable remedy which involves the imposition of the requirement of ratio-
hiring on a public agency in order to correct past discriminatory
conduct and to avoid repetition of any such conduct."[44] The
court went on to note that minority groups made up the following percentages of the population and of the police force:
blacks, 14 percent and 4.4 percent; Latinos, 15 percent and 4.0

percent; Asians, 14 percent and 0.9 percent. Combining all minorities, the corresponding figures were 43 percent and 9 percent. On this basis the court ordered the city thereafter to put qualified candidates for the police force on two lists—minority candidates on one list and others on a second list. And it ordered that three appointments be made from the minority list for every two from the other list until minority policemen comprised at least 30 percent of the total. Comparable findings, and a comparable order, applied to the promotion of patrolmen to the rank of sergeant.

A second illustration concerns the employment practices of the Detroit Edison Company.[45] The court found that the company had deliberately and blatantly discriminated against blacks. It based this finding both on testimony concerning the treatment of specific individuals and on statistics. It held that "statistical evidence is sufficient to establish a prima facie case of racial discrimination" in recruitment and in job assignments. Citing the fact that the proportion of blacks in Detroit's population, in its labor force, and among its skilled unemployed ranged from 41 to 47 percent of the total, the court found that they were grossly underrepresented in the work force of the Detroit Edison Company. On this basis it issued a series of orders, among them the following:

a. That "subject to the availability of qualified applicants," blacks be hired on an accelerated basis until they comprised 30 percent of the work force.

b. That one black employee be promoted to the position of foreman or supervisor for every white so promoted.

c. That individual black applicants or employees who had suffered loss be afforded an appropriate remedy. The remedy was to take any of various forms, such as back pay, first opportunity to apply for future vacancies, and the calculation of seniority from the time of the discrimination.

d. That substantial damages be paid.

Although the second of these cases included remedial action for the specific individuals who had been injured by discriminatory policies, the striking feature of both cases is that the

courts did not stick strictly to this rule. They both said in effect
that injury to one set of blacks in the past justifies the preferential hiring of another set of blacks in the future. And by
the same token they both said that a wrong done by one set of
whites in the past justifies the unequal and unfavorable treatment of another set of whites.

The same issue came up in the *Bakke* and *Weber* cases. The
Bakke case concerned admission to the Medical School of the
University of California at Davis. When Bakke applied to the
Medical School, it was admitting 100 students each year, 16 of
them under a special program for applicants who wanted to be
considered "economically and/or educationally disadvantaged"
or as members of a minority group. In fact, only minority applicants (black, Mexican-American, and Asian) were ever admitted under the special program, though large numbers of
whites asked to be considered disadvantaged. Bakke, considered under the regular program, was rejected, though his
"benchmark score" resulting from tests and interviews was
higher than that of a number of minority applicants admitted.
He sued, claiming that he was the victim of racial discrimination contrary to both the equal protection clause and Title
VI.

The Supreme Court split badly, just as it did in the case
concerning Mobile's at-large elections, its members writing six
different opinions. A majority found it possible to agree on the
rather narrow point that a fixed quota of minority admissions
was impermissible, and so Bakke won his case. But the more
significant fact is that the majority refused to rule racial considerations out of the admissions process. In effect the court
said that affirmative action based on race does not violate either
Title VI or the equal protection clause if race is only one of a
number of influencing considerations and if no fixed goal or quota
is set. This permitted Justice Brennan and three other justices
to join in saying that the central meaning of the *Bakke* opinion
is that "government may take race into account when it acts
not to demean or insult any racial group, but to remedy disadvantages cast on minorities by past racial prejudice...."[46]
Moreover, the same four justices agreed that remedial action
is justified by the record of general "societal discrimination,"

whether or not the individuals benefited have personally suffered discrimination and whether or not the individuals burdened have themselves engaged in discrimination. One of the justices spoke of the "inequity in forcing innocent persons in [Bakke's] position to bear the burdens of redressing grievances not of their making,"[47] but another spoke of the "ample support for the conclusion that a university can employ race-conscious measures to remedy past societal discrimination, without the need for finding that those benefited were actually victims of that discrimination."[48] To support their claim concerning congressional intent, four of the justices cited legislation relating to federal grants to support local public works projects. In this legislation (which the Court declared constitutional in a subsequent judgment)[49] Congress required that at least 10 percent of each grant be channeled to minority business enterprises, racially defined, the implication being that preferential treatment would occur if necessary.[50]

The Supreme Court took a comparable stand in *Weber*. Weber was a blue collar worker in a Kaiser aluminum plant. He sought appointment for in-plant training so as to qualify for a skilled craft, but he ran afoul of a collective bargaining agreement that the company had made with the United Steelworkers. The agreement reflected the fact that blacks, though comprising some 39 percent of the labor force in the local area, held less than 2 percent of the skilled craft jobs in the plant. Kaiser did not admit and the United Steelworkers did not allege prior discrimination, but their agreement called for affirmative action. It required the company to maintain two lists of applicants for entry into the training program for craft jobs (one for whites and one for blacks), to order those on each list by seniority, and to make appointments from the two lists alternately until 39 percent of the craftsmen were black. The result was that several white applicants with greater seniority were passed over so that blacks could be appointed. Weber was one of them, and he sued, claiming that the racial differentiation of which he was the victim was an unlawful employment practice under Title VII.

The lower courts supported Weber, but the Supreme Court did not. Five of the justices took views suggested above. They held that the intent of Congress in enacting the Civil Rights Act of 1964 was to promote "the integration of blacks into the mainstream of American society," and that the words of Title VII "cannot be interpreted as an absolute prohibition against all private, voluntary, race-conscious affirmative action efforts to hasten the elimination of [an unfortunate and ignominious page in this country's history]."[51] Thus, according to judicial interpretations of both the constitution and statutory law, preferential treatment based on race may in some circumstances legitimately occur.

Though basing their judgments on the idea of an equitable remedy and on the idea of a "compelling public interest," the courts are not explicit and precise in indicating what makes their judgments equitable or what makes a public interest compelling. It is nevertheless clear that a concern for groups operates in each connection. If discrimination against one set of blacks is equitably remedied by later differentiation in favor of another set of blacks, the obvious assumption is that blacks comprise an interrelated whole, a unit, an entity. The individual black is not considered simply as a person or as a citizen but as a member of a distinctive group with a collective identity. The assumption must be that injury to the group through one set of its members is compensated for by especially favorable treatment to another set of its members.

Similarly the emphasis on proportionality in the case described above puts the focus more on groups than on individuals. In the ratio-hiring cases the explicit effort is to get minorities hired in rough proportion to their number in the local population or in the relevant labor pool, and the requirement concerning 10 percent of the federal money granted to support local public works projects has an obvious relationship to the proportion of the population that is black. As Justice Stevens noted in the case in which the 10 percent set-aside was at issue, "A comparable approach in the electoral context would support a rule requiring that at least 10 percent of the candidates elected to the legislature be members of specified racial minorities."[52]

To emphasize the group is of course to challenge individualism, but the challenge has implicitly been of long standing.

As indicated above in the discussion of school integration, whites have always regarded blacks as a race apart. They have treated blacks not as so many individuals on the basis of their distinctive personal qualities but as members of a group. They kept the group in subordinate and second class status by discriminating against its members indiscriminately. To lynch one black was to intimidate them all, and to educate one was to encourage them all. To be sure, the group basis of the policies did not become a part of the ideology. An unacknowledged hypocrisy prevailed as whites proclaimed that all men are created equal, as if they were dedicated to non-racial universalism, and then denied the application of the principle outside the white group. Moreover, it is not at all farfetched to suppose that living blacks who may not personally have suffered specific acts of discrimination are nevertheless disadvantaged not only by the treatment of their parents and grandparents but also (and perhaps even more) by the tradition of attributing inferiority and second-class status to them. Affirmative action advancing blacks toward equality is at least as significant in symbolizing an attack on that tradition as in its material consequences.

The constitution is so written that the struggle against discriminatory laws and practices has had to be based on appeals to individual rights, but it would be surprising if generations of oppression directed at a group could now be remedied in timely fashion by action focusing entirely on individuals. The courts are implicitly acknowledging this. And, to anticipate a portion of the moral argument to be advanced shortly, they should. It would be a strange conception of justice that makes the advantage of the whites the governing rule—that permits preferential treatment as long as the benefits go to the whites and then prohibits it as soon as the benefits start going to the blacks.

The idea of a "compelling public interest" likewise reflects a concern for groups. Most obviously, it reflects a concern for the public—for the population of the country as a whole. The assumption is that the whole population has interests as a collectivity, and that some of these interests are substantial or compelling enough to override conflicting private rights. Although not using the expression "a compelling public interest," the federal district judge in the San Francisco case described above appealed to the underlying idea.

[A]ll citizens profit when the city achieves a racially integrated police force of qualified individuals who are knowledgeable of the diverse problems of different ethnic groups and who are not prey to destructive hostility from minorities who feel excluded from full participation in city government life. Clearly, the general harmony of the community is enhanced by the city's obtaining a police force representative of its population.[53]

A compelling public interest is equivalent to a right of the public, and a right of the public—of the many—may in some circumstances legitimately take precedence over a conflicting right of one or the few. The doctrine is obviously dangerous. It opens the way to serious and perhaps unjustified violations of individual rights. Few would today defend the application of the doctrine to American citizens of Japanese descent during World War II.[54] But a polity would jeopardize its survival if it extended a very extensive list of rights to individuals and gave them unquestioned priority. The appropriate principle is stated in Article 29 of the Universal Declaration of Human Rights:

In the exercise of his rights and freedoms, everyone shall be subject only to such limitations as are determined by law solely for the purpose of securing due recognition and respect for the rights and freedoms of others and of meeting the just requirements of morality, public order and the general welfare in a democratic society.

We will revert in a moment to this reference to the requirements of morality.

As noted, the interpretation of the equal protection clause described above centers on the reasonable classification principle. Owen M. Fiss is critical of that principle and offers a substitute, which he calls the group disadvantaging principle. He points out that the equal protection clause was adopted in the first place primarily out of concern for the blacks. He asserts that the blacks comprise a social group, and he defines a social group as having two characteristics in addition to being a collection of individuals:

(1) It is an *entity* (though not one that has a physical body). This means that the group has a distinct existence apart from its members, and also that it has an identity. It makes sense to talk about the group (at various points of time) and know that you are talking about the same group. You can talk about the group without reference to the particular individuals who happen to be members at any one moment. (2) There is also a condition of *interdependence*. The identity and well-being of the members of the group and the identity and well-being of the group are linked. Members of the group identify themselves—explain who they are—by reference to their membership in the group; and their well-being or status is in part determined by the well-being or status of the group.[55]

According to this definition, the whites of the United States, as well as the blacks, are a group; and so are the Indians, women, Jews, and certain language minorities. Fiss's concern is with "specially disadvantaged groups," and more particularly with "those laws or practices that particularly hurt a disadvantaged group."

Such laws might enhance the welfare of society (or the better-off classes), or leave it the same; what is critical . . . is that the state law or practice aggravates (perpetuates?) the subordinate position of a specially disadvantaged group. This is what the Equal Protection Clause prohibits.[56]

Fiss's emphasis is on the undesirability of aggravating or perpetuating the subordinate position of a group. The equal protection clause, he argues, should be interpreted to prohibit state action having that effect. In contrast, it should be interpreted to permit state action that enhances the status of a disadvantaged group even if at the expense of one that is advantaged.

The group-disadvantaging principle fits past practice in the United States at least as well as—and in some cases better than—the reasonable classification principle. With rare exceptions, the classifying that has been judged unreasonable has been the sort that works against the well-being of a disadvantaged group. What has been done to protect blacks and others from unequal treatment could just as well have been done under the group-disadvantaging principle. Moreover, the group-disadvantaging principle provides a better justification for some of the judgments that the courts have rendered than does the reasonable classification principle. Assuming that the concern is that the law should treat individuals equally, for example, it is not at all clear why the requirement that the race of candidates be indicated on ballots is unconstitutional. Further, the group-disadvantaging principle would presumably have led the courts in some instances to a different judgment; for example, in the *Moose Lodge* case it would presumably have led to the judgment that the state should not confer a scarce liquor license on a private club that refuses to serve blacks.[57] And had the group-disadvantaging principle been the guide, De-Funis, Bakke, and Weber would clearly have had no case, at least under the equal protection clause.

It might be noted that a number of countries that accept a rule of equal treatment like that of the United States attach a qualifier to it. Thus India amended its constitution rather than abide by a court decision prohibiting the use of caste and religious quotas in connection with admissions to colleges and universities. The amendment reads:

Nothing in this article [on equal protection] . . . shall prevent the state from making any special provision for the advancement of any socially or educationally backward class of citizens, or for the Scheduled Castes and the Scheduled Tribes.[58]

Similarly, New Zealand—in a law quoted above in Chapter 4—prohibits discrimination, but specifies that a measure that would otherwise violate the prohibition is permissible on two conditions: if the good faith purpose is to assist or advance persons or groups identified by color, race, or ethnic or national origin; and if those persons or groups can reasonably be supposed to need assistance or advancement in order to achieve an equal place with other members of the community. India's constitution and New Zealand's law reflect the requirements of the international convention on racial discrimination, quoted at the beginning of the chapter.

PREFERENTIAL TREATMENT: THE MORAL ISSUE

I assume that, as a rule, the courts that order certain practices, especially when they do it in equity, and the governments that follow those practices, believe that they are acting not only legally but also morally. At the same time, the moral issue needs to be debated as such, and to that we now turn.

Alan H. Goldman has examined that issue most thoroughly. He focuses on "preferential treatment for minority group members and women in job hiring, school admissions, or training-program policies."[59] His analysis is abstract and general, with few references to concrete cases. He obviously has the United States in mind, but states his judgments in unrestricted fashion, leaving it unclear how carefully he has considered the kinds of problems faced abroad. He shows little evidence of concern for the survival and well-being of the polity. His concerns, instead, are for the individual and society, and more particularly for equality and opportunity for the individual and the efficiency with which goods and services are provided to society.[60] These concerns, he believes, establish a *prima facie* case for awarding positions by competence, the question being in what circumstances, if any, deviation from this rule is justified in order to compensate for denials of equality of opportunity in the past or to overcome disadvantages that impair it for the future.

Goldman seeks moral perfection, above all where compensatory action is involved. Individuals who can demonstrate that they have been injured by discrimination are entitled to compensation, but the compensation must be appropriate to the injury, and no substitutions are allowed; that is, discrimination against one black in the past does not justify the preferential treatment of another black now or in the future. Goldman is markedly reluctant to grant that a group as a whole may suffer discrimination. When a group has no official representative body, when its members have no "formal" interaction, and when individual members may suffer harms that do not necessarily affect others, compensation "can be owed only to the individual members who have been harmed, and not to the group as a whole."[61] He grants, however, that group discrimination has occurred "in those geographical areas in which laws conferred a second-class citizenship in numerous important respects until recently."[62] But he argues that compensation for this should not go to individuals. Ideally it should go to an official body that represents all those harmed. In the absence of an official body it should go to "community projects and representative institutions—for example, colleges, businesses, etc.—with emphasis given to types of aid that would benefit large classes of blacks at once and thus approximate to general benefits."[63]

Goldman is similarly perfectionist in allocating the costs of compensatory action. When compensation goes to an individual, the cost should be borne by the perpetrator of the injury, and should not be imposed on one or more innocent third parties.[64] Group liability arises sometimes in that formally organized institutions, such as governments and corporations, are responsible for the actions of their agents, but individual persons should not be saddled with the consequent burdens. The liability should be discharged by drawing on general funds so as to spread the burdens equitably.[65] In no event should an innocent white suffer discrimination so that the grievance of a black can be redressed.

Goldman's argument goes in a different direction when he focuses not on compensation for past discrimination but on equal opportunity and the future. Attaching great importance to the rule that jobs should be "formally open to all strictly according to competence qualifications," he goes on to attach importance to the principle that people should have equal chances to acquire the qualifications. The principle does not require action to compensate for disadvantages due to inborn characteristics, but does require "correction for socially relative initial disadvantages," such as those stemming from a "deprived social background" or chronic poverty.[66] As in the case of compensation for past discrimination, however, he insists that correction for socially related disadvantages proceed on an individualistic basis. The correlation between race and chronic poverty is not close enough, as he sees it, to permit the use of race as a surrogate for the criterion that he wants to emphasize. The chronically poor are the ones entitled to corrective action, be they black or white. The corrective action may take different forms, and should be adjusted to the circumstances that cause the impairment of equal opportunity. It might, for example, take the form of special schooling. But in this context Goldman is also willing to accept preferential hiring. Thus a more competent and innocent person might be denied a job so that a less competent person from a deprived social background can be employed. Goldman would do this with regret, but he holds that hiring by competence "is not completely just until equality of opportunity has been achieved." He specifies, however, that the preferential hiring applies only to positions calling for "fixed levels of competence" and not to positions calling for "open-ended degrees of excellence."[67] Thus preferential hiring might be justified for a janitorial staff but not for a university faculty.

Goldman's position is well thought out, and appealing. I differ with him in part on matters of principle and in part on questions of practicality. The least significant of the differences of principle relates to his willingness to have innocent parties suffer in the name of affirmative action to promote equality of opportunity but not in the name of affirmative action to compensate for previous discrimination. Though I incline in his direction, I would put little emphasis on the distinction that he makes. If innocent individuals can be made to risk their lives in war in the name of the well-being of the country, and if they can be denied a job in the name of promoting equality of opportunity for persons who grow up in chronic poverty, I would not hesitate about requiring them to look elsewhere, if need be, so that a specific job can go to a person who has been a victim of discrimination. For that matter, it is not always clear—I do not believe that it is in the *Weber* case—whether preferential treatment should be regarded as compensatory or as contributing to equal opportunity.

The more significant difference of principle relates to what Goldman calls group desert and group liability. I am more inclined than he is to accept certain groups as entities with rights and obligations. He himself, be it recalled, does not rule this out. As noted above, he grants that in some parts of the United States the law has treated some as second-class citizens, creating both a group liability and a group desert. I would put more stress than he does on this fact, and I would go beyond it. When government treats members of a racial group with scorn and contempt it not only commits a wrong for which it is liable, but it puts a seal of approval on the scorn and contempt that private parties and agencies have been displaying and it encourages them to continue and perhaps to extend the injustice. This means that its obligation goes beyond redressing the wrongs that it has itself committed and includes a share of responsibility for the actions of private parties and agencies. Further, the responsibility is that of the whole community—of all the people in whose name the government acts; it is a collective responsibility that persists beyond the lifetime of the persons who committed the wrong. Ideally the burden of meeting the responsibility should of course be equitably shared, but concern for equity in the sharing should not be so meticulous as to indefinitely delay or restrict compensatory action. If some whites bear more of a burden than others, this is regrettable, but government would be paralyzed if it insisted that burdens be allocated in strict proportion to guilt or according to some other standard of individual justice. I do not suggest that whites be fired so that blacks can have jobs, but the line of thought that I am advancing suggests that preferential hiring is sometimes justified on grounds in addition to those that Goldman grants.

I am less inclined than Goldman to insist that, when redress goes to individual blacks, it shall go only to those who can prove that they personally have suffered discrimination. The most obvious problem is the practical one of determining on a case by case basis which of millions of persons have in fact suffered discrimination, especially when in many instances the acts of discrimination would have occurred years and perhaps decades previously. In truth, my own supposition is that literally all blacks born in the United States have suffered discrimination. Quite apart from the question whether discrimination is ever directed personally at them, they could scarcely escape the stigma associated with slavery and Jim Crow; and I am not inclined to dismiss psychological hurt and damage as somehow less serious than explicit discrimination. Goldman speaks of "vicarious harm" as so " 'remote and speculative' . . . that courts refuse, with good reason, to recognize [it] in compensation cases."[68] But I doubt whether the stigma is strictly vicarious, or that it is either remote or speculative. Even if this view is rejected, I would argue that so high a proportion of American blacks have suffered discrimination that the effort to identify them and to restrict compensatory action to them would not be worth the cost. If standards of proof were at all strict and if there were a serious effort to adjust the redress to the injuries individually suffered, the costs would be especially great, and delays and bitter resentments would be inevitable.

Another practical question concerns the method of obtaining preferential treatment where Goldman approves it as desirable. He does not prescribe a method. Where an employer has been persistently and egregiously discriminatory, I would not rely on simple admonitions or even on orders that left the employer with much discretion. Orders for ratio-hiring, such as those given to the San Francisco police department and to the Detroit Edison Company, seem to me to be imperative.

In addition to these practical questions, a larger question arises about the extent to which blacks comprise a community, a self-conscious entity, perhaps a nation within a nation. This is a question about the subjective attitudes of blacks, and is empirical. I have made no effort to assemble or otherwise obtain relevant evidence, but my assumption—the same one that underlies the court decisions described above—is already clear. I believe that to a significant extent blacks identify with each other, thinking that what happens to fellow blacks at the hands of whites also happens to them, good or bad. Whites have helped to create and reinforce this feeling by discriminating against blacks as such, regardless of distinctive personal qualities and solely on grounds of color. If my assumption is well-founded, it suggests that the courts have been justified in their obvious belief that the ratio-hiring of blacks can serve as compensation even when the set of blacks hired is not the same as the set that suffered discrimination at the hands of the specific employer involved. We can grant that it would be better if compensation could be finely adjusted to the experience of individual blacks, but we can also say that rough justice is better than none, and that it is better to do rough justice in a timely and economic way than to hold out for perfect justice that is both impractical and prohibitively costly.

The main weakness about the line of thought that I am advancing is its vagueness in indicating the action that should be taken, whether in the name of compensatory justice or in the name of promoting equality of opportunity. Goldman's position, though I think it impractical, has the merit of calling for a careful examination of individual cases, and this would do much to indicate the corrective action that would be appropriate. My position gives little guidance of a discriminating sort. I can, however, adopt Goldman's distinction between positions calling for "fixed levels of competence" and those calling for "open-ended degrees of excellence," though I would prefer to think of positions that range along a scale in terms of the demands they make and the opportunities that they offer with respect to a variety of qualities, such as knowledge, intelligence, creativity, and imagination. Ratio-hiring is most appropriate in positions where such demands and opportunities are relatively modest. In fact, the courts have ordered ratio-hiring only in positions of this sort.

CONCLUSION

As this chapter indicates at the beginning, Nathan Glazer speaks of the "simple and clear understanding, that rights attach to the individual, not the group." From earlier chapters, we know that understanding does not exist in many other countries, if any. Whether on grounds of language or religion or indigeneity, many other countries recognize groups, conceding them legal status and rights and presumably doing so on the basis of the belief that the groups have a good moral claim to what they get. Further, Glazer himself does not contend that the "simple and clear understanding" has prevailed during much of American history. Whatever the rhetoric, through most of

American history whites have arrogated rights to themselves both individually and collectively. So have those who speak English, those who are Protestant, and those who are male. Moreover, group rights have been conceded to the Indians and the Samoans. Glazer says that the understanding was fully reached in the 1960s, and that departures from it subsequently occurred. This chapter, however, casts doubt on the question whether such an understanding was ever reached in any full measure; even if so, it was certainly not "simple and clear."

Whereas Glazer decries evidence of any recognition of group rights, this book and this chapter go in the opposite direction. At the same time, the chapter does not argue for a recognition of group rights after the fashion of Belgium or Fiji, let alone Malaysia. The argument advanced is for the most part compatible with the dominant strain of thought currently guiding legislative, executive, and judicial policies. It makes explicit a feature of those policies that is ordinarily ignored: that even those who profess individualism are in some circumstances driven in the direction of a recognition of group rights. At the same time, the recognition is of a limited sort. The rhetorical tradition of the country is so fully individualistic, and the idea of the melting pot has taken such a hold, that the limits are not surprising. Moreover, the country has gone so far with its homogenizing policies that it would not be sensible to suggest an about face. My principal point is not that the United States should change its domestic policies, save in relatively minor ways, but that it should recognize the difficulties and the shortcomings of individualism and acknowledge that in a number of other countries, where cleavages between ethnic communities are sharper and deeper, individual rights must be supplemented by group rights, and conceptions of the meaning of equal and nondiscriminatory treatment must be adjusted accordingly. Conflicts between the two sets of rights are of course inevitable, requiring judgments and choices that are often difficult and doubtful. But complex problems do not always have simple solutions. An examination of the problems of South Africa will make this even clearer.

7

Race: South Africa

The population of South Africa is deeply divided: about 71 percent black, 16 percent white, 10 percent colored, and 3 percent Indian. To the racial differences are added others. The blacks divide into ten or so tribes or nations or peoples, speaking a number of different languages. The whites divide into those who speak Afrikaans (the Afrikaners, mainly of Dutch ancestry) and those who speak English—the Afrikaners comprising about 56 percent of the total. The Indians trace their ancestry to India and are mainly Muslim and Hindu in religion; a few other Asians are classified with them. The rest are the coloreds—mainly mulattoes. Though a degree of self-consciousness sets the Afrikaners and the English apart from each other, and though one encounters references to the Afrikaner nation, the dominant attitude among the whites is that they comprise one nation and not two. And, more importantly, the dominant view among the whites is a we/they view, coupled with an implacable determination to maintain what is called the white identity.

As a plural society, South Africa illustrates the problem of which Lewis wrote in *Politics in West Africa*, described in Chapter 1. The whites established the government originally and have always controlled it. Racial attitudes, and relationships among the races, have shifted somewhat through time, and it is no longer true that the whites regard the blacks as enemies; but nevertheless most of the whites believe that they face a black peril—a danger that the blacks may engulf and submerge them. In 1948 they voted the National Party into power, and have continued it in power ever since, supporting the policies of apartheid (racial separateness) that the party has championed. Among other things, these policies involved the elimination of the meager degree of political participation that had been allowed to the coloreds and the blacks, establishing a complete white monopoly.

The fact of a white monopoly and the methods that the government uses to maintain the white identity are the source of domestic opposition and of agitation that extends around the world. A minority of the whites have always opposed the apartheid system, and the National Party itself has come to accept the need for change. In 1983 it championed the adoption of a new constitution calling for a degree of power-sharing with the coloreds and the Indians. Even with the coloreds and the Indians included, however, the government will still be a minority government, looked on as illegitimate by a majority within the country (including many whites) and by a high proportion of the other governments in the world.[1]

We can approach the South African problem best by focusing first on the claim of the whites concerning their identity and on the methods that they employ to preserve that identity. Then we will describe and appraise the reforms in progress; and the judgment that they are inadequate will lead to the problem of outlining policies that are suitable in plural societies yet compatible with respect for human rights.

THE BASIC WHITE CLAIM

The appeal of the National Party and of the government is to the right of the white nation to preserve itself, or to the right of all peoples to self-determination. The chief architect of the apartheid system, Prime Minister Verwoerd, asserted some years ago that

it is a fundamental right . . . of the white man to protect his own nation from disaster. Every nation has the right to continued existence. That is the most basic human right. It is a fundamental right to preserve one's nation and to protect one's identity as a nation. That is the basis of our whole policy.[2]

The claim has been reiterated many times.[3]

Note that Verwoerd did not claim special privilege for the whites. He said that "every" nation has the right to continued existence, and he meant to include what he regarded as the black nations of South Africa. In describing the policy of separate development he said that it was a method "whereby one racial group will not permanently rule the other, but . . . every racial group will be given self-rule in respect of its own people, in an area of its own where possible."[4]

Further, spokesmen for the government do not claim racial superiority for the whites. "If we [engage in] discrimination," the South African delegate once told the Security Council, "it is not because the Whites . . . have any *Herrenvolk* complex. We are not better than the Black people, we are not cleverer than they are. What we can achieve, so can they."[5] And a National Party leader who later became prime minister, P. W. Botha, declared that "all people are equal before God; all peoples have the right to equal opportunity and self-determination. . . . "[6]

Neither do the whites attempt to justify their policies of discrimination or their domination over the other races. On the contrary, the delegate to the Security Council quoted above declared that "we shall do everything in our power to move away from discrimination based on race or color."[7] And a government publication, obviously prepared with thought and care, grants that "permanent White guardianship or supremacy over a number of Black peoples is not only impossible but also morally unjustifiable."[8]

Though National Party leaders deny claiming racial superiority and deny aiming at permanent white guardianship or supremacy, they refuse to take any steps that might give political domination to the blacks. This is the possibility that they dread. And the probability is that if they gave any sign of taking a course of action that might lead to black domination, they would be forced to hold an election, which (with only the whites voting) they probably would lose. They thus suffer a kind of paralysis. Unable to advance a reasoned case justifying their own dominance, they are unwilling to sponsor reforms that might reverse the situation and give domination to the blacks.

In Chapter 3 I spoke of the attitude of some Turks on Cyprus, who (before the partition) denied that the Turks there should be viewed as a minority, their contention being that to speak of a minority was to assume the existence of a single population—one whole community. The Turks in question denied the assumption, holding that the population of Cyprus consisted of different communities that stood in relation to each other as separate entities, not as parts of a single whole. The view assumed, in effect, that the two populations were potential candidates for separate statehood.

A similar point of view exists among whites in South Africa. Most of them stress the fact that South Africa is a plural society, not a single community. They speak of it as a multinational state, where it is as inappropriate to think of majority rule as it would be in the world as a whole. They think in terms of distinct peoples who want to preserve their separate identities but who face a problem in that they happen to find themselves intermixed in one geographic area, as the Turks and Greeks once did on Cyprus. Having no satisfactory solution to this problem, the party and government flounder, following policies in which they apparently do not believe but unable to replace them with other policies that meet the needs and are acceptable to the voters on whom the party depends.

METHODS OF PRESERVING IDENTITY

The most important fact about the policies followed—policies of apartheid, or policies of separate development—has already been indicated: they are the policies of the whites alone. The whites alone decide on the terms of the relationships among the races. To be sure, as will be noted more fully in a moment, some aspects of the policies depend for their implementation on cooperation from blacks, coloreds, and Indians, and the new constitution is designed to bring the last two of these groups within the political system. But the blacks are left out.

Table 4
Composition of the Population. South Africa, 1980

	Totals	Per cent	Resident in African homelands	Resident in the "White" homeland	Per cent of "White" homeland residents
Blacks	19,146,000	71	9,677,000	9,469,000	55
Whites	4,364,000	16	9,000	4,355,000	25
Coloreds	2,554,000	10	6,000	2,548,000	15
Asians	795,000	3	6,000	789,000	5
Totals	26,859,000		9,698,000	17,161,000	

Source: *South Africa 1982. Official Yearbook of the Republic of South Africa* (Johannesburg: Chris van Rensburg Publications, 1982), p. 33. This source gives 15,893,000 as the number of blacks (Africans). I have added 3,253,000 so as to include the populations of Transkei, Bophuthatswana, and Venda, which were officially independent when the *Yearbook* went to press. Subsequently Ciskei was also granted official independence. Its population in 1980 was 636,000.

Official policy relating to the blacks concerns the black homelands or Bantustans and what the whites choose to call the white homeland. Long ago the government set aside over 100 pieces of territory (13 percent of the total area of the country) as reserves for blacks. Now these pieces are grouped or consolidated into ten homelands, one for each of the "nations" into which the black population is said to divide. The aim has been to make the homelands self-governing, and this aim is now said to have been achieved in every case. Moreover, the aim has been to grant sovereign independence to each one, and in four cases this has been done (as of the end of 1983). Other countries, opposing the whole apartheid system, have refused to recognize the legitimacy of these grants of independence.

The 87 percent of the country not included in the black homelands is disingenuously called the white homeland. To appreciate the misleading character of that name, a knowledge of the racial composition of the population is essential. The figures are given in Table 4. Most notable is the fact that, although the whites speak of a "white" homeland, they comprise only a quarter of its population. Blacks living in the so-called white homeland outnumber the whites by more than two to one. The coloreds and Indians also live there and combine with the blacks to outnumber the whites by about three to one. In other words, in the so-called white homeland the blacks alone comprise 55 percent of the total, and the blacks, coloreds, and Indians combined comprise 75 percent. Further, population trends are against the whites; their proportion of the total is declining as the years go by.

On what basis, then, do those who support policies of separate development speak of a white homeland? There is an answer that was once officially espoused and that is still a basis for action; but it is no longer explicitly advanced, and it clearly leaves thoughtful white South Africans uncomfortable. It is that the blacks do not count. According to this view, blacks classify as temporary sojourners, as guests, and not as legitimate residents living where they do as a matter of right. Each black in the "white" homeland is said, on the basis of ancestral ties, really to belong in one of the black homelands, whether or not he has ever lived there; and so a black in the "white" homeland is in "another man's country."[9]

Further, in a procrustean way the government is seizing on independence for the homelands as a means of solving the problem of electoral discrimination against the blacks in the "white" area. The solution is to make them citizens of "their own" homeland whenever it becomes independent, and to strip them of South African citizenship.[10] Once they are aliens (and all blacks are slated eventually to be aliens), the denial of the vote to them will not be considered discriminatory. The position is that they can exercise their rights of political participation in their homeland rather than in the politicial system that affects their lives. It is as if Alex Haley, while living in the United States, were asked to exercise his political rights in Gambia. The government proves its concern for the political rights of the blacks by setting up polling booths for them in the "white" area when their homeland has an election.

That some whites, even in the highest councils of the government, do not support the above line of thought and action is clear. Among other things, the report of the Constitutional Committee of the President's Council (1982) speaks of the black population that is "permanently resident" in the "white" homeland.[11] Moreover, the government has adopted measures that are inconsistent with the guest worker theory. Most particularly, it no longer prevents blacks from acquiring property in officially accepted black enclaves within the "white" area; on the contrary, it permits them to acquire such property on the basis of a 99-year lease, with the probability of further change to make the 99-year period begin over again whenever the property changes hands. It is extending to blacks a substantial measure of self-government at the local level, ignoring the fact that many of those who vote in the local elections have been stripped of citizenship. It is permitting black trade unions to operate on the same basis as white trade unions, and is allowing dependence on black labor, including skilled labor, to increase year by year. And it is increasing its appropriations for education for blacks—and for coloreds and Indians—at every level, including the university level. Such measures suggest an assumption that the blacks are there to stay.

In the four homelands that have become independent, the government has obviously found blacks who are willing to cooperate, and the odds are that it will be able to do so in other black homelands as well; it is heady stuff to have the opportunity to become chief of state, or to occupy other high office. At the same time, the independence policy arouses opposition not only at the international level but also within South Africa. In fact, in 1976 leaders of seven of the homelands (including two of those that subsequently became independent) issued a statement declaring that they had "no intention whatsoever of opting for so-called independence." "We do not want," they said, "to abdicate our birthright as South Africans, as well as forfeiting our share of the economy and wealth, which we have jointly built."[12] And a comparable sort of statement followed in 1980.[13]

In 1981 the newly created President's Council, consisting of white, colored, and Indian members appointed by the state president, set up a Constitutional Committee, asking it to make recommendations for a new constitution. It made two reports.[14] It acknowledged the problem of the blacks, declaring it impossible "to design a form of government at the national level that does not take into account all population groups,"[15] but it nevertheless went on to recommend arrangements relating to the whites, coloreds, and Indians only. As might be expected, it found that "the *orthodox model of democracy* (simple majoritarianism or one man, one vote majoritarianism in a single system) *is not a viable option in South Africa in foreseeable circumstances.*"[16] The option is not viable because it "assumes that minorities can become majorities, and that governments and oppositions will alternate."[17] Underlying the committee's view was the assumption of racially polarized voting—more broadly, the assumption that politics would be a struggle not among shifting aggregations of individuals who choose the political party to support, but among permanently formed, coherent racial groups. Thus, given "one man, one vote majoritarianism," government would be the instrument of the blacks; the whites, coloreds, and Indians would be permanent minorities, futilely holding some seats in parliament, always outvoted. The committee quoted the following statement with obvious approval:[18]

One man, one vote is not a realistic goal: to solve ethnic conflicts, South Africa will have to institutionalise group rights. While democracies can allow power to pass from party to party, ethnically and racially diverse societies cannot do so. When a party loses power in a democracy, it does not have its basic rights endangered, whereas ethnic groups that lose political power often also lose everything else as well.

The committee also declared (I think correctly) that "the problem of accommodating ethnicity within the framework of democratic government . . . may . . . be described as one of the central problems of modern democracy. . . . "[19] This is the problem that so concerned W. Arthur Lewis in his *Politics in West Africa*, referred to in Chapter 1.

For its general approach to the problem, the committee claimed to look to Arend Lijphart's *Democracy in Plural Societies: A Comparative Exploration*[20] and thus to the idea of "consociational" democracy, to which we will give attention in the following chapter. It cited Lijphart's statement of the four essential characteristics of consociational democracy:[21]

a. Government by a "grand coalition" of the political leaders of all significant segments (groups) of the plural society;

b. The mutual veto or "concurrent majority" rule, which serves as an additional protection of vital minority interests;

c. The principle of proportionality in determining political representation, civil service appointments, and the allocation of public funds; and

d. A high degree of autonomy for each segment to run its own internal affairs.

But the appeal to consociational democracy was obviously qualified. Most notable was the failure to make any provision for the blacks. The "grand coalition" would include the whites and the less numerous colored and Indian population groups, but not the majority group.

Further, the proposals advanced were conditioned by the view of the Committee that

South Africa requires strong government, and any prospect of governmental paralysis must not be allowed to arise; accordingly, when consensus cannot be achieved, mechanisms for transcending dissent in order to ensure effective government must be employed.[22]

In other words, though "concurrent majorities" would assure the adoption of legislation, the veto of the coloreds and Indians should be qualified.

The constitution adopted in 1983 reflects the recommendations of the Committee. It provides for a strong president and makes no provision for a prime minister. The president is to be elected by an electoral college in which seats are assigned to the three racial groups on a 4:2:1 ratio, which means that the whites can make sure that the president is white. (They could of course also do this in a popular election in which only the three racial groups participated.) The parliament is to be tricameral—something new in the world. In addition to a chamber representing the whites, one is to be set up for the coloreds and another for the Indians. The president is to divide legislative matters into those that concern only one of the racial groups ("segmental") and those that are of general concern. The appropriate racial chamber is to consider bills in the first category, and all three are to consider bills in the second. Once adopted, bills in both categories go to the president, who may sign or veto.

The constitution permits each house to delay action on matters of common concern, but does not provide for anything that deserves to be called a mutual veto. If one chamber adopts a bill but does not get the concurrence of one or both of the others, the president may refer the bill to his Council, over which he will have great influence; and it may authorize him to sign it into law. The Council is to consist of 60 persons, of whom the president is to appoint 25; of the remainder, 20 are to be elected by the white chamber, 10 by the colored chamber, and 5 by the Indian chamber (the 4:2:1 ratio again). Assuming that the president is white and that whites comprise a majority of the President's Council, this means in effect that, if the white chamber enacts a bill, the bill can become law regardless of the action of the colored and Indian chambers. For that matter, the president could presumably arrange to have a bill made into law if he can get the support of any one of the three chambers.

Thus the whites and the National Party, while agreeing to power-sharing, impose safeguards. On the one hand, they apply the principle that the racial communities are distinct from each other, not making up a single community in which majority rule is appropriate. Moreover, the provision for separate chambers makes it impossible for the white opposition in parliament to form a coalition with the coloreds and Indians in order to wrest power from the National Party. On the other hand, especially in the light of the prospective composition and the powers of the President's Council, the coloreds and Indians will not be able to block action on matters of general concern. The whites can override their opposition—just as the whites could outvote them if all three races were more or less proportionately represented in the same chamber.

Whether the constitution will get enough support within the colored and Indian communities to be put into effect, and whether it will prove viable, remains to be seen. Obviously, nothing about it will be attractive to the blacks. Some whites support it on the ground that it will accustom whites to sharing power, or on the ground that one measure of reform, however flawed, is bound to lead to another. Those taking such views hope and expect that the incorporation of the blacks in the political system will somehow follow. In the debate on the adoption of the new constitution, the main white opposition party rejected such attitudes, denying that the proposed change would move the country in the right direction and instead condemning it as the capstone of a racial system that assures white supremacy and that freezes the blacks out for the indefinite future.

In addition to policies concerning the location of political control, "separate development" includes an array of other policies with various purposes. Some of them, such as restrictions on property ownership and on places of residence, are designed mainly to keep the races apart while permitting members of the subordinate races to take employment in white-owned enterprises. Some, such as those relating to influx control, are designed to exclude from the "white" homeland blacks who might become a problem, or to bring about their deportation if a problem develops. Some, such as those permitting arbitrary arrests and banning, are designed to prevent blacks, Indians, and coloreds (individually or collectively) from mounting an effective challenge to white control. For that matter, white opponents of the official policies on race may also be imprisoned arbitrarily or banned if their opposition takes a form or achieves a level of success that the government finds intolerable.

The adoption of the new constitution implies an acceptance of the need for change, as do other reform measures, such as the legal recognition of black trade unions and the grant to blacks of leasehold rights. In recent years a marked reduction in what is called petty apartheid has occurred. But grand apartheid continues. The fundamental fact of the supremacy of the whites and the subordination of the other races remains; and so does the fact that government spokesmen do not attempt a reasoned, moral justification of white control.[23] The best that they could do would be to seek justification on the basis of the claim that their policies will make an orderly rather than a violent transition to a new system more likely; but the government cannot even make this claim, for it denies that it has a plan for a new system that will include the blacks.

TRANSITION TO WHAT? IS THERE A SOLUTION?

If the main problem in South Africa is domination by one race over the others, and if even the National Party accepts the need for change, the aim should presumably be to set out on a course of action that, perhaps in an incremental and evolutionary way, provides for power-sharing on a fair basis while assuring respect for human rights.

The question is whether such a course of action has been established, and the answer is mixed. The very method of arriving at the present course of action is faulty, in that the crucial decisions are those of the whites alone. The new constitution, for example, is an in-house government document, presented to the white parliament and then to the white electorate for their approval, but without any conference or convention that included the leaders of the colored and Indian communities, let alone the leaders of the blacks.

Conceivably the course of action that the whites have set with respect to the black homelands could lead to a satisfactory outcome. At any rate, decentralization is one of the devices that can legitimately be employed to minimize domination by one set of people over another, and both the way in which the world is divided and the way in which a number of countries are divided set ample precedents for making political boundary lines coincide with ethnic boundary lines when this is feasible.

The least defensible (indeed the indefensible) feature of this policy is its corollary—that blacks in the "white" homeland are stripped of citizenship when "their" black homeland becomes independent. In the case of a high proportion of the blacks, this is an entirely arbitrary and therefore a discriminatory action. If this feature were eliminated, and if citizenship were restored to those who have been deprived of it, the remaining question would concern the fairness of the geographic allocations. The criticism that the whites have allocated only 13 percent of the land to 70 percent of the people is unjustified, for it assumes that all of the blacks belong in the black homelands. Nevertheless, it is questionable enough that 13 percent of the land has been allocated to about 35 percent of the people. Some of

the black homelands are simply not viable as independent econ-
omies. Further, of the four homelands that have been granted
independence, only one consists of a single block of territory.
The others consist of two, three, and six. That is, they consist
of separate, non-contiguous blocks, mostly enclaves in the
"white" area. Of the remaining six slated for independence,
two consist of a single block each, and the others of two, three,
six, and ten.[24] Now it is difficult to think that a small state
can be genuinely independent when it is economically dependent and when blocks of its territory are dispersed and
vulnerable.

The black leader of the first homeland to accept independence, Mantanzima of Transkei, faces such difficulties that he
speaks of abandoning independence and entering a federal South
African system. And leaders of the National Party speak of the
possibility of some kind of confederal system. Either a federation or a confederation might be both feasible and desirable.
It is imaginable that in some such system those blacks who
are geographically concentrated could retain what they speak
of as their birthright in South Africa and still enjoy autonomy
in handling their local affairs.

A counterpart for the whites is unlikely. As already indicated, the so-called white homeland is in fact far from white.
It is thinkable that a few restricted areas might be identified
as white, and that in them policies analogous to those applying
to the Aaland Islands and to the American Samoa might be
put into effect. If sovereign states can prohibit or restrict immigration, it does not seem totally out of the question that
some local communities would have an analogous power. There
are even precedents at the international level for the forced
exchange of populations. And it is thinkable that a racial war
or a radical breakdown of the present system might lead to a
sorting out of the races, with whites fleeing into certain restricted areas or completely out of the country. But those emphasizing respect for human rights must look forward to the
continued intermingling of the races in "white" South Africa,
with members of all races free to own property and reside wherever their financial resources permit. After all, as the Covenant
on Civil and Political Rights says, "everyone lawfully within

the territory of a state shall have . . . freedom to choose his residence."

With respect to the franchise the constitution is clear in fixing a course of action that could lead to a satisfactory outcome: it calls for universal adult suffrage for whites, coloreds, and Indians—that is, for a kind of rule that could easily be extended to the blacks.

The plan for a tricameral parliament and for the President's Council does not fix a promising course of action. To add a fourth chamber for the blacks would make an already cumbersome system quite impractical. And an abandonment of the system of separate racial parliamentary chambers would surely entail fundamental change in the composition and powers of the President's Council, if not its abolition. The blacks cannot be expected to accept a council, controlled by the whites, that can authorize the enactment of legislation that the blacks oppose, as it can do in the case of the coloreds and Indians.

Governmental leaders have proposed to the blacks that, instead of being brought fully into the government, they should have a Representative Council that the government could consult. Understandably, the blacks have rejected the proposal. Nothing about the situation in South Africa suggests that a satisfactory accommodation can be reached that excludes the blacks who reside in the "white" homeland from the formal governmental structure.

It would be much more promising if South Africa had a conventional type of parliament, perhaps bicameral. It would then be possible to adopt a number of devices that are compatible with democracy and respect for human rights and that nevertheless provide safeguards for the vital interests of different communities. I assume that racial rolls would be used in the elections, after the examples set in Fiji and New Zealand. And there might be a general roll on which anyone could register, giving an opportunity for voters to de-emphasize race if they wish to do so. Seats in multi-member bodies such as parliament might then be allocated to those on the different rolls in proportion to their turn-out at the polls. It might or might not be made permissible for voters of one race to elect a member of

another race as their representative. And it might or might
not be required (as in Fiji) that some of those representing a
given race be elected on an interracial basis.

There are, of course, other potentially relevant precedents.
South Africa might simply add a quota for the blacks to the
quota system that the new constitution applies to the whites,
coloreds, and Indians—which would presumably lead to ratios
of from 9:4:2:1 to 19:4:2:1, depending on which blacks are
counted. Theoretically it might follow any of various practices
found at the international level. The members of the General
Assembly vary tremendously in population, but they all have
one vote. Five members of the Security Council have a veto
whereas the others do not. Votes in some of the international
financial institutions are allocated to member states in proportion to the capital that they provide, which means that votes
are assigned in proportion to the importance of the various
members to the functioning of the institution. In the European
parliament, the quota of seats for each member state is more
favorable the smaller the population of the state. It works out
that Luxembourg gets one member for every 60,000 persons,
Ireland one for every 220,000, Italy one for every 700,000, and
the Federal Republic of Germany one for every 760,000. One
person in Luxembourg thus counts for as much as 12.3 persons
in the Federal Republic. A justification for this seemingly unequal treatment is fairly obvious. It is that the smaller and
weaker a people the more representation it should have, for
both symbolic and practical reasons. Symbolically the "over-
representation" indicates a repudiation of the idea that justice
is the interest of the strong; it indicates the intent of the strong
to respect the interests of the weak. And practically it gives
the weak a slightly better chance of commanding that respect.
The more populous a state the less it needs such reassurance,
especially when greater numbers carry with them greater economic and military power.

We might note incidentally that when the European states
set up their parliament, they did not go for individualism. That
is, they did not go for the idea that the populations of the
various states should all be lumped together into one mass,

with the majority ruling. Instead, they went for a form of communalism, with the population of each state as the entity to be represented, each entity getting its quota of seats.

And we might add another incidental note: that few countries are as strict as the United States in insisting on the equal population principle—that is, on the principle that members of a legislature shall represent equal numbers of people; and the United States does not apply the principle to the Senate.[25]

A reference was made earlier to Lijphart's acceptance of the principle of proportionality in representation. Here we might add that Lijphart goes on to accept a significant qualification on the principle: that small communities might be deliberately overrepresented, up to the point of parity.[26] He thus opens the way to an arrangement that would prevent a small community, such as the whites of South Africa, from obtaining representation that goes beyond parity, and prevent a large community, such as the blacks, from achieving domination.

Whatever the basis for representation in parliament, special majorities might be required if certain kinds of changes are proposed, and one or more communities might be enabled to delay or veto action. Recall, for example, that Belgium gives special powers to the parliamentary delegation of each of the two main communities. Either delegation may veto changes in linguistic boundary lines, and either may sound an alarm, delaying action, if it thinks that a bill under consideration seriously threatens relations between the communities.

Arrangements like those just described might or might not be coupled with comparable arrangements relating to a second chamber. Recall that in Fiji proposals to change the law concerning land ownership can be adopted only if supported by not less than three quarters of the members of the House and by at least six of the eight senators appointed on the advice of the Fijian Great Council of Chiefs. This permits the Fijians in each house to block action.

Special measures to assure each group that its interests will be considered and protected might well extend beyond the legislature. Recall that ministries in the Belgian cabinet are divided half and half between those who speak French and those who speak Dutch, and that the parity rule is also followed in filling posts in the civil service. And recall the arrangement in the Federal Republic of Germany under which a cabinet minister and his deputy are to be of different faiths. More or less comparable rules are followed, formally or informally, in a number of other countries, including the United States.

The possibilities listed above all belong in the political sphere. In plural societies, adjustments are also likely to be necessary and justifiable in other fields as well. For example, rules can legitimately be adopted concerning the schools so as to permit them to be instruments for preserving a culture while at the same time making some degree of racial integration highly probable. Mandatory segregation on a racial basis would violate Unesco's Convention Against Discrimination in Education, but that convention permits the adoption of the neighborhood school or the freedom of choice rule. Similarly, differentiation as to language and religion in the schools is permissible. Recall that a number of countries, especially in Europe, administer schools of a given religious character, not fixing religious criteria for admission but nevertheless expecting that parents will want their children to attend the school that supports their faith.

South Africa now prohibits miscegenation. The law has its counterpart in the social pressures that groups all over the world bring to bear, especially religious groups, to keep members within the fold, and it is to be expected that social pressures would operate in South Africa whatever the provisions of the law. Nevertheless, the law violates an individual right recognized in the Universal Declaration: "Men and women of full age, without any limitation due to race, nationality or religion, have the right to marry. . . . " Neither of the Covenants includes an explicit provision to the same effect, but freedom to marry across racial lines is surely implied by the guarantee of equality before the law and the equal protection of the law. If a black may marry a black, but a white may not, then equal protection is denied. This was the judgment of the Supreme Court of the United States when it struck down Virginia's law forbidding miscegenation.[27] So far as I am aware, no government on earth other than that of South Africa now forbids miscegenation. Here is a case where the right of the individual is of so precious a nature that it surely overrides any conflicting right that the group may have to preserve its special character.

South Africa has been notorious for racial discrimination relating to labor and trade unions. Significant changes in this respect have occurred since 1979. So far as the law is concerned, blacks may now organize into trade unions on the same basis as whites, and trade unions may be interracial in their membership. The statutory reservation of jobs by race has been terminated. The principle of equal pay for equal work is accepted, though its significance is limited by the fact that whites and blacks generally do different kinds of work. Nevertheless, in recent years the unconscionable gap in average wages between white and black workers has been narrowing. An Industrial Court exists that is authorized to hear complaints of unfair labor practices, and the law leaves it free to find that racial discrimination is unfair. All of these changes indicate a course of action going in the direction of respect for human rights, including the right to equal treatment. But discrimination remains. Some of the white trade unions obtain collective bargaining agreements through which they enlist the cooperation of employers in racial discrimination—for example, closed shop agreements. And black workers are generally handicapped by their relatively inadequate education and training.

WILL CHANGE MEAN IMPROVEMENT?

Those who demand change in the name of respect for human rights need to ask with what degree of assurance they can expect the change to bring improvement. The adage about the frying pan and the fire applies.

The problem is difficult. Although the new constitution fixes the details of immediately impending change, no one can be entirely confident in predicting even its consequences, and anyone who advocates more extensive changes faces greater difficulties. Much depends, no doubt, on the circumstances surrounding the incorporation of the blacks into the system. The prospect of respect for human rights is no doubt best if the incorporation occurs on a negotiated basis, with the black share of power increasing through a transition period of some years. In contrast, the prospect is much more doubtful if incorporation occurs quickly after a prolonged, violent struggle, for this would give power to the inexperienced, and presumably they would be under their more extreme leaders.

The whites have been so successful in repressing political activity by blacks that we have to grasp at straws in attempting to anticipate what the blacks will do politically when they get the opportunity. It would be rash to assume that the record of the states between South Africa and the Sahara indicates what the blacks of South Africa itself will do, but that record is nevertheless among the straws; and it is not encouraging. Although the states to the north have not as a rule engaged in racial discrimination, most of them have discriminated on a tribal basis. A high proportion of the refugees of the world are in Africa, these refugees having fled across international boundaries in fear of their lives; and black Africa has provided the world with examples of genocide. Uganda expelled its Indian minority from the country. Few of the black African states have maintained freedom and democracy. The Organization of African Unity (OAU) has developed a charter on "Human Rights and Peoples' Rights," but was slow in doing so; and how much impact it will have remains to be seen. Further, quite apart from the question of respect for human rights, the level of competence displayed by most of the governments between South Africa and the Sahara has been low.

The black African states have been vocal in denouncing and agitating against the apartheid system in South Africa. They may or may not ever achieve significant influence over the course of events in South Africa, but again we can grasp briefly at straws in an effort to anticipate the kind of changes they would seek. Ali A. Mazrui and David F. Gordon make comments on this question that are worth noting. They say that it is naive to think that these other states have in common a commitment to human rights, and almost as naive to assert that they are committed to the principle of "majority rule" if that is taken to imply free elections. Instead, according to them, the black

African states are committed to the principle of "racial sovereignty," and Mazrui and Gordon elaborate on this principle as follows:

This [racial sovereignty] does involve a concept of "majority rule," but not a liberal one. Under the principle of racial sovereignty, the people in a given society should not be dominated by a racially alien minority. The rulers of each society should as far as possible be racially or ethnically representative. Foreign rule is not merely rule by a nation-state from abroad but rule by a foreign racial or ethnic minority. White rule in Southern Africa is illegitimate partly because it violates this principle of racial sovereignty.[28]

With some strain this statement might be taken to mean that in South Africa each racial group should have appropriate representation in government, and if that is the meaning intended it fits with the thrust of the present chapter. But various features of the statement are disquieting: the admission that the black African states that criticize South Africa do not act out of a commitment to human rights or to majority rule if that is taken to imply free elections; the apparent reference to the whites as a "foreign" minority; and the reference to "racial sovereignty." The words intimate that the goal is to set up "black sovereignty" in place of "white sovereignty," and that the black sovereigns, once in power, can be expected to turn the tables and treat the whites as if they are in another man's country. One wonders what the gain would be for human rights and for the rule of equal and nondiscriminatory treatment if this outlook should come to prevail.

The Lusaka Manifesto stands in contrast to the analysis of Mazrui and Gordon. The Fifth Summit Conference of East and Central African States proclaimed the manifesto in 1969. The states involved denounced "systems of minority control which exist as a result of, and in pursuance of, doctrines of human inequality." Although they accepted "transitional arrangements while a transformation from group inequalities to individual equality is being effected," they denied that "the liberation of Africa for which we are struggling [means] a reverse racialism." In fact, they promised opposition to "a racialist majority government which adopted a philosophy of deliberate and permanent discrimination between its citizens on grounds of racial origin." They said that "without a commitment to . . . human equality and self-determination . . . there can be no basis for peace and justice in the world." They did not speak out for democracy, but nevertheless the stress on humane concerns stands in sharp contrast to the attitudes that Mazrui and Gordon perceive.[29]

The General Assembly has adopted many resolutions on South Africa. In one of them the General Assembly

16. *Reaffirms* the legitimacy of the struggle of the oppressed people of South Africa and their national liberation movement by all available means, including armed struggle, for the seizure of power by the people, the elimination of the *apartheid* regime and the exercise of the right of self-determination by the people of South Africa as a whole.

23. *Reaffirms* the commitment of the United Nations to the total eradication of apartheid and the establishment of a democratic society in which all the people of South Africa as a whole, irrespective of race, colour, sex, or creed, will enjoy equal and full human rights and fundamental freedoms and participate freely in the determination of their destiny.[30]

So far as goals are concerned, these statements for the most part reflect the requirements of the Universal Declaration and of the Covenant on Civil and Political Rights. But each paragraph refers to the people "as a whole," which seems to deny self-determination to component groups and to preclude the adoption of any guarantees of "balanced" participation in government. A winner-take-all system seems to be envisaged, and in deeply divided societies such a system makes the equal enjoyment of human rights unlikely.

Pronouncements of the African National Congress should be noted, though they are badly dated. At the end of World War II it listed its demands in a Bill of Rights, and in 1955 it joined with other groups in formulating a Freedom Charter.[31] Both documents endorse mainstream western liberalism, calling for the equal participation of all in the political system regardless of race. Both permit the view that what is anticipated is "majority rule" in a winner-take-all system, with no special arrangements to assure consideration of the interests of minorities. Several more recent pronouncements of black groups seeking liberation are quite vague about the type of political system that they envisage.[32]

The principal legal black political organization operating within South Africa is Inkatha, led by Gatsha Buthelezi, the Zulu leader. Buthelezi is concerned about white fears, and seeks to allay them. He urges the government to allow experimentation in political power-sharing between all groups on a regional basis so as to build up mutual trust. He contemplates the incorporation of the blacks in the political system on a stage by stage basis during a transition period of unspecified duration. He wants a constitutional convention, and would participate in it "in a spirit of compromise, rather than as the bearer of a long list of non-negotiable demands." And he speaks of safeguards for minorities.[33]

Inkatha was joined in 1983 by an interracial organization, the United Democratic Front. It stands for "a united democratic South Africa based on the will of the people," and for "a single non-racial, unfragmented South Africa." Its original pronouncement did little more to indicate the type of regime that it favors.

CONCLUSION

In a deeply divided plural society, the problem of arranging for the equal enjoyment of human rights is difficult. In such a society the strong tendency is for one of the ethnic groups to achieve and maintain political domination, and for the different groups to be mutually hostile. The dominant group then fears the consequences if it accepts reforms that might lead to the transfer of domination to another group. Such a situation does not make for the equal enjoyment of human rights.

South Africa is such a society. The whites dominate the government, and the government admittedly discriminates as to race. It has been reducing discrimination in the area of "petty apartheid," and the constitution adopted in 1983 looks in a qualified way toward reducing grand apartheid where the coloreds and Indians are concerned. But grand apartheid with respect to 70 percent of the population continues. The constitution of 1983 might turn out to be a break in a log jam and lead to the incorporation of the blacks in the political system, but it does not fix a course of action that offers any real promise of leading to this outcome. The prospect instead is for continued struggle, and the danger is that concern for human rights and equal treatment will continue to be a secondary consideration.

8

Standards of Judgment

A mistaken conception of discrimination—mistaken because of its individualism and its inattention to groups—is illustrated in a case developed against South Africa before the International Court of Justice in the 1960s. An American counsel represented Liberia and Ethiopia in presenting the case. His accusation was that, in exercising its mandate in what is now called Namibia, South Africa "distinguished by race . . . in establishing the rights and duties of the inhabitants." The accusation was naive. According to widespread practice, and in the eyes of most of those who examine the question, it is not necessarily either immoral or illegal to distinguish by race— or by language or religion; it is thus not surprising that the counsel was asked to clarify his case.

What he then did was to accuse South Africa of violating what he described as "a generally accepted international human rights norm of non-discrimination or non-separation." Here he was on good ground, at least potentially. Such a norm exists, and South Africa was violating it. But in connection with the accusation, the counsel offered a definition of nondiscrimination and non-separation, and in doing so he went wrong.

[S]tated negatively the terms refer to the absence of governmental policies or actions which allot status, rights, duties, privileges or burdens on the basis of membership in a group, class or race rather than on the basis of individual merit, capacity or potential: stated affirmatively, the terms refer to governmental policies and actions the objective of which is to protect equality of opportunity and equal protection of the laws to individual persons as such.[1]

Every chapter of this book demonstrates that this definition is bad. As one bit of the relevant evidence, recall the provisions of the international convention on racial discrimination. According to it the question is not whether "status, rights, duties, privileges, or burdens" are alloted on the basis of race, but what the purpose or effect is. If the purpose or effect is to nullify or impair the enjoyment of human rights on an equal footing, the practice is discriminatory. Otherwise (with minor qualifications) it is not. In particular, measures that differentiate "to ensure the adequate development and protection of certain racial groups" are not discriminatory. By the same token, measures that differentiate on the basis of language, religion, or indigeneity are not necessarily discriminatory either. It is not the fact of differentiation that counts, but its purpose or effect.

The American counsel's definition of discrimination showed a lack of knowledge of American constitutional law. As noted before, that law permits classification and differentiation on racial and other grounds so long as what is done is not unreasonable or invidious. What no doubt misled the counsel, however, is the fact that Western rhetoric, which reflects the Western liberal-democratic tradition, is so individualistic, encouraging the assumption that where the allocation of rights and duties is concerned, ethnic and racial differences should simply be ignored.

We come here to a serendipitous consequence of our inquiry. The focus has been on the requirement of the United Nations Charter that members promote human rights "without distinction as to race, . . . language, or religion," the effort being to work out a sensible meaning for the requirement. The effort has led again and again to the fact that many groups identified by the characteristics named want differential treatment in order to preserve cherished features of their culture; and it has led again and again to the fact that the less advanced and the weak are often thought to need differential treatment so as to promote and defend their equal enjoyment of human rights.

And when differentiation occurs the question is automatically raised whether it is justified and thus not discriminatory or whether it should be classified as a violation of the Charter requirement. Seeking an answer to that question, we had to probe into relevant portions of traditional Western liberal-democratic theory, with unsatisfactory results. Now we will focus on that theory, seeking to pinpoint its weakness and to applaud the few who have offered correctives.

I have come to believe that the individualism of that theory is arbitrary and unjustified, and that the theory needs to be modified so as to recognize the just claims of certain kinds of groups—that is, so as to concede them rights that are distinct from and not reducible to individual rights. I want to present a list of the criteria to employ in deciding on the kinds of groups that ought to be recognized as right-and-duty-bearing units, to restate the criteria for deciding when differentiation on a group basis is acceptable and when it should be considered discriminatory, and to review the question of the problems and benefits associated with group rights and communalism. Out of all this, I hope, will come a sounder conception of equal and nondiscriminatory treatment—a conception applicable within the United States and around the world.

THE INDIVIDUALISM OF LIBERAL-DEMOCRATIC THEORY

Though the individualism of liberal-democratic theory traces far back in the history of political thought, we will begin here with the thought of Hobbes and Locke. Their eyes were for the individual, and this was a matter of their choice, not a matter of being true to a historical record or even to plausible conjecture. To be sure, the question whether the individual or the group came first has about it a chicken and egg aspect, and need not be argued, but surely groups of some sort—if nothing more than different family groups—would have come into existence before anything like a social contract was needed, providing the succor and the protection on which the lives of the young depended. These groups, in the interest of their own survival and well-being, would surely have imposed rules on the young—socializing them willy-nilly. And in some respects rules would surely have governed the behavior of adults as well, the notion of the consent of the governed (or the equivalent) having no more operational significance than it does today, if as much. Not that individuals necessarily had to go through life accepting all group customs and norms unquestioningly, but if they wanted change they surely would have been required to seek it in ways that the group found acceptable. Whether or not a group right was ever articulated in a state of nature, it was surely in practice asserted.

Hobbes and Locke could well have chosen the above perspective, but did not. Instead they imagined a state of nature peopled by adult men in full liberty, not beholden to each other or to anyone else. These men, each acting for himself, get together and make a social contract, creating the state. As Hobbes put it, "A commonwealth is said to be instituted when a multitude of men do agree. . . . "[2] Agreement thus brings one major group into existence, the commonwealth, but nothing is said about groups intermediate between the individual and the commonwealth. As Sabine puts it, "There is [for Hobbes] no middle ground between humanity as a sand-heap of separate organisms and the state as an outside power. . . . "[3] Similarly Locke spoke of an "original compact [through which] any number of men . . . make one community or government wherein the majority have a right to act and conclude the rest."[4] Later, Rousseau too spoke of a number of men establishing the state through a social compact; and he was explicit about eliminating associations intermediate between the individual and the state, holding that "if . . . the general will is to be truly expressed, it is essential that there be no subsidiary groups within the State. . . . " Each citizen was to "voice his own opinion and nothing but his own opinion."[5] Rights, then, according to traditional theory, are to exist at two levels, the level of the individual and the level of the state, but none are to go to groups intermediate between the two.

Other liberal writers have built the tradition up and carried it along. John Stuart Mill is among them, favoring democracy and concerned about the conditions prerequisite to it. Among the prerequisite conditions, he thought, is the absence of cleavages that the presence of differing nationalisms would imply.

Free institutions are next to impossible in a country made up of different nationalities. Among people without fellow-feeling, especially if they read and speak different languages, the united public opinion, necessary to the working of representative government, cannot exist. . . . [I]t is in general a necessary condition of free institutions that the boundaries of governments should coincide in the main with those of nationalities.[6]

Ernest Barker took a similar line. He was so eager to have homogeneity that he engaged in wishful thinking. "[M]ost States," he said, "are what we call 'national states.'" The assertion was surely untrue when he made it (his book was published in 1951), and it is egregiously untrue today. It is even questionable whether the United Kingdom is a national state. Speaking of the United Kingdom, however, Barker equated it with England. He spoke of the "general structure of English life," and said that "we start from the primary fact of the existence of a national society."[7]

The reason why the nation is generally the basis of a State is simple. There must be a general social cohesion which serves as it were, as a matrix, before the seal of legal association can be effectively imposed on a population. If the seal of the State is stamped on a population which is not held together in the matrix of a common tradition and sentiment, there is likely to be a cracking and splitting, as there was in Austria-Hungary.[8]

Barker acknowledged that "the modern State is not always a unitary national society. It may contain national minorities. . . ."[9] But rather than adjusting his theory to this fact, he treated it as an "addition," tacked on and left as an anomaly.

John Rawls fits into the tradition, seeing society as composed of individuals entitled to justice. He imagines individuals not in a state of nature but in an "original position," where they work out the principles of justice. Rawls shows concern for social classes (that is, for "the least advantaged"), but he does not raise the question whether ethnic communities or national minorities should be considered as entities with claims to justice. The individuals in the original position speak only for a narrowly restricted set of persons—for themselves, their immediate families, and their nearest descendants—and not for any group identified by race, language, religion, or culture. Rawls does not even mention the fact that people speak different languages, and he is much more concerned about differences in talent and industry than in differences of race or religion. The justice for which he is concerned is justice for individuals in a substantially homogeneous society.[10]

In a book entitled *Democratic Political Theory*, published in 1979, Roland Pennock carries the tradition on. He devotes a chapter to "individualism and collectivism," and he makes a few brief references to groups and communities; but his collectivism is essentially the collectivism of the state or of "society." To him "a collectivist is primarily concerned about the whole and he may believe that groups within the state . . . threaten the unity of the whole."[11] He treats the possible presence of "a large intransigent minority" not as a circumstance raising questions about the rights of intermediate groups but as a circumstance that might make democracy unworkable.[12] Similarly, he recognizes the possibility of "communalism," but he treats it as "a formidable barrier to social mobilization, to nation-building, and to democracy."[13] His "case for equality"[14] is a case for equality among individuals. He speaks of the representation not only of individuals and of the nation, but also of interests; but the interests that he thinks of (for example, the interest of the individual in education) are not those of any intermediate group.[15] He does speak of proportional representation as a possible method of providing for the representation of "religious or ethnic minorities,"[16] but this is inadequate as a treatment of the problem of intermediate groups. The book has little to offer a country whose population is seriously divided by race, language, religion, indigeneity, or, more broadly, by culture. It thus carries on the weakness that liberal-democratic theory has traditionally shown.

As indicated above in the comments on the choice that Hobbes and Locke made, and as this whole book attests, nothing is necessary or foreordained about any of these positions. It is highly improbable that a state of nature ever existed like the one that Hobbes and Locke imagined. In a state of nature individuals could not have been self-sufficient any more than they can be in other circumstances. Far from being free to make or not to make a contract, individuals would from birth have automatically been members of some kind of group; otherwise, they would not have survived. And the odds are that the group would have been larger than what we think of today as a nuclear family. If a contract was ever deliberately made, it would probably have been among groups rather than among individuals; and the groups might well have differed as to race, language, or religion, or more broadly as to culture. On these kinds of assumptions, those making the contract would not have been speaking only for themselves and their immediate relatives. They would have been concerned with the community on which so much depended and with interrelationships among individuals, communities, and states. Consent would have come not so much from individuals as from collectivities, and obligations would have been undertaken by them. And it is plausible to assume that their contract would have reflected an awareness of heterogeneity rather than an assumption of homogeneity. We should resist the tendency to think of the Mayflower Compact as a model and project it back into an imaginary state of nature.

The case against an overweening emphasis on individual rights does not rest entirely on rejecting the arbitrary assumptions on which liberal theory depends. It also rests on a contemplation of factual circumstances and associated values. The factual circumstance is that humankind does not divide simply into sovereign states. Once so divided, it goes on dividing into various sorts of groups: into nations or peoples, into national minorities, and into ethnic communities. The number of states with cultural cleavages is far higher than this book itself suggests, for it simply gives illustrations and does not claim to present an exhaustive survey. Counting 132 states as of 1972, Walker Connor finds that only 12 (9.1 percent) can be described as "essentially homogeneous from an ethnic viewpoint."

An additional 25 states (18.9 per cent of the sample) contain an ethnic group accounting for more than 90 per cent of the state's total population, and in still another 25 states the largest element accounts for between 75 and 89 per cent of the population. But in 31 states (23.6 per cent of the total), the largest ethnic element represents only 50 to 74 per cent of the population, and in 39 cases (29.5 per cent of all states) the largest group fails to account for even half of the state's population. Moreover, this portrait of ethnic diversity becomes more vivid when the number of distinct ethnic groups within states is considered. In some instances the number of groups within a state runs into the hundreds, and in 53 states (40.2 per cent of the total), the population is divided into more than *five* significant groups.[17]

Neither the sovereign state nor the groups within it are eternal, of course. Both come and go. Nevertheless, many of them are enduring, lasting far longer than individual persons. Further, although both the sovereign state and groups within it are sometimes malign, they are also sometimes beneficent, contributing more to human well-being than individual persons are likely to do. That they go unrecognized and unsung, if not condemned, is incredible. In fact, as the evidence of this book attests, in a number of countries different kinds of groups are recognized and given status and rights—groups identified by language, by religion, by indigeneity, and by race. This is not done covertly, of course, but as a rule it is not done on the basis of avowed principle either; rather, more often than not, it occurs on a pragmatic ad hoc basis, agreed to as a means of solving a specific problem. It occurs not simply without benefit of a supporting theory but in seeming violation of liberal theory, and may well attract condemnations or excuses. Moreover, the lack of supporting theory makes for difficulties in interpreting the requirement that human rights be promoted without discrimination, and measures are condemned that ought to be lauded as giving appropriate recognition to group rights.

THEORIES CONCERNING GROUP RIGHTS

I have spoken so far only of political theories that focus on the individual, or on the individual and the state, but now wish briefly to note theories that include group rights or interests and in some cases focus on them.

In recent years the term *consociationalism* has come to be associated with a concern for groups. The term traces back at least to Althusius, who wrote that "politics is the art of associating (*consociandi*)" and that the subject matter is therefore association (*consociatio*).[18] Althusius went along with the idea of the social contract, but in his eyes the contracting parties were not individual men, as Hobbes and Locke assumed, but communities: "cities, provinces, and regions agreeing among themselves" and establishing an essentially federal arrangement.[19] In the writing of Althusius, I see little other than this basic idea that is potentially helpful in connection with contemporary needs. He assumed that the communities making the contract were territorially delimited, whereas today it is necessary to think of the possibility that individuals might belong to this or that community depending not on their place of residence but on their ethnic affiliation. And Althusius proposed a central government that would deal only with units of government at the next lower level in the hierarchy, whereas experience has now made it clear that a more flexible arrangement is both possible and desirable.

Interestingly enough, an American writer, John C. Calhoun, deserves a mention. He did not speak in terms of either individualism or the social contract. To him, the basic units in politics are not individuals but interests, and he argued that to give a controlling voice to "numerical majorities" of individuals was to invite social conflict: ganging up to gain a "numerical majority," individuals would then aggrandize and enrich some interests at the expense of others. What Calhoun wanted was a system operating on the basis of "concurrent majorities." That is, he proposed that the consent of each interest should be necessary "either to put or to keep the government in action," each interest deciding "separately through its own majority or in some other way" whether to give its consent or to veto.[20] The effect, he argued, would be "to unite and harmonize conflicting interests—to strengthen attachments to the whole community."[21] He did not attempt to list the interests that should be recognized, nor did he say whether a person might share in more than one interest.

Writers espousing nationalism are necessarily concerned with the nation, but this usually means a concern only for the dominant group in a given country. Ideally the nationalist wants the state to consist of one homogeneous nation. Thoughts along these lines led John Stuart Mill to make the statement quoted above, that "it is a necessary condition of free institutions that the boundaries of governments should coincide in the main with those of nationalities." And when the population of a state is not homogeneous, the more chauvinist members of the dominant nationality are likely to espouse oppressive policies toward minorities. Lord Acton in Britain is among those who have challenged these tendencies while seeking to preserve nationalism in a milder form. In his view:

The greatest adversary of the rights of nationality is the modern theory of nationality. By making the State and the nation commensurate with each other in theory, it reduces practically to a subject condition all other nationalities that may be within the boundary. It cannot admit them to an equality with the ruling nation which constitutes the State, because the State would then cease to be national.... [22]

Acton favored multinational states. He thought that "the coexistence of several nations under the same State is a test, as well as the best security of its freedom. . . . [A] State which is incompetent to satisfy different races [ethnic communities?] condemns itself; a State which labors to neutralize, to absorb, or to expel them, destroys its own vitality."[23] He favored federal arrangements in the state, permitting "self-government in the whole and in all the parts."[24]

Like Hobbes, Otto Gierke advanced a form of the contract theory, but he differed from Hobbes in that he refused to limit the individuals involved to one contract. He held that if they could create a "sovereign Commonwealth" by contract, they could also create "Fellowships and local communities" in the same way. The fellowships and local communities would be group-persons with "their own inherent rights, which were not abolished by the fact of inclusion in a higher sovereign group."[25]

Gierke influenced the English pluralists, John N. Figgis being prominent among them. Figgis spoke of the "natural associative instincts of mankind,"[26] and he believed that group-persons or corporate personalities develop naturally and inevitably, existing in their own right and not at the pleasure of the sovereign.[27] He observed that society is a collection of individuals, but held that to stop with that observation is "woefully to misconceive the actual facts of social life. . . . " "What we actually see in the world is not on the one hand the state, and on the other a mass of unrelated individuals; but a vast complex of gathered unions . . . ," a *communitas communitatum*.[28] Figgis wanted especially the recognition of the church as a group with natural authority over its members, limited by the sovereign yet not dependent on the sovereign for its status and rights. "Instead of an iron uniformity, we need more and more a reasonable distinction of groups, all of which should be honorable. . . . The real question of freedom in our day is the freedom of the smaller unions to live within the whole."[29]

A few more theorists might be named, but even an exhaustive list would not be long, and none of those on the list belong in what is ordinarily thought of as the mainstream of Western political theory. As Kenneth D. McRae says, "Western political thought in general has shown little understanding or respect for the cultural diversity of mankind and has made scant allowance for it as a possible concern of government."[30]

The situation has changed in recent decades with the appearance of various works dealing explicitly with the problems of divided or plural societies. Consociationalism is the focal term, and it is associated mainly with Arend Lijphart. As noted in the preceding chapter, he defines consociational democracy in terms of four characteristics:

The first and most important [characteristic] is government by a grand coalition of the political leaders of all significant segments of the plural society. . . . The other three basic [characteristics] are (1) the mutual veto or "concurrent majority" rule, which serves as an additional protection of vital minority interests, (2) proportionality as the principal standard of political representation, civil service appointments, and allocation of public funds, and (3) a high degree of autonomy for each segment to run its own internal affairs.[31]

As Lijphart points out, and as the earlier chapters of this book show, all of these characteristics are found in practice in one or more political systems, and in appropriate circumstances all of them are surely desirable as possible options. Yet they are out of keeping with the spirit if not with the explicit requirements of traditional competitive individualistic liberalism. They reflect a recognition of the rights and interests of communities as such—communities that might well be identified by race, language, or religion. To have a cabinet that is a grand coalition, members would have to be selected not simply on the basis of their individual qualities and their party membership but also on the basis of their communal affiliation. The very idea of a mutual veto recognizes the community as such, and so does the proportionality principle. And segmental autonomy (under which each segment might, for example, operate its own schools and have its own separate churches) obviously calls for differentiation among persons depending on the segment to which they belong.

An interrelationship is patent between these theories acknowledging group rights and the definition of discrimination one finds acceptable. Consociationalism, for example, would be ruled out by the definition of discrimination submitted in the case against South Africa referred to above. Those who would like some form of consociationalism to be among the possible options must perforce accept some kinds of differentiation among individuals, even if it is based on race, language, or religion. And the standards for judging when differentiation is discriminatory need to be adjusted accordingly.

WHY GIVE STATUS AND RIGHTS TO COMMUNITIES?

All of the preceding chapters cite circumstances in which communities have legal status and rights, and all of them offer reasons for thinking that the legal situation is or is not morally justified. Here the object is to offer a coherent summary.

We can imagine differing circumstances. At the one extreme we can imagine a homogeneous society—literally "one nation, indivisible." At the other extreme, we can imagine a plural society, consisting of two or more ethnic or national communities that differ sharply from each other, that are historic enemies, and that seem destined to remain sharply different and hostile for the indefinite future. And we can imagine all sorts of gradations in between.

Given a homogeneous society, the idea of communal rights is simply irrelevant. People may be divided territorially for a variety of reasons, as the United States is divided into states; but homogeneity offers no reason to abandon individualism and the territorial principle in favor of communalism and the principle of personality.

In contrast, if we imagine a plural society with deep and enduring ethnic or national divisions, the idea of communal rights is highly relevant. It is relevant on the assumption that the goal is the equal enjoyment of human rights, and on the additional assumption that equal enjoyment is difficult to achieve in such a society. One of the implications of deep divisions is that politics tends to be a struggle between the different communities, and the question who controls government takes on fateful significance, for government is potentially a powerful instrument in communal struggles. If democratic processes are attempted, the record shows that political parties tend to organize along communal lines, and that victory at the polls is therefore a communal victory. Or, if it is a question of seizing power militarily, as it usually is in much of the third world, the odds are that the group seizing power will come largely or entirely from one of the communities.

Once a community achieves domination in government, the incentive to maintain that domination at any cost is powerful, if only in self-defense. Those dominant in government have a considerable range of choice open to them. They may be benign in their policies, but even benignity may take on a character offensive to other communities, for it is likely to be associated with paternalism and therefore with humiliation. Moreover, even those who intend to be benign may be especially sensitive to and considerate of the needs and interests of their own kind, and thus biased in their policies. Beyond that, it is easy for the dominant to be neglectful of the needs and interests of other communities, and beyond neglect are numerous possibilities going in the direction of scorn, contempt, oppression, exploitation, and even extermination.

Given this perspective, a community that becomes dominant has reason to maintain its dominance. Whatever its own intentions, it has reason to fear what might follow if a reversal of the situation gave dominance to the historic enemy. The situation, then, is not one that is likely to make for the equal enjoyment of human rights; and the usual liberal-democratic political prescription is unsuitable. As the quip goes, that prescription leads to "one man one vote—once."

The problem as just described is the one on which W. Arthur Lewis dwells in *Politics in West Africa*, cited in the first chapter, and the solution must surely be sought more or less along the lines that he proposes: an effort to secure the participation of all the communities in all decision-making bodies, and a change in political rhetoric and the associated thought. The political rhetoric that is objectionable speaks of winning and losing, and of the ins and the outs. Lewis would see to it that leaders of all communities are invited to participate not only in legislative activities but also in the executive and judicial branches of government, the effort being to give every group visible evidence of fair consideration of its interests and desires and thus to give every group reason to be loyal to the system and supportive of it. No sizeable community should have reason to regard government as the instrument of an enemy. To be sure, issues come up in politics that have to be resolved, and the decisions made are bound to be more favorable to some than to others. And experience in Cyprus and Lebanon demonstrates that even when governmental offices are shared out among communal leaders, paralysis and breakdown may occur. Further, some distinct ethnic communities are so small that proportional representation—even if it extends into the executive—will still leave them weak. These considerations are reminders of the extreme difficulties that deeply divided societies face, suggesting that in some circumstances the effective choice is between breakdown and domination by one group over the others. But those concerned about the equal enjoyment of human rights will want to look for alternatives.

Plural societies within the state are comparable to the world society, and reasoning by analogy may be instructive. Few if any want to throw humankind into one common society in which the majority rules or in which some kind of authoritarian regime exercises power. When people think of all humanity, they want to acknowledge the many differences and to arrange political life accordingly. They want to acknowledge differences of race, of language, of religion, of values, of tradition, of social customs and mores—differences in ways of life, differences of national sentiment. They think it good that people should govern themselves or at least be governed by others of their own kind. They think that alien rule is bad. But when the boundaries of sovereign states are drawn the tendency (especially the tendency of those who are dominant within the state) is to shift to a different stance. Instead of recognizing differences, they want to deny them or at least to give them no political significance. Knowing that individualism and majority rule would be disastrous to most if applied on a world scale, they nevertheless want to apply it at the domestic level regardless of racial and ethnic divisions. The attitudes are not consistent.

This is not to say that every group that wants recognition as a right-and-duty-bearing unit should get it, or that those recognized should get all the rights they might want. These matters remain to be examined.

GROUP RIGHTS AND INDIVIDUAL RIGHTS

In this book I sometimes speak of the moral rights of groups or communities as a shorthand way of speaking of the rights of the several individuals composing the group or community. In such instances no significant issue of political theory is raised. But more often I speak of a group or community as a collective entity, meaning that it comprises one unit, one whole, with a collective right of its own—a right that cannot be reduced to the rights of individuals; and here a question is legitimate. Can a group or community have moral rights as a collective entity?

My answer is obviously in the affirmative. I assume that

groups and communities can exist in the same sense that corporations exist, it being understood that a corporation is an entity that has rights and obligations distinct from those of individual stockholders. The rights of the corporation are of course created by human decision, but they do not derive from the rights of individuals and cannot be reduced to the rights of individuals. They are original to the corporation, and disappear when the corporation disappears.

I might speak of group-persons, like one of the authors cited above, or of moral persons, but refrain in order to avoid any suggestion that the groups or communities should be regarded as organic, as possessing a mind or will of their own. This is the feature of the thought of Gierke and the English pluralists that Barker criticizes. He says that if the state is regarded "as a *personne morale* with a *volonté générale* transcending and reconciling individual wills, [this] fosters *étatisme.* . . . "[32] The idea of group rights, however, does not necessarily have anything to do with the idea of a group mind or a general will. It simply assumes that a group or community may have interests, and that some of the interests are compelling enough that they ought to be (and are) classified as rights. The existence of the interest and the right does not depend on awareness of it in a group mind, or on the existence of a group mind. The right can be claimed on behalf of the group by anyone who wants to do it, and others may or may not concede the claim. It can be attributed to the group by anyone who wants to make the attribution, and again others may or may not concur. Judgment and choice are involved, of course, but they rest on common sense and not on mysticism.

Thought about the problem may be advanced by considering statements made in connection with the American and French revolutions. In the same Declaration in which Jefferson and his associates proclaimed the inalienable rights of all men, they also proclaimed the right of "one People to dissolve the Political Bands which have connected them with another, and to assume . . . the separate and equal station to which the Laws of Nature and of Nature's God entitle them. . . ." The wording is not entirely clearcut on the issue at hand. Jefferson spoke of "one People" and of "them." Those impressed by the reference to "one People" can say that Jefferson had a collective entity in mind; and regardless of Jefferson's wording, they can point out that the "one People" acted and were accepted as a corporate entity. On the contrary, those impressed by Jefferson's reference to "them" can say that the Laws of Nature and Nature's God conferred the right on individuals severally, who then agreed to act through representatives in exercising it and to accept a majority decision of the representatives.

The difficulty with the second position is that it involves an obvious fiction. Although some persons no doubt did agree to act through representatives and to accept majority decision, not all did, leaving the question unanswered how the majority got the right to impose its will on the rest, forcing some kind of change on them. The most likely alternative, which I accept, is to assume that the "one People" to whom Jefferson referred had an aboriginal collective right to do what it did and that, except for those who voted for the Declaration, individual members had little choice. On the personal level, they could of course approve or condemn, and they could decide whether to remain in the country or to flee. As members of the group, however, their rights (if they had any) did not extend beyond some kind of participation in the decision-making process, the decision itself being made by the Continental Congress as a body, on behalf of the collectivity.

The French revolutionaries were clearer. They proclaimed the rights of man, but they also proclaimed that "all sovereignty resides essentially in the nation." The statement presumably means that the nation has a collective right to act as a unit, and the word "essentially" suggests that the right is aboriginal, reflecting the interests of individuals, no doubt, but not delegated by individuals or reducible to the rights of individuals.

It may also be helpful to consider the question whether the holder of the right of self-determination is a collectivity or a set of separate persons, and for this purpose we should note a contrast in the Covenant on Civil and Political Rights. The Covenant includes an article on minorities, the statement being that "persons belonging to . . . minorities" shall not be denied certain rights. The clear intent is to avoid giving minorities any basis for a claim of a collective right. But no such intent appears in connection with the assertion of the right of self-determination. This right is attributed to "all peoples" as such, not to persons belonging to peoples. Further, the General Assembly describes the possible outcomes of self-determination as "the establishment of a sovereign and independent state, the free association or integration with an independent state, or the emergence into any other political status freely determined by a people"—language that does not suggest a reference to the rights of individual persons.[33]

Practices associated with self-determination likewise suggest a group right and not an individual right. Self-determination sometimes takes place simply on the basis of agreements among political leaders, private persons playing no role. If private persons play a role, it is to participate in the decision of the group, and those who oppose the decision have no basis for claiming that action going against their will violates their personal rights. It may be possible as a matter of humane policy to shift a boundary this way or that to accommodate the preferences of individuals living along the border, and individuals who oppose the outcome of self-determination may be permitted to leave the territory involved and take up residence elsewhere, but these are supplementary and peripheral matters, not necessary features of self-determination. External self-determination has to do with the political status of a people as a collectivity and with jurisdiction over the associated territory, so the right has to be a collective one.[34]

I am aware of assertions to the contrary, but such assertions have no reasonable basis that I can see. For example, a note in the *Yale Law Journal* says that "in its broad meaning self-determination must be viewed as the basic right of an individual to form his own associations in order to maximize his preferred interests."[35] But can any set of persons decide to associate together so as to form a people entitled to self-determination? So far as I am aware, no champion of the idea of self-determination has ever made such a claim, and it seems highly unlikely that any state or any international organization would concede it. I see no way of formulating a persuasive argument in support of such a claim. A people is historically constituted, and does not come into existence on the basis of ad hoc decisions of many persons to associate together. It is enough of a threat to the integrity of existing states that historically constituted peoples should have a right of self-determination, and it would be intolerable if any set of persons were entitled to claim the right at will. Moreover, freedom of association can scarcely imply for every person the right to choose the sovereignty under which to live, for that would imply a right to immigrate into the country of one's choice. To repeat the statement made above: if individuals have any right in connection with self-determination, it is to participate in the decision of the group. The right belongs to the group, and it is the fate of the group and its territory that is determined.

Dov Ronen reflects a view similar to that of the *Yale Law Journal* when he says that "the 'self' in self-determination is the singular, individual being and not any aggregation of human beings."[36] Now I grant that individuals have interests that are served by the right. The individual has an interest in being grouped with his own kind for purposes of government—an interest in being governed by those who share his values, who accord him respect, and who fully accept him as an equal human being. But the fact that interests of individuals are served does not necessarily mean that any related right should go to individuals. Sometimes a person's interests can be best served, or only served, by allocating the related right to a group, and this is the case with self-determination. Those concerned with the well-being of individuals sometimes need to abandon individualism and emphasize the group, endowing it with status and rights. One of the reasons why some governments objected to the inclusion of the article on self-determination in the Covenants was that in their view the Covenants should be limited to spelling out the rights of individuals. They correctly held that the right of peoples to self-determination is a group right.

A different perspective on the same point is obtained by contemplating the people of a political dependency that has just become sovereign and thus has become a collective juridical personality. Those who approve the development are in an odd position if they say that up to the moment of independence no collective entity existed that had a moral claim.

Reasoning on the question whether group rights are reducible to individual rights can helpfully be addressed also to numerous legal arrangements described in earlier chapters. We noted that the Belgian constitution, after saying that the country consists of three cultural communities, goes on to say that "each community enjoys powers invested in it," and powers are in fact invested. Further, the Belgian cabinet must be made up of an equal number of French-speaking and Dutch-speaking ministers, and the law requires that a just equilibrium (interpreted as parity) be maintained between the two principal communities in the civil service. We noted that in the province of Alberta, Canada, schools are organized on a religious basis, with the minority religious community entitled to establish its own schools and impose a school tax on its members. We noted that in West Germany religious communities are formally accepted as corporate bodies with the power to tax, and that in the United States the courts accept Indian tribes as semi-independent corporate bodies. We noted instances of communalism for purposes of political representation—the Fijian and the Indian communities of Fiji, for example, each being assigned a quota of seats in parliament. In none of these cases (and others like them could be recalled) does it seem sensible to say that what is plainly a group right is reducible to rights at the level of the individual. In all of these cases (and in others) the concern is with a collective entity, a community that is treated literally and figuratively as a corporate body. To seek to reduce the rights to the individual level is to seek to maintain a paradigm that does not fit.

Finally, I might refer to what I take to be the obvious fact that it is common to hold the whole people collectively accountable in a moral and legal sense for the behavior of their government. To be sure, those in public office do the acting and may deserve credit for what they do or be personally culpable, but their powers and duties go with the office that they hold. They are agents of a principal, and it is the principal that is accountable.

For some purposes it may not matter whether group rights are reducible to individual rights. But sound and correct conceptions are to be preferred to those that are unsound and incorrect. More to the point is the probability, which the record establishes, that those who unthinkingly assume that all rights are ultimately the rights of individuals will fail to see and to pursue questions about the implications of group rights for individual rights. The implication on which I am dwelling, obviously, is the proposition that the rights of individuals to equal and nondiscriminatory treatment must be interpreted in the light of the impinging rights of groups.

WHY SOME GROUPS AND NOT OTHERS?
THE RELEVANT CRITERIA

The idea that "groups" or "communities" have rights is troublesome in that these crucial terms are so vague. I have been referring to a selected list of groups: the population of sovereign states; nations and peoples; racial and ethnic communities; national minorities; indigenous populations; and those disadvantaged by prior discrimination. But many other kinds of groups also exist, raising an obvious question about the criteria of selection. On what basis do we decide which groups should be recognized as collective entities?

The following criteria are implicit in current practices; that is, they are derived by analyzing circumstances surrounding the groups that are in fact treated as collective entities in one or more countries and that thus have special status and rights. The criteria do not point unerringly to the judgment to be made in every instance, but they identify the considerations to be taken into account.

1. A group has a stronger claim the more it is a self-conscious entity with a desire to preserve itself. Its members should have a sense of belonging together, a we/they sense, a sense of solidarity vis-à-vis outsiders, a sense of sharing a common heritage and a common destiny, distinct from the heritage and destiny of others.

2. A group has a stronger claim the deeper are the cleavages between it and other groups. The question is how enduring the cleavages are. If reason exists to suppose that they will go away in time, or can be rendered insignificant by deliberate effort, a strong argument can be made to pursue public policies going

in this direction. Conversely, if the cleavages are so deep as to be permanent, thought and policy should be adjusted to this circumstance.

In connection with this point, it is interesting to note a shift in Nathan Glazer's position. Recall that he ended his book on *Affirmative Discrimination* with an assertion of the "simple and clear understanding, that rights attach to the individual, not the group, and that public policy must be exercised without distinction of race, color, or national origin."[37] Later Glazer took a different line:

I believe the key principle, that does in fact and should determine for a multi-ethnic state—including the United States—whether it elects the path of group rights or individual rights, is whether it sees the different groups as remaining permanent and distinct constituents of a federated society or whether it sees these groups as ideally integrating into, eventually assimilating into, a common society.[38]

3. A group has a stronger claim the more evident it is that it has a reasonable chance to preserve itself. It should be of sufficient size to make long-term survival possible.

4. A group has a stronger claim the more significant it is in the lives of its members and the more the members tend to "identify themselves—explain who they are—by reference to their membership."[39] Although a group may have great significance in the lives of its members if it is distinguished by only one characteristic, the chance of this is increased if it is distinguished by several—for example, not only by race but also by cultural characteristics such as language and religion.[40] The claim is especially strong if the group serves as a major socializing agency, shaping the personalities and values of the members, and when not only their identity but also their well-being and pride depend at least in part on their membership.

5. A group has a stronger claim the more important the rights that it seeks are to the interests of its members, and the less costly or burdensome the grant of the rights is to others.

6. A group has a stronger claim the clearer are the tests or criteria of membership, permitting all to know who are members and who are not. It may or may not be possible for a person

to transfer membership from one group to another. Where it is possible, the person attempting the transfer must meet whatever conditions the receiving group fixes. Among the tests or criteria are race, language, religion, citizenship, and, more generally, adherence to a given set of cultural norms and social mores.

7. A group has a stronger claim the more clearly and effectively it is organized to act and to assume responsibilities. Formal organization, however, should not be regarded as imperative. Many a group—many a people—has succeeded in establishing its claim through the more or less spontaneous and uncoordinated actions of individual members.

8. A group has a stronger claim the more firmly established is the tradition of treating it as a group. By definition, groups with legal status as corporate entities have established their legal claim, however good their moral claim may be. And groups that historically have been victims of discrimination have a prescriptive basis for any claim they choose to make for continued differential treatment designed to advance them toward the equal enjoyment of human rights.

9. A group has a stronger claim the more clearly the status and rights that it seeks can be granted compatibly with the equality principle. The central requirements of that principle are that those affected get equal consideration, that like cases be treated in like manner, that the purpose pursued in differentiating between groups be legitimate, and that differences in treatment be justified by relevant differences and be proportionate to them.

Although these criteria permit varying degrees of decisiveness in judging whether a group is entitled to status and rights, they do not suggest any great proliferation of the kinds of groups to be recognized. In truth, I do not see that any kinds qualify other than those I have been discussing. What are commonly described as interest groups are clearly excluded. The question whether social classes might qualify is troublesome, but I would argue that their claims—and particularly those that are likely to be associated with an upper or privileged class—are rendered doubtful by the first criterion and are ruled out by the second, fourth, fifth, sixth, and ninth.

THE EQUALITY PRINCIPLE

The ninth criterion—the equality principle, requiring that like cases be treated in like manner—calls for comment. First, I am assuming that "like cases" may include those of groups as well as those of individuals. Thus, if the grant of a certain status and a certain set of rights to one group means that like groups cannot have a like status and a like set of rights, then the requirement of the equality principle is not met. No group in a plural society, for example, could be conceded monopoly control over government, such as the whites have had in South Africa.

Second, given the need to consider whether like cases are treated in like manner, comparisons are necessary, and this requires a choice of the universe within which the comparisons should be made. When it is a question of a right under a constitution or law, the universe includes those in the relevant jurisdiction. Or, to put it more broadly, when it is a question of a right vis-à-vis an authoritative actor, the universe includes those to whom the authority extends. This principle is applicable even in connection with rights assured by treaty, such as those assured in the Covenant on Economic, Social, and Cultural Rights. In binding the parties to recognize the right of everyone to education, for example, and to guarantee that the right is exercised without discrimination, the Covenant is assuming comparisons within the national framework. If a person in Ecuador has educational opportunities inferior to those available to a person in England, no violation of the legal right to equal treatment occurs. Whether the same proposition holds with respect to moral rather than legal rights is a question. Moral rights are supposed to be general and universal, and in the long run the proposition that people in Ecuador should be treated equally with those in England is surely the ideal. Even now it makes a difference whether the inferior treatment of people in Ecuador results from deliberate choices of the government there or from the exigencies of relevant circumstances, such as the scarcity of necessary resources in Ecuador as compared to England. On the one hand, not even a moral right exists to what is impossible or impracticable. On the other hand, given the equality principle, the question is whether those receiving inferior treatment may not have a just claim to some kind of international action—for example, a transfer of resources—designed to advance them toward equality of treatment according to an international standard.

The third comment on the equality principle overlaps with the second. It is that different standards are employed around the world in interpreting the principle, and that caution is indicated in any attempt to say what it means. The situation is illustrated in the field of voting and political representation. I take for granted Article 25 of the Covenant on Civil and Political Rights, providing that every citizen shall have the right to equal suffrage in genuine, free elections. But the article does not say how voters are to be grouped for electoral purposes—whether territorially or communally; and, although every vote is no doubt to count as one in a numerical sense, the requirement of "equal" suffrage may or may not mean that the votes must have equal weight or value. If so, some violations of the requirement are obvious—as in electing United States senators from, for example, Nevada and California. Even the meaning of equal weight or value is uncertain. In the United States we compute the weight or value of votes in terms of the total population of electoral districts, but some other countries do it in terms of the number of eligible or actual voters. Further, granting that precise equality is unachievable, countries vary widely in the deviations that they permit, deviations of up to one-third being not at all uncommon.[41]

The problem of the relationship between the equality principle and rules relating to voting and representation is complicated still more if practices at the international level are considered. They are listed in the preceding chapter. Recall that in elections to the European parliament, for example, the vote of one person in Luxembourg counts for as much as the vote of twelve persons in the Federal Republic of Germany.

It is difficult enough to say precisely what the equality principle calls for when the reference is exclusively to individuals; and in the light of the practices at the international level it is even more difficult to say precisely what it means when the reference is to collective entities. What seems to happen is that in some instances other principles are taken into account too, and lead to practices that the equality principle alone does not suggest. For example, the principle is widely accepted that special concessions should be made to the weak, which may be the full explanation of the seeming "overrepresentation" of the weaker countries in the European parliament. Similarly, the principle is good that the voting power and influence of any unit should be more or less proportionate to its importance to the functioning of the system of which it is a part, or to its ability to defy or disrupt the system. Gross disparities between voting power and other kinds of power are dangerous to any system, for those with other kinds of power will be tempted to use it instead of relying on a voting system that only brings defeat.

In calling attention to problems with the equality principle, I do not mean to attack the principle. I leave it as the ninth criterion, as stated above. But neither the ninth nor any of the other criteria is stated in unconditional terms. The statement is that the claims of intermediate groups will be stronger the more fully they meet the criteria.

WHEN DOES DIFFERENTIATION AMOUNT TO DISCRIMINATION?

We now come back to the central question of the book: the meaning that it is sensible to give to the requirement of the Charter that members shall promote human rights without distinction as to race, language, or religion. The problem, noted many times, is that groups identified by these characteristics, or perhaps by indigineity, sometimes need and want special status and rights; and if they are conceded special status and rights, the implication is that differentiation must occur among persons depending on whether they are members. This raises the question whether or when the differentiation should count as discrimination.

As indicated in Chapter 1, the internationally agreed touchstone is the equal enjoyment of human rights. When the purpose or effect of the differentiation is to promote the equal enjoyment of human rights, it is justifiable and therefore nondiscriminatory. When the purpose or effect is to maintain or extend special privilege, the reverse holds true. These criteria should be construed to permit preferential treatment and perhaps other special measures during a transitional period, provided it is reasonable to suppose that they may contribute to the goal of equal enjoyment. Admittedly, the reference to the "purpose or effect" of differentiation is a potential source of trouble, for purpose and effect are not necessarily correlated; but they are both potentially significant to a judgment.

In speaking of the equal enjoyment of human rights, I mean to include the right of peoples to self-determination, recognizing that by virtue of that right peoples may "freely pursue their economic, social and cultural development." That is, peoples may seek to preserve their culture and shape its development. And it is to be expected that measures adopted for this purpose will raise questions about discrimination. In previous chapters I have given illustrations, and need not go over them again here. The crucial generalization is that, important as the right of self-determination is, it is not absolute and unconditional; actions taken on the basis of the right must reflect due concern for other rights and interests that may be affected. Admittedly again, the reference to "due concern" makes for uncertainty, but once more I see no acceptable way of getting away from the need for judgment in individual cases. I reject the thought that the rights and interests of the many should always prevail over the rights and interests of the one or the few. On the contrary, on the theory that weakness deserves special protection, I would be inclined to say that the presumption should be in favor of the rights of the individual, with the burden of the argument placed on those who believe that in specific cases the right of the individual should give way to the collective right of the group. At the same time, an emphasis on the rights of the individual should not be extreme. It is perhaps an odd way to put it, but those who believe in the dignity and the equal worth of individuals may in some circumstances need to endorse status and rights for groups, for the protection and advancement of the interests of the individual are sometimes possible only through the group of which the individual is a part. An insistence on individualism may well mean that the minority individual is done in.

Similarly, those who believe in the dignity and worth of the individual should look with skepticism on the assumption that in deeply divided societies their belief dictates "majority rule." People have a pronounced tendency to be especially sensitive to the needs and interests of their own kind, and to be scornful or at least neglectful of the needs and interests of lesser breeds; and majorities have a number of ways of favoring their own kind without violating the requirement of the equal protection of the laws. Even if the members of the majority are committed to upholding the dignity and equality of all and justice for all, somehow it usually works out that what dignity and equality and justice require is also compatible with their own interests. They can champion democracy, knowing that democracy assures and sanctions their dominance. They can deplore appeals to ethnic or racial consciousness on the part of others, without acknowledging that they serve their own ethnic or racial purposes naturally and quietly in the day to day decisions that they make. They can champion nationalism and patriotism, for by this means they can call for loyalty to the system that is good for them and undermine competing provincial or segmental loyalties that are good for others. They are likely to be more educated and skilled than others, and so can be confident of winning out wherever competitive individualism is maintained. They can be proud, and can enjoy the satisfaction of treating others with paternalism, condescension, scorn, disdain, or contempt.

The other side of the coin is fairly obvious. In most societies the nondominant, the minorities, have not done well. In the United States we get an illustration of the fact by looking at the fate of the blacks through the period of Jim Crow. The record is clear in indicating that white men, mainly Anglo-Saxon and mainly Protestant, were individualistic only in a limited way. They could stand individualistic competition among each other, and they thought it good to concede civil rights and liberties to each other, but when it came to the blacks they closed the ranks on a communal basis and used government to keep the blacks down. And they did something comparable with the Indians, the Orientals, and women. The rule that persons are to be treated on the basis of their individual merit went by the board. Similarly, as previous chapters indicate, the history of a number of other countries provides illustrations of the oppression of minorities.

What I am saying is that a perversion of individualism is common—that those who favor individualism tend to favor it only among their own kind; they confine treatment according to merit mainly to people who count. And when it comes to relationships with people from other ethnic or racial communities, their own ethnic or racial consciousness wells up and becomes controlling. Ostensible individualism thus becomes an enemy of the individual—or at least the enemy of the individual who is regarded as different and alien. And measures of a communal sort may then be justifiable in order to safeguard individual rights and in order to give greater assurance that the interests of the minority are taken into account as well as the interests of the majority.[42]

PROBLEMS AND BENEFITS

The course of action under scrutiny involves problems and offers benefits. The right of self-determination is potentially explosive, going counter to the right of states to preserve their integrity. How the conflict between these principles is worked out is necessarily a matter of political struggle, with its possibilities for disaster as well as for liberation. Even in an ideal world, no fixed order of priority for the two principles would always hold. More specifically, it should not be assumed that humankind ought to be divided into precisely the sovereign states that now exist, and that all existing states must therefore be preserved with their boundaries intact. Neither should it be assumed that every ethnic community that wants sovereign independence should be granted it regardless of the costs and burdens that this would entail for others. Of course, an exercise of self-determination does not necessarily mean that the choice will be for independence. One of the potential choices is for autonomy within the framework of the state, and given reasonableness on both sides this is the choice, or the compromise, that in many instances will be made. Vital to this is a willingness on the part of existing states to accept some degree of decentralization so as to make autonomy possible.

The idea of putting communalism on the list of possible options is likewise open to question. The adoption of communalist measures marks the absence of significant hope of assimilation or fusion and implicitly emphasizes social cleavages, perhaps even encouraging the emergence of new collectivities that demand status and rights. It is scarcely compatible with the idea of one nation, indivisible—or at least it calls for a reinterpretation of that idea. The record of communalism in Ceylon and India under the British is generally deplored, and communalism obviously has failed to solve the problems of Cyprus and Lebanon. In South Africa its distinctive application is morally indefensible. In other countries where some form of communalism is practiced—in Belgium, Canada, the Federal Republic of Germany, Fiji, Finland, Malaysia, New Zealand, Switzerland, and Zimbabwe, for example—the record is mixed. Obviously, communalism is not a panacea. But a solution that is not one hundred percent successful should not be blamed for the problem. After all, Northern Ireland has not achieved peace by insisting on individualism and by pretending that the population is homogeneous; and if the kind of communalism tried in Cyprus and Lebanon has not worked, this does not prove that individualism and majority rule would have worked better.

Acceptance of affirmative action also has problems, with which American readers are likely to be familiar—epitomized by the idea that the undeserving may be favored at the expense of the innocent. At the same time, problems also arise (if only moral problems) from a failure to make any attempt to undo a wrong or to promote for disadvantaged minorities the equal enjoyment of human rights.

The problems sketched in the above paragraphs are real and are not to be dismissed. Nevertheless, considerations going in the opposite direction need to be taken into account too. After all, problems also arise from a refusal to acknowledge that certain kinds of groups are right-and-duty-bearing units. The idea that every state should be a nation-state is clearly preposterous, given the multitude of nations and peoples and racial and ethnic groups into which humankind divides. It is also preposterous to think that the dignity and worth of individuals can be respected while the group and culture in which they take pride are obliterated.

Denial of justice is the danger that a recognition of group rights seeks to counter. A system of competitive individualism based ostensibly on merit is a system that favors those who are already more advanced and more powerful, for they can serve their interests more effectively than, and perhaps at the expense of, the less advanced and the weaker. Equality of opportunity is, as someone has said, equal opportunity to leave others behind, and perhaps to do them in. If the more advanced and powerful group is also the group with the most votes, then the principle of one person one vote and "majority rule" becomes a means of promoting the advantage of that group and maintaining or accentuating the disadvantage of others. Members of the dominant race can oppose racism, knowing that their own race will prevail in an ostensibly non-racial system, and members of dominant national or ethnic groups can do the same. The perspective of John C. Calhoun is sometimes proved to be well-founded.

The inherent flaw of an individualistic system based on non-discrimination is especially obvious in democratic political systems: there is no way to prevent discrimination on the part of voters. Elections that are free and open are elections in which voters are free to discriminate, free to vote for their own kind. Voters do not always do this. Sometimes they support members of an ethnic community other than their own. But bloc voting along racial, linguistic, religious, or national lines also occurs, condemning some groups to the status of permanent minorities without significant political influence. To questions thus raised about justice are added questions about order and stability in the system, for permanent minorities may or may not go on accepting arrangements that deny them consideration and respect.[43]

Those who believe that rights come from the Creator or are dictated by natural law or come from some other source beyond human control may or may not find it possible to accept the idea of group rights. My own assumption is that it is a matter of human decision what kinds of units are accepted as right-

and-duty-bearing units and what kinds of rights they shall have. General agreement exists that live persons are such units, and the Covenants on human rights register general agreement on the list of rights to which they are entitled. Debate is under way on the question of classifying the fetus, and on classifying animals, as such units and, if so, on the list of rights to concede to them. It comports with both past practice and common sense to hold that we are free to make comparable decisions with respect to groups.

Notes

1. EQUAL TREATMENT: THE INDIVIDUAL AND THE GROUP

1. Vernon Van Dyke, "Human Rights Without Discrimination," *American Political Science Review*, 67 (December 1973), 1267–1269.

2. The texts of the Covenants, and of most of the other treaties on human rights to be cited, are conveniently assembled in Ian Brownlie, ed., *Basic Documents on Human Rights* (2nd ed. New York: Oxford University Press, 1981).

3. W. Arthur Lewis, *Politics in West Africa* (New York: Oxford University Press, 1965), Chapter 3.

4. *Ibid.*, p. 66.

5. *Ibid.*

6. *Ibid.*, p. 71.

7. *Ibid.*, p. 67.

8. United Nations. Commission on Human Rights. Sub-Commission on Prevention of Discrimination and Protection of Minorities. *The Main Types and Causes of Discrimination* (1949.XIV.3), p. 2.

9. United Nations. *Study of Discrimination in the Matter of Political Rights*, by Hernán Santa Cruz (New York, 1962; 63.XIV.2), pp. 96-99.

10. Unesco. General Conference. 14C/Res. 8.1. 4 November 1966. See also 17C/Res. 4.111, Declaration of Guiding Principles on the Use of Satellite Broadcasting, 15 November 1972. Vernon Van Dyke, "The Cultural Rights of Peoples," *Universal Human Rights*, 2 (April-June 1980), 1-2.

2. DISTINCTION AS TO LANGUAGE

1. Cf. E. M. Vierdag, *The Concept of Discrimination in International Law* (The Hague: Nijhoff, 1973), p. 93.

2. United Nations document A/Res.181 (II). Future Government of Palestine. 29 November 1947.

3. Joseph Tussman and Jacobus tenBroek, "The Equal Protection of the Laws," *California Law Review*, 37 (September 1949), 344-364. "The Supreme Court, 1975 Term," *Harvard Law Review*, 90 (November 1976), 114-120. "Developments in the Law. Equal Protection," *Harvard Law Review*, 82 (March 1969), 1077-1132.

4. Great Britain. Parliamentary Papers. Palestine Royal Commission. *Report.* July, 1937. Cmd. 5479 (1937), p. 333.

5. League of Nations. *Protection of Linguistic, Racial and Religious Minorities by the League of Nations.* Geneva, 1927. I. B. Minorities 1927. I.B.2. P. 17. Cf., Jan-Magnus Jansson, "Language Legislation," in Jaakko Uotila, ed., *The Finnish Legal System* (Helsinki: The Union of Finnish Lawyers Publishing Co., 1966), p. 66.

6. Pierre Maroy, "L'évolution de la législation linguistique belge," *Revue du Droit Public et de la Science Politique en France et à l'Etranger*, 82 (May-June 1966), 453, 456-458; A. Lagasse, "Le droit de parler sa langue," *Journal des Tribunaux* [Belgium], 83 (November 30, 1968), 708; Val R. Lorwin, "Belgium: Religion, Class, and Language in National Politics," in Robert A. Dahl, ed., *Political Oppositions in Western Democracies* (New Haven: Yale University Press, 1966), pp. 159-161; Eur. Court H.R. Series B, "Linguistic" Case, I, 312, and II, 114-115, 122, 130-132; H. Vanderpoorten, "Le point de vue Flamand sur les relations culturelles et linguistiques," *Res Publica*, Vol. 5, No. 1 (1963), pp. 10-11, 14. Pierre L. van den Berghe, *The Ethnic Phenomenon* (New York: Elsevier, 1981), p. 203.

7. R. E. M. Irving, *The Flemings and Walloons of Belgium* (London: Minority Rights Group, Report No. 46, 1980).

8. Robert Senelle, "The Revision of the Constitution, 1967-1971," *Memorandum from Belgium*, Nos. 144-145-146, January-February-March, 1972 (Ministry of Foreign Affairs, External Trade and Cooperation in Development), p. 12.

9. *Ibid.*, pp. 12-15.

10. Maroy, *loc. cit.*, p. 486.

11. André Molitor, "The Reform of the Belgian Constitution," in Arend Lijphart, ed., *Conflict and Coexistence in Belgium* (Berkeley: Institute of International Studies, The University of California, 1980), pp. 148-149. *Keesing's Contemporary Archives*, May 16, 1980, 30249A; August 22, 1980, 30423B; November 7, 1980, 30559B.

12. *Keesing's Contemporary Archives*, November 7, 1980, 30560A.

13. Guy Héraud, "Pour un droit linguistique comparé," *Revue Internationale de Droit Comparé*, 23rd Year, No. 2 (April-June, 1971), 324-325. Maroy, *loc. cit.*, pp. 469-470. Eur. Court H.R. Series B, "Linguistic" Case, I, 249, and II, 182.

14. Franz Coppieters, *The Community Problem in Belgium* (Brussels: Belgian Information and Documentation Institute, n.d. [1971?]), pp. 26, 29; André Philippart, "The University in Belgian Politics since the Contestation of 1968," *Government and Opposition*, 7 (Autumn 1972), 461-462.

15. *Keesing's Contemporary Archives*, December 24-31, 1973, p. 26260; Maroy, *loc. cit.*, pp. 489–490.

16. Eur. Court H.R. Series B, "Linguistic" Case, II, 127, 185. Eur. Court H.R., Case "relating to certain aspects of the laws on the use of languages in education in Belgium" (merits), Judgment of 23rd July 1968, pp. 25, 34.

17. Eur. Court H.R., Case "relating to certain aspects of the laws on the use of languages in education in Belgium" (merits), Judgment of 23rd July 1968, p. 44.

18. Eur. Court H.R. Series B, "Linguistic" Case, I, 325, 358, and II, 45, 47-48, 81-82, 97-98, 178.

19. India. Office of the Registrar General. Language Division. Census of India 1971. *Language Handbook on Mother Tongues in Census.* Census Centenary Monograph No. 10. See also Jyotirindra Das Gupta, *Language Conflict and National Development, Group Politics and National Language Policy in India* (Berkeley: University of California Press, 1970), pp. 34-35, 46. Julian Dakin, Brian Tiffen, and H. F. Widdowson, *Language in Education, The Problem in Commonwealth Africa and the Indo-Pakistan Sub-continent* (London: Oxford University Press, 1968), p. 13.

20. Baldev Rah Nayar, *National Communication and Language Policy in India* (New York: Praeger, 1969), p. 12.

21. *Ibid.*, p. 15.

22. Articles 29 and 30.

23. Nayar, *op. cit.*, p. 120.

24. Das Gupta, *op. cit.*, pp. 244-245.

25. Nayar, *op. cit.*, pp. 122-123.

26. Gopi Nath Srivastava, *The Language Controversy and the Minorities* (Delhi: Atma Ram, 1970), pp. 47-51.

27. Nayar, *op. cit.*, pp. 113-121, 136.

28. India. Constituent Assembly. *Report of the Linguistic Provinces Commission.* 1948 (New Delhi: Government of India Press, 1948), p. 29.

228   *Notes*

29. *Ibid.*, p. 28.

30. Ivo D. Duchacek, *Comparative Federalism: The Territorial Dimension of Politics* (New York: Holt, Rinehart & Winston, 1970), p. 296. Hugh Tinker, "Is There an Indian Nation?" in Philip Mason, ed., *India and Ceylon: Unity and Diversity* (New York: Oxford University Press, 1967), p. 290.

31. Dakin, Tiffen, and Widdowson, *op. cit.*, pp. 12, 34.

32. *Ibid.*, p. 33.

33. *Ibid.*, pp. 39-40. Mohammad Ghouse, "Safeguards of Linguistic Minorities," *Journal of Constitutional and Parliamentary Studies*, 7 (April-June 1973), 45-47.

34. U.S. Department of Commerce. Bureau of the Census. *Ancestry and Language in the United States: November 1979.* Current Population Reports. Special Studies. Series P-23, No. 116. Issued March 1982. P. 14. The 1980 census shows that 89 percent of those 18 and over speak only English at home, with 5 percent speaking Spanish and 6 percent speaking other languages. See U.S. Department of Commerce. Bureau of the Census. *1980 Census of Population and Housing.* Supplementary Report. Provisional Estimates of Social, Economic, and Housing Characteristics. Issued March 1982. P. 14, Table P-2.

35. U.S. Congress. Senate. Committee on the Judiciary. Subcommittee on Constitutional Rights. *Literacy Tests and Voter Requirements in Federal and State Elections. Hearings.* 1962. 87th Cong., 2d Sess. Pp. 315-325. U.S. Congress. House. Committee on the Judiciary. Subcommittee No. 5. *Voting Rights Act Extension. Hearings.* 1969. 91st Cong., 1st Sess. Pp. 90-91.

36. *Katzenbach v. Morgan*, 384 U.S. 641 (1966).

37. *Cardona v. Power*, 384 U.S. 672 (1966), at 676.

38. *Castro v. State*, 466 P.2d., 244 (1970).

39. PL 91-285 (June 22, 1970), 84 Stat. 315. PL 94-73 (August 6, 1975), 89 Stat. 400.

40. U.S. Congress. House. Committee on the Judiciary. Subcommittee on Civil Rights and Constitutional Rights. *Extension of the Voting Rights Act. Hearings.* 1975. 94th Cong., 1st Sess. Vol. I, pp. 9-10. (Hereafter cited as: *House Hearings, 1975, Voting.*)

41. Franco Garcia, Jr., "Language Barriers to Voting: Literacy Tests and the Bilingual Ballot," *Columbia Human Rights Law Review*, 6 (Spring 1974), 86-87. Arnold H. Leibowitz, "English Literacy: Legal Sanction for Discrimination," *Notre Dame Lawyer*, 45 (Fall 1969), 36-38.

42. *House Hearings, 1975, Voting.* I, 177. U.S. Commission on Civil Rights. *Mexican Americans and the Administration of Justice in the Southwest* (March 1970). P. 67.

43. *Puerto Rican Organization for Political Action v. Kusper*, 350 F. Supp. 606 (1972) and 490 F.2d 565 (1973). *Coalition for Education in District One v. Board of Elections of the City of New York*, 370 F. Supp. 42 (1974). *Arroyo v. Tucker*, 372 F. Supp. 764 (1974). *Torres v. Sachs*, 381 F. Supp. 309 (1974).

44. PL 94-73 (August 6, 1974), 89 Stat. 400.

45. *House Hearings*, 1975, *Voting*, I, 177.

46. U.S. Commission on Civil Rights. *Mexican Americans and the Administration of Justice in the Southwest* (March 1970). P. 96.

47. *Ibid.*, p. 67.

48. Heinz Kloss, *The National Minority Laws of the United States of America* (Honolulu: East-West Center, Institute of Advanced Projects, Translation Series No. 16, 1966), p. 62.

49. Arnold H. Leibowitz, "Educational Policy and Political Acceptance: The Imposition of English as the Language of Instruction in American Schools" (Washington, D.C.: Center for Applied Linguistics, ERIC Clearinghouse for Linguistics, March 1971), p. 4.

50. *Ibid.*, p. 67.

51. *Ibid.*, pp. 50-53.

52. *Ibid.*, pp. 84-104.

53. Leibowitz, "English Literacy: Legal Sanction for Discrimination," *loc. cit.*, pp. 17–19.

54. *Ibid.*, p. 42.

55. *Meyer v. Nebraska*, 262 U.S. 390 (1923). *Bartels v. Iowa*, 262 U.S. 409 (1923).

56. *Federal Register*, Vol. 35, No. 139 (July 18, 1979), pp. 11594-11595.

57. *United States v. State of Tex.*, 506 F. Supp. 405 (1981).

58. PL 93-380 (August 21, 1974), 88 Stat. 484, Title IX, Section 904.

59. *Lau v. Nichols*, 414 U.S. 563 (1974).

60. Cf. *Otero v. Mesa County Valley School District No. 51*, 308 F. Supp. 162 (1975), at pp. 169, 170.

61. U.S. Commission on Civil Rights, *A Better Chance to Learn: Bilingual Bicultural Education*. Clearinghouse Publication No. 51 (May 1975), p. 169.

62. *Ibid.*, pp. 213, 218, 226, 235. N.J. Stat. Ann. 585 (1974) 18A:35-18.

63. Erica Black Grubb, "Breaking the Language Barrier: The Right to Bilingual Education," *Harvard Civil Rights/Civil Liberties Law Review*, 9 (January 1974), 52-94; William E. Johnson, "The Constitutional Right of Bilingual Children to an Equal Educational

Opportunity," *Southern California Law Review*, 47 (May 1974), 943-997; Jorge C. Rangel and Carlos M. Alcalo, "De Jure Segregation of Chicanos in Texas Schools," *Harvard Civil Rights/Civil Liberties Law Review*, 7 (March 1972), 307-391; Gerald M. Birnberg, "Desegregation—Brown v. Board of Education Applies to Mexican-American Students and Any Other Readily Identifiable Ethnic-Minority Group or Class," *Texas Law Review*, 49 (January 1971), 337–346.

64. Kloss, *The National Minority Laws of the United States of America*, pp. 34, 36, 38-39.

65. Kenneth D. McRae, *Switzerland, Example of Cultural Coexistence* (Toronto: Canadian Institute of International Affairs, Contemporary Affairs No. 33, 1964). James A. Dunn, Jr., "Consociational Democracy and Language Conflict. A Comparison of the Belgian and Swiss Experiences," *Comparative Political Studies*, 5 (April 1972), 3-40. Kurt Mayer, "Cultural Pluralism and Linguistic Equilibrium in Switzerland," in Pierre van den Berghe, ed., *Intergroup Relations: Sociological Perspectives* (New York: Basic Books, 1972), pp. 71-81.

66. *Acts of New Brunswick 1981*. Third Session of the Forty-ninth Legislature. 30 Eliz II (1981). Chapter O-1.1 I wish to thank Kenneth D. McRae for calling this measure to my attention.

3. DISTINCTION AS TO RELIGION

1. ECOSOC, OR, 1981, Sup. No. 5. E/CN.4/1475. Cf. Roger S. Clark, "The United Nations and Religious Freedom," *New York University Journal of International Law and Politics*, 11 (Fall 1978), 197-225.

2. Great Britain. Parliamentary Papers. East India (Constitutional Reforms). *Report on Indian Constitutional Reforms*. Cd. 9109. 1918. P. 189. Martin Wight, *The Development of the Legislative Council, 1606-1945* (London: Faber & Faber, 1946).

3. Khalid B. Sayeed, *The Political System of Pakistan* (Boston: Houghton Mifflin, 1967), pp. 13-14. J. K. Mittal, "Right to Equality in the Indian Constitution (Part I)," *Public Law*, Spring 1970, 76.

4. Sayeed, *op. cit.*, p. 22.

5. Great Britain. Parliamentary Papers. *Report of the Special Commission on the Constitution*. July 1928. Cmd. 3131. P. 39.

6. *Ibid.*, p. 94.

7. A. H. Hourani, *Syria and Lebanon* (London: Oxford University Press, 1946), pp. 181-182.

8. *Ibid.*, p. 182.

9. J. C. Hurewitz, "Lebanese Democracy in its International Set-

ting," in Leonard Binder, ed., *Politics in Lebanon* (New York: Wiley, 1966), p. 215.

10. Michael C. Hudson, *The Precarious Republic: Political Modernization in Lebanon* (New York: Random House, 1968), p. 23.

11. *Report by the United Nations Mediator on Cyprus to the Secretary-General.* 26 March 1965. S/6253, pp. 236-237. Cf. Great Britain. Parliamentary Papers. *Constitutional Proposals for Cyprus.* December 1956. Cmd. 42, p. 13.

12. Consultative Assembly of the Council of Europe, Resolution 290 (1965).

13. A/Res 32/15. 9 November 1977.

14. Frederic Spotts, *The Churches and Politics in Germany* (Middletown, Conn.: Wesleyan University Press, 1973), pp. 203-205. Cf. Gerhard Loewenberg, *Parliament in the German Political System* (Ithaca: Cornell University Press, 1967), pp. 99-100.

15. Joachim Matthes, "Religionszugehörigkeit und Gesellschaftspolitik über Konfessionalisierungstendenzen in der Bundesrepublik Deutschland," *International Yearbook for Sociology and Religion*, Vol. I (1965), p. 44.

16. Spotts, *op. cit.*, p. 192. Appendix to the Basic Law, Article 137. Cf. Francesco Capotorti, *Study of the Rights of Persons Belonging to Ethnic, Religious and Linguistic Minorities* (United Nations, E/CN.4/Sub.2/384), Add. 4, para. 69. Cf. John Golay, *The Founding of the Federal Republic of Germany* (Chicago: University of Chicago Press, 1958), p. 255.

17. Spotts, *op. cit.*, pp. 190-207.

18. Gordon P. Means, "Public Policy Toward Religion in Malaysia," *Pacific Affairs*, 51 (Fall 1978), 399.

19. Stanley Rothman, "The Politics of Catholic Parochial Schools: An Historical and Comparative Analysis," *Journal of Politics*, 25 (February 1963), 49-55.

20. Daniel H. Levine, *Religion and Politics in Latin America: The Catholic Church in Venezuela and Colombia* (Princeton: Princeton University Press, 1981), pp. 70-71.

21. J. Lloyd Mecham, *Church and State in Latin America* (Rev. ed.; Chapel Hill: University of North Carolina Press, 1966), pp. 126-135. Charles D. Ammoun, *Study of Discrimination in Education* (United Nations, 1957.XIV.3), p. 46.

22. Ammoun, *op. cit.*, p. 64.

23. William O. Lester Smith, *Education in Great Britain* (London: Oxford University Press, 1958), p. 128.

24. Stanley J. Curtis, *History of Education in Great Britain* (7th ed.; London: University Tutorial Press, 1967), p. 571.

25. Spotts, *op. cit.*, p. 186.

26. Golay, *op. cit.*, p. 196.

27. J. Goudsblom, *Dutch Society* (New York: Random House, 1967), p. 102. N. R. Wilson, "Dutch Schools and Religious Segmentation," *Comparative Education Review*, 3 (October 1959), 19-24. Arend Lijphart, *The Politics of Accommodation: Pluralism and Democracy in the Netherlands* (Berkeley: University of California Press, 1968), pp. 110-111, 127. *Moniteur Belge*, June 19, 1959. Law of 29 May 1959. Bernard E. Brown, "Religious Schools and Politics in France," *Midwest Journal of Political Science*, 2 (May 1958), 160-178.

28. Charles Bruce Sissons, *Church and State in Canadian Education* (Toronto: Ryerson Press, 1959), p. 344.

29. *Schmidt v. Calgary Bd.*, 6 W.W.R. (1976), 717, at 721.

30. *Ibid.* Cf. *Schmidt v. Calgary Bd.*, 6 W.W.R. (1975), 279.

31. Gordon P. Means, "State and Religion in Malaya and Malaysia," in M. M. Thomas and M. Abel, eds., *Religion, State and Ideologies in East Asia* (Bangalore: East Asian Christian Conference, 1965), p. 113.

32. Laws of the State of Israel, Vol. 19 (1964/65), 5725-1965, p. 113.

33. Macabee Dean, "Israel's New Antimissionary Law," *Liberty*, 73 (July-August 1978), 14-15. Sefer Hachukkim No. 880, 4738 (1977), p. 50.

34. *New York Times*, April 15, 1979, 12:3.

35. *Statesman's Yearbook*, 1977-78, p. 1000.

36. *New York Times*, November 27, 1979, A3:1.

37. U.S. Senate. Committee on the Judiciary. Subcommittee on Constitutional Rights. Amendments to the Indian Bill of Rights. *Hearings . . . on Title II of the Civil Rights Act of 1968*. 91st Cong., 1st Sess. April 11, 1969. Pp. 59-60.

38. *Santa Clara Pueblo v. Martinez*, 436 U.S. 49 (1978), at 62-63.

39. Steven Runciman, *The Orthodox Churches and the Secular State* (Auckland: Auckland University Press, 1971), pp. 27-33. J. A. Laponce, *The Protection of Minorities* (Berkeley: University of California Press, 1960), pp. 84-85.

40. Isaac S. Shiloh, "Marriage and Divorce in Israel," *Israel Law Review*, 5 (October 1970), 482-483.

41. *Ibid.*, p. 494.

42. *Wisconsin v. Yoder*, 406 U.S. 205 (1972), at 212.

4. EQUAL TREATMENT AND THE INDIGENOUS

1. See, however, Pierre L. van den Berghe, "Protection of Ethnic Minorities: A Critical Appraisal," in Robert G. Wirsing, ed., *Protection*

of Ethnic Minorities, Comparative Perspectives (New York: Pergamon Press, 1981), pp. 343-354.

2. Text in International Commission of Jurists *Review,* No. 27 (December 1981).

3. International Labor Organization. *Conventions and Recommendations Adopted by the International Labor Conference, 1919-1966* (Geneva, 1966), Convention No. 107.

4. The documents quoted, along with others, are conveniently assembled in United Nations document E/CN.4/Sub.2/476/Add.5, Annexes. This is part of the following report: José R. Martinez Cobo, Special Rapporteur, *Study of the Problem of Discrimination Against Indigenous Populations.* Sub-Commission on Prevention of Discrimination and Protection of Minorities. 34th Session. Item 10 of provisional agenda. E/CN.4/Sub.2/476. 30 July 1981. And E/CN.4/Sub.2/476/Add.1-6. 17 June to 30 July 1981.

5. See *American Indian Journal,* 3 (November 1977), 4-5.

6. Unesco, 14C/Res. 8.1. 4 November 1966. 17C/Res.4.111. 15 November 1972.

7. Frances Svensson, *The Ethnics in American Politics: American Indians* (Minneapolis: Burgess, 1973), p. 39. Cf., United States Commission on Civil Rights. *Indian Tribes, A Continuing Quest for Survival.* June 1981. Pp. 39-40.

8. Vine Deloria, Jr., *Behind the Trail of Broken Treaties* (New York: Dell, 1974), p. 262.

9. Vine Deloria, Jr., *We Talk, You Listen* (New York: Dell, 1970), p. 136.

10. *Ibid.,* p. 17. Cf. Deloria, *Behind the Trail of Broken Treaties,* pp. 162ff. George C. Lodge, *The New American Ideology* (New York: Knopf, 1975).

11. *Congressional Record,* July 27, 1978, p. H7458.

12. Robert Ericson and D. Rebecca Snow, "The Indian Battle for Self-Determination," *California Law Review* 58 (March 1970), 445-490.

13. *Worcester v. Georgia,* 6 Pet. 515 (1832), at 559-560.

14. *Cherokee Nation v. Georgia,* 5 Pet. 1 (1831), at 17.

15. *United States v. Kagama,* 118 U.S. 375 (1886), at 381.

16. *Talton v. Mayes,* 163 U.S. 376 (1896), at 384.

17. *Native American Church v. Navajo Tribal Council,* 272 F.2d 131 (1959), at 134-135.

18. *Williams v. Lee,* 358 U.S. 217 (1959).

19. Quoted by Svensson, *op. cit.,* p. 27.

20. Monroe E. Price, *Law and the American Indian* (Indianapolis: Bobbs-Merrill, 1973), p. 683.

21. *Ibid.*, pp. 684-687. Charles Wilkinson and Eric Biggs, "The Evolution of the Termination Policy," *American Indian Law Review*, 5 (No. 1, 1977), 143.

22. Commission on the Rights, Liberties, and Responsibilities of the American Indian, established by the Fund for the Republic. O. Meredith Wilson, Chairman. *A Program for Citizens*, A Summary Report (Albuquerque, 1961), p. 5. Wilkinson and Biggs, *loc. cit.*, pp. 150-162.

23. 25 U.S.C., sections 1301-1303 (1970).

24. Edward Ward, "Minority Rights and American Indians," *North Dakota Law Review*, 59 (Fall 1974), 179. *Santa Clara Pueblo v. Martinez*, 436 U.S. 49 (1978), at 63.

25. "The Indian Bill of Rights and the Constitutional Status of Tribal Governments," *Harvard Law Review*, 82 (April 1969), 1359.

26. *Santa Clara Pueblo v. Martinez*, 436 U.S. 49 (1978).

27. Cf. Ward, *loc. cit.*, p. 180. Alvin J. Ziontz, "In Defense of Tribal Sovereignty: An Analysis of Judicial Error in Construction of the Indian Civil Rights Act," *South Dakota Law Review*, 20 (Winter 1975), 1-58. *O'Neal v. Cheyenne River Sioux Tribe*, 482 F.2d 1140 (1973), at 1146. Frances Svensson, "Liberal Democracy and Group Rights: The Legacy of Individualism and its Impact on American Indian Tribes," *Political Studies*, 37 (September 1979), 430-434, 438.

28. U.S. President. *Public Papers of the Presidents of the United States*. Richard Nixon. 1970 (Washington, 1971), p. 567.

29. P.L. 93-638.

30. Felix S. Cohen, *Handbook of Federal Indian Law* (Albuquerque: University of New Mexico Press, 1971), pp. 221-227.

31. *United States v. Holliday*, 70 U.S. (3 Wall), 407 (1865). *United States v. 43 Gallons of Whiskey*, 93 U.S. 188 (1876). *United States v. Sandoval*, 231 U.S. 28 (1913). *State v. Rorvick*, P.2d 566 (1954).

32. Cohen, *op. cit.*, pp. 159-162. *American Indian Civil Rights Handbook—A Guide to the Rights and Liberties, Under Federal Law, of Native Americans Living On and Off Reservations* (Washington: Government Printing Office, 1972), pp. 48-49. *Morton v. Mancari*, 417 U.S. 535 (1974), at 545, 548.

33. *Morton v. Mancari*, 417 U.S. 535 (1974), at 545.

34. *Academe* [American Association of University Professors], 9 (April 1975), 51.

35. *Morton v. Mancari*, 417 U.S. 535 (1974), at 553, footnote 24. Cohen, *op. cit.*, 159.

36. Norman Vieira, "Racial Imbalance, Black Separatism, and Per-

missible Classification by Race," *Michigan Law Review,* 67 (June 1969), 1577-1580. *United States v. Williams,* 523 F.2d 400 (1975), at 403.

37. *Morton v. Mancari,* 417 U.S. 535 (1974), at 553-554. Cf. *Fisher v. District Court,* 424 U.S. 382 (1976), at 390. *United States v. Antelope,* 430 U.S. 641 (1977) at 646.

38. Nathan Glazer, *Affirmative Discrimination: Ethnic Inequality and Public Policy* (New York: Basic Books, 1975), p. 28.

39. Article 1, Section 3. Text in: U.S. Congress. House. Committee on Interior and Insular Affairs. *Texts of the . . . Constitution of American Samoa.* Committee Print No. 1. 87th Cong., 1st Sess. March 6, 1961. P. 39.

40. William J. Stewart, "American Law Below the Equator," *ABA Journal,* 59 (January 1973), 52. United Nations, Department of Political Affairs, Trusteeship and Decolonization, *Decolonization.* Issue on American Samoa, No. 13, October 1978, p. 13.

41. On Maori representation, see W. K. Jackson and G. A. Wood, "The New Zealand Parliament and Maori Representation," *Historical Studies, Australia and New Zealand,* 11 (October 1964), 383-396.

42. United Nations document A/7200/Add.7, para. 63. 31 October 1968.

43. Ahmed Ali, "The Emergence of Muslim Separatism in Fiji," *Plural Societies,* 8 (Spring 1977), 67-68.

44. Great Britain. Parliamentary Papers. *Fiji Constitutional Conference 1965.* October 1965. Cmnd. 2783. P. 6.

45. United Nations document A/7200/Add.7, #63. 31 October 1968. Report of the Special Committee on Colonialism, Chapter XVI. Fiji, pp. 24-25.

46. Parliament of Fiji. *Report of the Royal Commission Appointed for the Purpose of Considering and Making Recommendations as to the Most Appropriate Method of Electing Members to and Representing the People of Fiji in the House of Representatives.* Parliamentary Paper No. 24 of 1975, pp. 9-11, 16. Cf. R. K. Vasil, "Communalism and Parliamentary Representation in Fiji," *International Studies,* 17 (April-June 1978), 247-276.

47. A/Res/1951 (XVIII). 11 December 1963.

48. A/Res/2068 (XX). 12 December 1965.

49. A/Res/2185 (XXI). 12 December 1966.

50. General Assembly, XXI Session, Annexes. Addendum to Agenda Item 23. A/6300/Rev.1, p. 554, paras. 34-38.

51. R. K. Vasil, "Communalism and Constitution-Making in Fiji," *Pacific Affairs,* 45 (Spring 1972), 35, 38.

52. CERD/C/64/Add.4. 24 July 1981.

5. THE *BUMIPUTRA*: MALAYSIA

1. Gordon P. Means, "Public Policy Toward Religion in Malaysia," *Pacific Affairs*, 51 (Fall 1978), 403. Mahathir bin Mohamad, *The Malay Dilemma* (Singapore: Donald Moore for Asia Pacific Press, 1970), p. 135.

2. Great Britain. *Report of Brigadier General Sir Samuel Wilson . . . on his Visit to Malaya 1932*. Cmd.4276. London, 1933. P. 6.

3. *Ibid.*, p. 12.

4. Gordon P. Means, " 'Special Rights' as a Strategy for Development," *Comparative Politics*, 5 (October 1972), 40-41, fn. 23. B. Simandjuntak, *Malayan Federalism 1945-1963* (Kuala Lumpur: Oxford University Press, 1969), p. 134.

5. Alvin Rabushka, "The Manipulation of Ethnic Politics in Malaya," *Polity*, 2 (Spring 1970), 346.

6. R. K. Vasil, *Politics in a Plural Society. A Study of Non-Communal Political Parties in West Malaysia* (New York: Oxford University Press, 1971), p. 6.

7. Simandjuntak, *op. cit.*, pp. 53, 130-131. Edward McWhinney, *Federal Constitution-Making for a Multi-National World* (Leyden: Sijthoff, 1966), p. 66.

8. Gordon P. Means, "Malaysia," in Robert N. Kearney, ed., *Politics and Modernization in South and Southeast Asia* (New York: Wiley, 1975), p. 179.

9. Milton J. Esman, *Administration and Development in Malaysia* (Ithaca: Cornell University Press, 1972), p. 30. Vasil, *op. cit.*, p. 290.

10. H. P. Lee, "Constitutional Amendments in Malaysia," *Malaya Law Review*, 18 (July 1976), 117-119. Vasil, *op. cit.*, pp. 8-10.

11. Karl von Vorys, *Democracy Without Consensus: Communalism and Political Stability in Malaysia* (Princeton: Princeton University Press, 1975), pp. 206-210. Margaret Roff, "The Politics of Language in Malaya," *Asian Survey*, 7 (May 1967), 316-328.

12. Cf. Richard Allen, *Malaysia, Prospect and Retrospect: The Impact and Aftermath of Colonial Rule* (London: Oxford University Press, 1968), p. 256.

13. *New York Times*, September 18, 1974, 12:1.

14. Gordon P. Means, "The Role of Islam in the Political Development of Malaysia," *Comparative Politics*, 1 (January 1969), 280. Gordon P. Means, "State and Religion in Malaya and Malaysia," in M. M. Thomas and M. Abel, eds., *Religion, State and Ideologies in East Asia* (Bangalore: East Asian Christian Conference, 1965), pp. 101-126.

15. David S. Gibbons and Zakaria Haji Ahmad, "Politics and Selection for Higher Civil Service in New States, The Malaysian Example," *Journal of Comparative Administration [Administration and Society]*, 3 (November 1971), 334.

16. *Ibid.*, p. 338.

17. Tanzania. *Report of the Presidential Commission on the Establishment of a One-Party State* (Dar es Salaam: Government Printer, 1965), p. 2. Julian R. Friedman, "The Confrontation of Equality and Equalitarianism: Institution-Building through International Law," in Karl W. Deutsch and Stanley Hoffman, eds., *The Relevance of International Law* (Cambridge: Schenkman, 1968), p. 196. Judith Listowel, *The Making of Tanganyika* (New York: London House & Maxwell, 1965), pp. 416–417. Henry Bienen, *Tanzania, Party Transformation and Economic Development* (Princeton: Princeton University Press, 1967), pp. 123-124, 268.

18. Donald Rothchild, *Racial Bargaining in Independent Kenya, A Study of Minorities and Decolonization* (New York: Oxford University Press, for the Institute of Race Relations, 1973), pp. 192-193, 225-231.

19. von Vorys, *op. cit.*, pp. 98-99. Esman, *op. cit.*, p. 25. Robert S. Milne, *Government and Politics in Malaysia* (Boston: Houghton Mifflin, 1967), pp. 38-39.

20. Mahathir bin Mohamad, *op. cit.*, pp. 121, 126.

21. *Ibid.*, p. 75.

22. R. K. Vasil, *The Malayan General Election of 1969* (Singapore: Oxford University Press, 1972), pp. 4-5.

23. von Vorys, *op. cit.*, p. 28.

24. Means, "Malaysia," *loc. cit.*, pp. 189-191.

25. Ahmad Ibrahim, "Constitutional and Legal Trends," in Patrick Low, ed., *Proceedings and Background Paper of Seminar on Trends in Malaysia* (Singapore: Institute of Southeast Asian Studies, 1971), p. 19.

26. *Ibid.*, p. 21.

27. Constitution (Amendment) Act, 1971, A30, 10 March 1971. von Vorys, *op. cit.*, p. 418. Lee, *loc. cit.*, pp. 72, 106.

28. James Osborn, "Economic Growth with Equity? The Malaysian Experience," *Contemporary Southeast Asia*, 4 (September 1982), 159.

29. *Ibid.*, p. 167.

6. RACE: THE UNITED STATES

1. Nathan Glazer, *Affirmative Discrimination: Ethnic Inequality and Public Policy* (New York: Basic Books, 1975) , p. 5.

2. *Brown v. Board of Education*, 347 U.S. 483 (1954), at 494, 495.

3. *Green v. County School Board*, 391 U.S. 430 (1968).

4. *United States v. Texas Ed. Agency*, 532 F.2d 380 (1976), at 390-391.

5. *Swann v. Board of Education*, 402 U.S. 1 (1971), at 16, 25, 26. *United States v. Montgomery Bd. of Education*, 394 U.S. 225 (1969).

6. Jon M. Van Dyke, *Jury Selection Procedures* (Cambridge: Ballinger, 1977), pp. 48-49.

7. *Hernandez v. Texas*, 347 U.S. 475 (1954). *Cisneros v. Corpus Christi Indp. School District*, 324 F. Supp. 509 (1960). *United States v. Texas Ed. Agency*, 467 F.2d 848 (1972).

8. *United States v. State of Texas*, 321 F. Supp. 1043 (1970). *Bradley v. School Board of City of Richmond* 462 F.2d 1058 (1972). *Milliken v. Bradley*, 418 U.S. 717 (1974). U.S. Commission on Civil Rights, *Report, Statement on Metropolitan School Desegregation*, February 1977.

9. Norman Vieira, "Racial Imbalance, Black Separatism, and Permissible Classification by Race," *Michigan Law Review*, 67 (June 1969), 1618-1625.

10. M. Glenn Abernathy, *Civil Liberties Under the Constitution* (3rd ed.; New York: Harper & Row, 1977), pp. 571-600.

11. *Sims v. Baggett*, 247 F. Supp. 96 (1965), at 109, 110.

12. Italics supplied. *Bussie v. Governor of Louisiana*, 333 F. Supp. 452 (1971), at 456.

13. *Cousins v. City Council of City of Chicago*, 466 F.2d 830 (1972), at 843, 851.

14. *United States v. Carolene Products Co.*, 304 U.S. 144 (1938), at 153, footnote 4.

15. Mr. Justice White, in *Beer v. United States*, 425 U.S. 130 (1976), at 143.

16. Letter from J. Stanley Pottinger, Civil Rights Division, Department of Justice, to George D. Zuckerman, dated April 1, 1974.

17. *United Jewish Org. of Williamsburgh v. Wilson*, 510 F.2d 512 (1974) at 514, 517, 527.

18. Brief for Appellants, submitted by Nathan Lewin and Dennis Rapps to the U.S. Court of Appeals for the Second Circuit, in the case of United Jewish Organizations of Williamsburgh v. Wilson, No. 74-2037, p. 37.

19. *United Jewish Organizations v. Carey*, 430 U.S. 144 (1977), at 165-166.

20. *Ibid.*, p. 175.

21. *Ibid.*, p. 178.

22. *Ibid.*, p. 186.

23. *Ibid.*, p. 181.

24. *Hernandez v. Texas*, 347 U.S. 475 (1954), at 478-480. Cf. *Cisneros v. Corpus Christi Independent School District*, 324 F. Supp. 599 (1970), at 606.

25. *Klahr v. Williams*, 339 F. Supp. 922 (1972).

26. *Ince v. Rockefeller*, 290 F. Supp. 878 (1968), at 883, quoting *Wells v. Rockefeller*, 281 F. Supp. 821 (1968), at 825.

27. *Washington v. Davis*, 426 U.S. 229 (1976), at 240.

28. *Mobile v. Bolden*, 446 U.S. 55 (1980).

29. *Ibid.*, at p. 67.

30. *Ibid.*, at p. 121, fn. 21.

31. *Lodge v. Buxton*, 639 F. 2d 1358 (1981).

32. *Ibid.*, at p. 1377.

33. *Rogers v. Lodge*, 458 U.S. 613 (1982).

34. Chandler Davidson and George Korbel, "At-Large Elections and Minority-Group Representation: A Re-Examination of Historical and Contemporary Evidence," *Journal of Politics*, 43 (November 1981), 982-1005.

35. Edwin Dorn, *Rules and Racial Equality* (New Haven: Yale University Press, 1979).

36. Alan H. Goldman, *Justice and Reverse Discrimination* (Princeton: Princeton University Press, 1979). Carl Cohen, "Why Racial Preference is Illegal and Immoral," *Commentary*, 67 (June 1979), 40-52. Joel Kassiola, "Compensatory Justice & the Moral Obligation for Preferential Treatment of Discriminated Groups," *Polity*, 11 (Fall 1978), 46-66.

37. *University of California Regents v. Bakke*, 438 U.S. 265 (1978), at 329. Cf., p. 287.

38. *Steelworkers v. Weber*, 443 U.S. 193 (1979), at 204.

39. Joseph Tussman and Jacobus tenBroek, "The Equal Protection of the Laws," *California Law Review*, 37 (September 1949), 341-381. Owen H. Fiss, "Groups and the Equal Protection Clause," *Philosophy & Public Affairs*, 5 (Winter 1976), 107-177.

40. *Barbier v. Connolly*, 113 U.S. 27, 31 (1885), as quoted by Tussman and tenBroek, *loc. cit.*, p. 343.

41. Tussman and tenBroek, *loc. cit.*, p. 358.

42. *Bridgeport Guardians v. Members of the Bridgeport Civil Service Commission*, 482 F.2d 1333 (1973), at 1340.

43. *NAACP v. Allen*, 340 F. Supp. 703 (1972), at 705.

44. *Officers for Justice v. Civil S. Com'n, C. & C. San Francisco*, 371 F. Supp. 1328 (1973), at 1339.

45. *Stamps v. Detroit Edison*, 365 F. Supp. 87 (1973).

46. *University of California Regents v. Bakke*, 438 U.S. 265 (1978).

47. *Ibid.*, p. 298. Opinion of Justice Powell.

48. *Ibid.*, p. 400. Opinion of Justice Marshall. Cf., opinion of Justice Brennan, pp. 377-378.

49. *Fullilove v. Klutznick*, 448 U.S. 448 (1980).

50. *University of California Regents v. Bakke*, 438 U.S. 265 (1978), at 348, 349. Opinion of Justice Brennan.

51. *Steelworkers v. Weber*, 443 U.S. 193 (1979), at 203.

52. *Fullilove v. Klutznick*, 448 U.S. 448 (1980).

53. *Officers for Justice v. Civil S. Com'n, C. & C. San Francisco*, 371 F. Supp. 1328 (1973) at 1331.

54. *Korematsu v. United States*, 323 U.S. 214 (1944).

55. Fiss, *loc. cit.*, p. 148.

56. *Ibid.*, p. 157.

57. *Moose Lodge No. 107 v. Irvis*, 407 U.S. 163 (1972).

58. Alan Gledhill, *Fundamental Rights in India* (London: Stevens, 1956), pp. 50-51. A. P. Barnabas and Subhash C. Mehta, *Caste in Changing India* (New Delhi: The Indian Institute of Public Administration, 1965), pp. 70-71.

59. Goldman, *op. cit.*, p. 4.

60. *Ibid.*, pp. 31, 33, 144, 183.

61. *Ibid.*, p. 88.

62. *Ibid.*, p. 85.

63. *Ibid.*, p. 86.

64. *Ibid.*, pp. 62, 70.

65. *Ibid.*, p. 112.

66. *Ibid.*, pp. 171, 176, 185.

67. *Ibid.*, pp. 65, 198.

68. *Ibid.*, p. 79.

7. RACE: SOUTH AFRICA

1. The General Assembly has adopted a resolution declaring that "the racist regime of South Africa is illegitimate and has no right to represent the people of South Africa." A/Res 31/61. 9 November 1976.

2. South Africa. House of Assembly. *Debates*. Vol. 2 (23 January 1962), col. 92. (Hereafter cited as: *Assembly Debates*.)

3. United Nations document A/PV.1857 (1 October 1970).

4. *Assembly Debates*, Vol. 107 (14 April 1961), col. 4618.

5. United Nations document S/PV. 1800 (24 October 1974), p. 43.

6. *Assembly Debates*, Vol. 55 (6 February 1975), col. 296.

7. United Nations document S/PV.1800 (24 October 1974), p. 43.

8. South Africa. Department of Information. *Multi-National Development in South Africa: The Reality* (Pretoria: 1974), p. 12. (Hereafter cited as South Africa, *Multi-National Development.*)

9. South African Institute of Race Relations, *A Survey of Race Relations in South Africa, 1976* (Johannesburg, 1967), p. 147.

10. South Africa. Statutes. Status of the Transkei Act No. 100, 1976. Status of Bophuthatswana Act No. 89, 1977. Willie Breytenbach, "The Transkeian Constitution in the African Context," *Africa Institute Bulletin*, 14 (Nos. 7 & 8, 1976), 248; cf. p. 239. London *Economist*, Vol. 281, No. 7214 (December 5, 1981), p. 47.

11. South Africa. President's Council. Constitutional Committee. *Second Report . . . on the Adaptation of Constitutional Structures in South Africa.* P.C.4/1982 (Cape Town, 1982), p. 89. (Hereafter cited as: Constitutional Committee, *Second Report.*)

12. Keesing's *Contemporary Archives*, October 22, 1976, col. 28010.

13. *Ibid.*, May 29, 1981, cols. 30884-30885.

14. South Africa. President's Council. Constitutional Committee. *First Report.* P.C.3/1982 (Cape Town, 1982). (Hereafter cited as: Constitutional Committee, *First Report.*) And see note 11 above.

15. Constitutional Committee, *First Report*, p. 15.

16. *Ibid.*, p. 19.

17. *Ibid.*, p. 69.

18. *Ibid.*, citing L. H. Gann and Peter Duignan, *Why South Africa Will Survive* (Tafelberg, 1981), p. 279.

19. Constitutional Committee, *First Report*, p. 27.

20. New Haven: Yale University Press, 1977.

21. Constitutional Committee, *First Report*, p. 33.

22. Constitutional Committee, *Second Report*, p. 11.

23. United Nations. Unit on Apartheid. *Repressive Legislation of the Republic of South Africa*, 1969. ST/PSCA/Ser.A/7. John Dugard, *Human Rights and the South African Legal Order* (Princeton: Princeton University Press, 1978).

24. South Africa. Bureau for Economic Research re Bantu Development (Benbo). *Black Development in South Africa: The Economic Development of the Black Peoples in the Homelands of the Republic of South Africa* (Pretoria, 1976), p. 23. Table 3.4.

25. Vernon Van Dyke, "One Man One Vote and Majority Rule as Human Rights," *Revue des Droits de l'Homme [Human Rights Journal]*, Vol. VI, Nos. 3-4 (1973), 454-456.

26. Arend Lijphart, *Democracy in Plural Societies* (New Haven: Yale University Press, 1977), p. 41.

27. *Loving v. Virginia*, 388 U.S. 1 (1967).

242   *Notes*

28. Ali A. Mazrui and David F. Gordon, "Independent African States and the Struggle for Southern Africa," in John Seiler, ed., *Southern Africa Since the Portuguese Coup* (Boulder: Westview, 1980), p. 185.
29. J. Ayo Langley, ed., *Ideologies of Liberation in Black Africa 1856-1970* (London: Rex Collings, 1979), pp. 782-788.
30. A/Res/37/69A. 9 September 1982.
31. Texts in Gwendolen M. Carter, *The Politics of Inequality. South Africa Since 1948* (London: Thames and Hudson, 1958), Appendix IV.
32. Hendrik W. van der Merwe, Nancy C. J. Charton, D. A. Kotze, & Ake Magnusson, eds., *African Perspectives on South Africa: A Collection of Speeches, Articles and Documents* (Stanford: Hoover Institution Press, 1978), pp. 91-93, 97-101.
33. John Kane-Berman, "Inkatha: The Paradox of South African Politics," *Optima*, 30 (February 26, 1982), 144-177.

8. STANDARDS OF JUDGMENT

1. International Court of Justice. Pleadings, Oral Arguments, Documents. *South West Africa Cases.* 1966. Vol. I, p. 4; and Vol. IV, p. 493.
2. *Hobbes' Leviathan* (Oxford: Clarendon Press, 1909), Chap. XVIII, 133.
3. George H. Sabine, *A History of Political Theory* (New York: Holt, 1950), p. 475.
4. Ernest Barker, ed., *Social Contract: Essays by Locke, Hume, and Rousseau* (New York: Oxford University Press, 1962), pp. 56-57.
5. *Ibid.*, p. 194.
6. John Stuart Mill, *Considerations on Representative Government* (Indianapolis: Bobbs-Merrill, 1958), pp. 230, 233.
7. Ernest Barker, *Principles of Social and Political Theory* (Oxford: Clarendon Press, 1951), pp. 3, 42.
8. *Ibid.*, p. 55.
9. *Ibid.*, p. 56.
10. John Rawls, *A Theory of Justice* (Cambridge: The Belknap Press of Harvard University Press, 1971), pp. 128, 136-150. Vernon Van Dyke, "Justice as Fairness: For Groups?" *American Political Science Review*, 69 (June 1975), 607-614.
11. J. Roland Pennock, *Democratic Political Theory* (Princeton: Princeton University Press, 1979), p. 201.
12. *Ibid.*, p. 207.
13. *Ibid.*, p. 252.
14. *Ibid.*, p. 143.

15. *Ibid.*, pp. 352-355.

16. *Ibid.*, p. 358.

17. Walker Connor, "Nation-Building or Nation-Destroying?" *World Politics*, 24 (April 1972), 320. Cf. Walker Connor, "The Politics of Ethnonationalism," *Journal of International Affairs*, 27 (No. 1, 1973), 1. Marie R. Haug, "Social and Cultural Pluralism as a Concept in Social System Analysis," *American Journal of Sociology*, 73 (November 1967), 299.

18. *The Politics of Johannes Althusius.* An abridged translation of the third edition. Translated, with an Introduction by, Frederick S. Carney (Boston: Beacon Press, 1964), p. 12.

19. *Ibid.*, p. 62.

20. John C. Calhoun, *A Disquisition on Government* (New York: Political Science Classics, 1947), pp. 24-25.

21. *Ibid.*, p. 104.

22. Lord Acton, *Essays on the Liberal Interpretation of History, Selected Papers* (Chicago: University of Chicago Press, 1967), p. 157.

23. *Ibid.*, pp. 150, 158.

24. *Ibid.*, p. 137.

25. Otto Gierke, *Natural Law and the Theory of Society, 1500 to 1800*, Tr. with an Introduction by Ernest Barker (Cambridge: At the University Press, 1934), I, 77, 138, 164.

26. John Neville Figgis, *Churches in the Modern State* (London: Longmans, Green, 1913), p. 47.

27. *Ibid.*, pp. 42, 64.

28. *Ibid.*, pp. 68, 80, 87.

29. *Ibid.*, pp. 90, 91, 51-52.

30. Kenneth D. McRae, "The Plural Society and the Western Political Tradition," *Canadian Journal of Political Science*, 12 (December 1979), 685. Cf. Frances Svensson, "Liberal Democracy and Group Rights: The Legacy of Individualism and its Impact on American Indian Tribes," *Political Studies*, 37 (September 1979), 421-439.

31. Arend Lijphart, *Democracy in Plural Societies* (New Haven: Yale University Press, 1977), p. 25. Cf. Arend Lijphart, "Consociation and Federation: Conceptual and Empirical Links," and Comment: "Federation, Consociation, Corporatism," by Kenneth D. McRae, *Canadian Journal of Political Science*, 12 (September 1979), 499-522.

32. Ernest Barker, *Principles of Social and Political Theory* (Oxford: Clarendon Press, 1951), p. 71.

33. United Nations document A/Res.2625 (XXV). 14 October 1970. Declaration on Principles of International Law Concerning Friendly Relations and Cooperation Among States. . . .

34. United Nations document E/CN.4/Sub.2/404 (Vol. I). 3 July 1978. Aureliu Cristescu, Special Rapporteur, The Historical and Current Development of the Right to Self-determination . . . , paras. 31, 46, 213-214, 228. And E/CN.4/Sub.2/405 (Vol. I). 20 June 1978. Hector Gros Espiell, Special Rapporteur, Implementation of United Nations Resolutions Relating to the Right of Peoples . . . to Self-determination, paras. 54-56.

35. *Yale Law Journal*, "The United Nations, Self-determination, and the Namibia Opinions," 82 (January 1973), 534.

36. Dov Ronen, *The Quest for Self-determination* (New Haven: Yale University Press, 1979), p. 8.

37. Nathan Glazer, *Affirmative Discrimination: Ethnic Inequality and Public Policy* (New York: Basic Books, 1975), p. 221.

38. Nathan Glazer, "Individual Rights Against Group Rights," in Eugene Kamenka and Alice Erh-Soon Tay, eds., *Human Rights* (London: Edward Arnold, 1978), p. 98.

39. Owen M. Fiss, "Groups and the Equal Protection Clause," *Philosophy and Public Affairs*, 5 (Winter 1976), 148.

40. Svensson, *loc. cit.*, pp. 434-435.

41. Vernon Van Dyke, "One Man One Vote and Majority Rule as Human Rights," *Revue des Droits de l'Homme [Human Rights Journal]*, 6 (Nos. 3-4, 1973), 453-459.

42. See the Draft International Convention on the Protection of National or Ethnic Minorities, sponsored by the Minority Rights Group, in: James Fawcett, *The International Protection of Minorities* (Report No.41, Minority Rights Group, London, 1979), Appendix G.

43. Herbert J. Gans, "We Won't End the Urban Crisis Until We End Majority Rule," *New York Times Magazine*, August 3, 1969, pp. 12ff. Cf., Herbert J. Gans, *More Equality* (New York: Pantheon, 1973), pp. 127-148.

Bibliographical Essay

Writing that relates somehow to the subject of this book is abundant, though little of it is specifically about the relationship between equality and discrimination and the rights of groups. Good materials are available on (1) the general idea of equality and discrimination; (2) minorities and their rights; (3) the plural society, ethnonationalism, consociationalism, and self-determination; and (4) the policies and problems of various individual countries.

The best brief discussion of equality of which I am aware is Isaiah Berlin's "Equality" (*Proceedings of the Aristotelian Society*, LVI [1955-1956], 301-326). I have benefited greatly also from Morris Ginsberg's *On Justice in Society* (Ithaca, N.Y.: Cornell University Press, 1965).

An examination of the problem of equality and discrimination as it is attacked at the international level is to be found in a book of which I became aware only after completing my own: Warwick McKean, *Equality and Discrimination Under International Law* (Oxford: Clarendon, 1983). The book is especially good on international definitions of equality and discrimination and on the formulation of provisions relating to equality and discrimination in a number of international conventions and declarations.

On special measures to promote the equal enjoyment of human rights, books that I cite in the text are stimulating: Alan H. Goldman, *Justice and Reverse Discrimination* (Princeton, N.J.: Princeton University Press, 1979), and Nathan Glazer, *Affirmative Discrimination* (New York: Basic, 1975). (Note that the words used to identify the problem may or may not be neutral.) Those who read Glazer's book should also read his article, "Individual Rights Against Group Rights," in Eugene Kamenka and Alice Erh-Soon Tay, eds., *Human Rights*

(London: Edward Arnold, 1978). Of special interest, too, is *Equality and Preferential Treatment*, edited by Marshall Cohen and others (Princeton, N.J.: Princeton University Press, 1977); in it, note the article by Owen M. Fiss, "Groups and the Equal Protection Clause."

On language policies, see Brian Weinstein, *The Civic Tongue: Political Consequences of Language Choices* (New York: Longman, 1983). Weinstein does not focus on equal and nondiscriminatory treatment, but the subject keeps coming up implicitly. The book includes a bibliography.

Books focusing on minorities reflect different perspectives. The perspective of Inis L. Claude, in *National Minorities*, is suggested by his subtitle, *An International Problem* (Cambridge, Mass.: Harvard University Press, 1955; Greenwood reprint, 1969). Claude's focus is on international actions relating to minorities before, during, and since World War II, though he also includes a chapter on the solution of the problem through assimilation or through the acceptance of a depoliticized cultural pluralism. His book includes a bibliography.

Several other books treat minorities mainly as a domestic problem. One is J. A. Laponce, *The Protection of Minorities* (Berkeley: University of California Press, 1960). Laponce focuses on the constitutional and civil rights of minorities in various countries, and on the impact on minorities of differing arrangements relating to (a) the structure of the state and government and (b) parties and elections. The minorities with which Claude deals are mainly European, but Laponce ranges over a wider field.

Protection of Minorities, Comparative Perspectives, edited by Robert G. Wirsing (New York: Pergamon, 1981) likewise reflects a domestic perspective. It contains chapters on countries in each of the major regions of the world. And it contains a provocative chapter by Pierre L. van den Berghe, arguing that "that government is best which pays least official attention to ethnicity."

The authors of *The Future of Cultural Minorities*, edited by Antony E. Alcock and others (New York: St. Martin's, 1979) seem to be guided by different, largely unavowed, concerns. Like most writers about minorities, some are concerned with political issues—issues relating to the policies that are or might be followed. Basically the concern is with political justice. Others have concerns of a more sociological sort, asking about the relationship between policies toward minorities and the prospect that the minorities will be able to maintain their cultural distinctiveness.

The publications of the Minority Rights Group in London deserve special mention, and so does a book edited by its executive director,

Ben Whitaker, *The Fourth World, Victims of Group Oppression* (New York: Schocken, 1973). The fourth world is the world of minorities. The Minority Rights Group is willing to view a minority as a unit, an entity, with collective rights. So is Yoram Dinstein, in "Collective Human Rights of Peoples and Minorities," *International and Comparative Law Quarterly*, 25 (January 1976), 102-120.

Jay A. Sigler's *Minority Rights: A Comparative Analysis* (Westport, Conn.: Greenwood, 1983) treats both the international and the domestic aspects of the subject. The book gives a good history of minority rights, describes arrangements both within and among countries for the protection of minorities, discusses both affirmative action and anti-discrimination policies, and ends with a chapter on the future of minority rights. Sigler differs from most authors in treating a numerical minority as a minority even if it is politically dominant, and so includes a chapter on political systems in which the minority rules. He provides an extensive, annotated bibliography.

Books and articles focusing on the idea of a plural society, or on ethnonationalism, consociationalism, or self-determination, contrast in an interesting way with books on minorities. The term minorities suggests the existence of majorities, and thus suggests weakness in the face of strength, perhaps together with paternalism. The other concepts get away from intimations of subordination and domination, and instead suggest groups of whatever size that live side by side, all of them with legitimate claims to equal treatment in terms of status and rights.

Harold R. Isaacs, *Idols of the Tribe, Group Identity and Political Change* (New York: Harper and Row, 1975) provides a good background for studies that focus on the plural society and related concepts. Isaacs examines the elements that go together to give a sense of group identity—the "soft stuff of which group identities are made." He speaks of the existence of varied cultures as "life-giving," though with some "death-dealing consequences."

J. S. Furnivall coined the expression "plural society" in *Colonial Policy and Practice, A Comparative Study of Burma and Netherlands India* (Cambridge, Eng.: At the University Press, 1948). Alvin Rabushka and Kenneth A. Shepsle focus on the concept in *Politics in Plural Societies, A Theory of Democratic Instability* (Columbus, Ohio: Merrill, 1972), reaching pessimistic conclusions about the prospects of democracy and stability in such societies. Walker Connor has been a leader in calling attention to what he calls ethnonationalism ("Self-Determination. A New Phase," *World Politics*, 20 [October 1967], 30-53; "Ethnology and the Peace of South Asia," *World Politics*, 22 [October 1969], 51-86; "Nation-Building or Nation-Destroying?" *World Politics*, 24 [April 1972], 319-355), and he has published an extended treatment of one aspect of the subject: *The National Question in Marx-ist-Leninist Theory and Strategy* (Princeton, N.J.: Princeton University Press, 1984). Eric A. Nordlinger, in *Conflict Regulation in Divided Societies* (Cambridge, Mass.: Harvard University, Center for International Affairs, 1972), focuses on societies in which ethnic divisions make it likely that violence or repression, or both, will occur; he states his goal as "the development of a theoretical statement which can explain when, why, and how such intense conflicts are successfully regulated."

Ethnicity, edited by Nathan Glazer and Daniel P. Moynihan (Cambridge, Mass.: Harvard University Press, 1975), subtitled *Theory and Experience*, includes five chapters of a general and theoretical sort, and eleven on ethnicity in various countries and regions of the world.

Joseph Rothschild, *Ethnopolitics, A Conceptual Framework* (New York: Columbia University Press, 1981), discusses "the causes, options, and consequences of bringing ethnicity into the political arena." He examines the reasons for an emphasis on ethnicity and the functions that it serves; the different organizational arrangements within the state that take ethnicity into account; the dynamics of interethnic relations; the goals and strategies associated with ethnicity; the consequences of ethnic divisions for international politics; and the ways in which the government or the state, and the dominant elites, may react when confronting ethnic divisions. His book includes an extensive bibliography, and so does the book by Rabushka and Shepsle.

The Mobilization of Collective Identity: Comparative Perspectives, edited by Jeffrey A. Ross and Ann Baker Cottrell (Lanham, Md.: University Press of America, 1980) describes policies and problems relating to minority and ethnic groups in a number of different countries. It includes a chapter on the American Indians. *Ethnicity and Nation-Building: Comparative, International, and Historical Perspectives*, edited by Wendell Bell and Walter Freeman (Beverly Hills, Calif.: Sage, 1974), contains some chapters that are general and theoretical and others that focus on one or another country. Cynthia H. Enloe, *Ethnic Conflict and Political Development* (Boston: Little, Brown, 1973) likewise combines a general, theoretical treatment with illustrations from particular countries. *Ethnic Separatism and World Politics*, edited by Frederick L. Shields (Lanham, Md.: University Press of America, 1984) treats the Ibos, the Bengalis and Bangladesh, the French-speaking people of Canada, the Basques, and several nationalities in Yugoslavia.

The idea of consociationalism is advanced mainly in the writings of Arend Lijphart, Gerhard Lehmbruch, Val Lorwin, and Kenneth D. McRae. The fullest coherent exposition of the idea is in Lijphart's *Democracy in Plural Societies, A Comparative Exploration* (New Haven, Conn.: Yale University Press, 1977). Implicitly arguing for consociational democracy in certain kinds of circumstances, Lijphart nevertheless remains formally descriptive and analytical. He describes the idea of consociational democracy, lists conditions favorable to it, and describes applications of the idea in different countries. Similar materials are included in *Consociational Democracy, Political Accommodation in Segmented Societies*, edited by Kenneth D. McRae (Toronto: McClelland and Stewart, 1974).

Arend Lijphart's more recent contribution is *Democracies: Patterns of Majoritarian and Consensus Government in Twenty-One Countries* (New Haven, Conn.: Yale University Press, 1984). Note the reference to "consensus government" rather than to "consociationalism." The twenty-one countries are those that have maintained democracy since about the end of World War II. Concerned with minority participation in the political process, with power-sharing, Lijphart describes rules and practices relating to the executive and legislative branches of government, to party systems and elections, to centralization-decentralization, and to the use of referenda.

Pierre L. van den Berghe's *The Ethnic Phenomenon* is outstanding (New York: Elsevier, 1981; distribution by Greenwood). The chapters that provide "an explanatory framework" for ethnicity and that comment on consociationalism are especially good. The book includes an extensive bibliography.

Rupert Emerson, *Self-Determination Revisited in the Era of Decolonization* (Cambridge, Mass.: Harvard University, Center for International Affairs, 1964) is excellent on the subject indicated. Lee C. Buchheit, *Secession. The Legitimacy of Self-Determination* (New Haven, Conn.: Yale University Press, 1978) and Dov Ronen, *The Quest for Self-Determination* (New Haven, Conn.: Yale University Press, 1979) are also to be commended. I have already registered a dissent from Ronen's view that the right of peoples to self-determination is basically the right of individual persons. I might call attention, too, to the chapter on self-determination in my own book, *Human Rights, the United States, and World Community* (New York: Oxford University Press, 1970).

Books dealing with the problems and policies of individual countries or regions are so numerous that I will not try to list them all, and in particular will not repeat references to books cited in my notes.

For Cyprus, I suggest Stanley Kyriakides, *Cyprus: Constitutionalism and Crisis Government* (Philadelphia: University of Pennsylvania Press, 1968); Thomas Ehrlich, *Cyprus, 1958-1967* (New York: Oxford University Press, 1974); Kyriacos C. Markides, *The Rise and Fall of the Cyprus Republic* (New Haven, Conn.: Yale University Press, 1977); and Polyvios G. Polyviou, *Cyprus, Conflict and Negotiation 1960-1980* (New York: Holmes and Meier, 1980).

For Lebanon, David R. Smock and Audrey C. Smock, *The Politics of Pluralism: A Comparative Study of Lebanon and Ghana* (New York: Elsevier, 1975); and Walid Khalidi, *Conflict and Violence in Lebanon: Confrontation in the Middle East* (Harvard University, Center for International Affairs, 1979).

For Malaysia, R. K. Vasil, *Ethnic Politics in Malaysia* (New Delhi: Radiant Publishers, 1980) and Karl von Vorys, *Democracy Without Consensus, Communalism and Political Stability in Malaysia* (Princeton, N.J.: Princeton University Press, 1975). R. S. Milne deals with Guyana, Malaysia, and Fiji in his *Politics in Ethnically Bipolar States* (Vancouver: University of British Columbia Press, 1981).

Sri Lanka is treated in Robert N. Kearney, *Communalism and Language in the Politics of Ceylon* (Durham, N.C.: Duke University Press, 1967), and Bangladesh, India, Indonesia, Malaysia, Pakistan, and Thailand are treated in Robert N. Kearney, ed., *Politics and Modernization in South and Southeast Asia* (New York: Wiley, 1975).

For New Zealand, see W. A. McKean, ed., *Essays on Race Relations and the Law in New Zealand* (Wellington: Sweet and Maxwell, 1971).

Those interested in black Africa will get help from Leo Kuper and M. G. Smith, eds., *Pluralism in Africa* (Berkeley: University of California Press, 1971); from Donald Rothchild, *Racial Bargaining in Independent Kenya, A Study of Minorities and Decolonization* (New York: Oxford University Press, 1973); and from Leo Kuper, *The Pity of It All: Polarisation of Racial and Ethnic Relations* (Minneapolis: University of Minnesota Press, 1977). *State Versus Ethnic Claims: African Policy Dilemmas*, edited by Donald Rothchild and Victor A. Olorunsola (Boulder, Colo.: Westview, 1983), includes one set of chapters on claims of the state, another on claims of ethnic groups, and a third on the management of competing claims, with illustrations relating to various African countries.

Leading the field with respect to South Africa is John Dugard, *Human Rights and the South African Legal Order* (Princeton, N.J.: Princeton University Press, 1978). The Report of the Study Commission on U.S. Policy Toward Southern Africa, *South Africa: Time Running Out* (Berkeley: University of California Press, 1981) gives a comprehensive analysis of the problem indicated by the title. Both of these books contain extensive bibliographies. Nic Rhoodie has edited several books dealing mainly with South Africa, including *Intergroup Accommodation in Plural Societies* (New York: St. Martin's, 1978), and *Conflict Resolution in South Africa, The Quest for Accommodationist Policies in a Plural Society* (Pretoria: Institute for Plural Societies, 1980). The current ferment in South Africa shows up particularly in Edwin S. Munger, ed., *The Afrikaners* (Cape Town: Tafelberg, 1979); Robert Schrire, ed., *South Africa, Public Policy Perspectives* (Cape Town: Juta, 1982); D. J. van Vuuren et al., *Change in South Africa* (Pretoria: Butterworths, 1983); and D. J. van Vuuren and D. J. Kriek, eds., *Political Alternatives for Southern Africa, Principles and Perspectives* (Pretoria: Butterworths, 1983).

For Latin America, the principal relevant book of which I am aware— an excellent one—is Leo A. Despres, *Cultural Pluralism and Nationalist Politics in British Guiana* (Chicago: Rand McNally, 1967).

Those interested in Canada will do well to look at the various volumes of the *Report* of the Royal Commission on Bilingualism and Biculturalism (Ottawa, 1967-70) and the subsequent reports of the Commissioner of Official Languages. Also to be recommended are the three volumes of Quebec's Commission of Inquiry on the Position of the French Language and on Language Rights in Quebec (Montreal, 1972). McRae's book on *Consociational Democracy*, cited above, includes five chapters relating to Canada.

On questions concerning equality and discrimination in the United States I have relied mainly on the opinions of various courts. Those wanting the references will find them in the notes for Chapters 2 and 6.

Index

Leibowitz, Arnold H., 41
Lewis, W. Arthur, 7-9, 31, 58, 169, 176, 206
Lijphart, Arend, 176, 184, 203
Locke, John, 195-196, 199
Lusaka Manifesto, 188

McRae, Kenneth D., 203
Majority rule: and communalism, 55; and ethnic domination, 58, 176; and Jim Crow, 58; and Lewis, W. Arthur, 7; not sacred, 147-148; in South Africa, 105, 176, 189; versus humankind, 207
Malapportionment, 137; and "over-representation," 183
Malaysia: and the *bumiputra*, 113-117, 130; composition of the population, 111-112; constitutional contract, 126-127; and Islam, 123; language policies, 121-123; Malays as "rightful owners," 127; national ideology, 128-129; political communalism, 119-121; and proselytism, 70-71; and Singapore, 118-119; the "special position" of Malays, 113, 124-126; support for religion, 65
Maldive Republic, and communalism, 61
Mantanzima, George, 181
Maoris, 94-97
Mazrui, Ali A., 187-188
Means, Gordon, 115
Mexican-Americans, and the language of instruction, 42
Mill, John Stuart, 196, 202
Millets, 74
Minorities: exclusion of, 55; "identifiable," 134-135, 139-

140; protection of, 10; representation of, 10; rights of, 129; special rights for, 220. *See also* Cultural rights
Miscegenation, 185
Mobile, Alabama, and at-large elections, 144
Moose Lodge case, 160

Namibia, 193
New Brunswick, language legislation, 47
New Mexico, language policies, 39, 40, 42, 50
New Zealand, Maori policy, 94-97
Nixon, Richard M., 90
Nyerere, Julius K., and racial preferences, 125

Old Order Amish, 75, 77
Organization of African Unity, 187
Ottoman Empire, and religious communalism, 74

Pakistan, 57
Palestine, 20-21
Parents' rights, 68
Peoples: definition, 11; indigenous groups as, 83-84, 88; right to survive, 81-82. *See also* Self-determination
Pennock, Roland, 198
Personality, principle of, 25, 205
Preferential treatment: of American Indians, 92, 149, 151; in Belgium, 26; and the *bumiputra* of Malaysia, 113-117, 124-126; claimed by American whites, 132; a constitutional problem, 148-161; endorsed or required by trea-

258   *Index*

ties, 10; and the equal enjoyment of human rights, 219; in
India and New Zealand, 160-
161; a moral problem, 161-
166; and religion, 68, 149; in
Tanganyika, 125. *See also* Affirmative action
Proselytism, protections
against, 70-72
Puerto Rico, language of instruction, 42; and status for
Spanish, 46

Rabushka, Alvin, 116
Race: as a basis for differentiation, 133-134; and the indigenous, 84, 94-95, 113
Racism, 105
Ratio-hiring, 125; justification
of, 125-126; its justifiability,
165-166; ordered by U.S.
courts, 152-154. *See also* Affirmative action; Preferential
treatment
Rawls, John, 197-198
Religion: and communalism, 54-
63; draft convention concerning, 54; and preservation of
the religious community, 69,
72; as a qualification for office, 53-54; state support for,
65-66, 123-124. *See also*
Proselytism
Representation: by appointment, 115, 120; "balanced,"
10, 125; in a consociational
democracy, 184; of ethnic
communities, 26, 53-63, 96,
99, 101, 182-183; of interests,
54-55; in international institutions, 183; possibilities in
South Africa, 183-184; propor-

tional, 8, 106, 140, 141, 184,
198
Rights: absolute, 13, 19, 23, 47-
48; collective, 15, 32, 47, 127-
131; individual, 208-213; and
interests, 32, 158, 208, 211;
moral and legal, 24, 31;
source or origin, 15-16, 32,
209, 223-224; of units, 207.
See also Equal population
principle
Ronen, Dov, 211
Roosevelt, Franklin D., 42
Rousseau, J. J., 196

Sabine, George H., 196
Samoa, American, 23, 93-94
Scotland, and religion in
schools, 68
Segregation, and the indigenous, 83
Self-determination: an absolute
right, 13, 219; and the American Indians, 91; and autonomy for religious groups, 74;
and the equal enjoyment of
human rights, 219; explosive
potential, 221; the holder of
the right, 209-211; for the indigenous, 80, 83, 116, 130; interpreted, 11-13; and New
Brunswick, 47; possible outcomes, 210; and secession, 12;
within South Africa, 170-171,
187
Separate but equal, 21, 133-134
Separatism, black, 136-137
Singapore: language policy, 123;
and Malaysia, 118-119
Social contract, 196, 197-198,
201, 202
Societies, plural, 7, 13, 172; and

About the Author

VERNON VAN DYKE is Carver Professor of Political Science Emeritus at the University of Iowa. He is the editor of *Teaching Political Science: The Professor and the Polity*, the author of *Human Rights, the United States, and World Community, Pride and Power*, and articles which have been published in journals such as *Politikon, South African Journal of Political Science, Journal of Politics, World Politics*, and *American Political Science Review*, among others.